THE REAL ESTATE DICTIONARY

THIRD EDITION

PUBLICATION NO. 510, REV.

By
John Talamo, J.D.

FINANCIAL
PUBLISHING
COMPANY

82 Brookline Avenue
Boston, Massachusetts 02215
(617) 262-4040

PUBLICATION NO. 510, REV.
COPYRIGHT © 1975, 1979, 1984 BY
FINANCIAL PUBLISHING COMPANY

PRINTED IN THE
UNITED STATES OF AMERICA

Buying a home can be one of the most valuable and significant investments an individual can make. Laws and contracts regulating one's rights and obligations as a property owner form the foundation of our legal system.

Because of this long history, many terms used in real estate may have implications that are not at first apparent. This dictionary provides you with functional, working definitions of all the terms commonly encountered.

These terms were prepared by John Talamo, J.D., who works in real estate and teaches at Fullerton College in Fullerton, California. A graduate of Notre Dame, he received his law degree from Detroit College of Law.

A

A.B.A. (AMERICAN BAR ASSOCIATION) — A national organization composed of member state and local bar associations, which control the licensing of attorneys.

ABANDONMENT — The voluntary relinquishment of rights of ownership or another interest (such as an easement) by failure to use the property, coupled with an intent to abandon (give up the interest).

ABANDONMENT OF HOMESTEAD — A recorded document, executed by those claiming a homestead exemption, giving up said homestead. Not applicable to all states and procedure must be according to local statutes.

ABATEMENT — A reduction or decrease. Usually applies to a decrease of assessed valuation of ad valorem taxes after the assessment and levy.

ABC SOIL — Soil having distinct A (upper), B (middle), and C (lower) horizons (layers of soil).

ABSCISSA — The horizontal axis of a curve; the vertical axis being the ordinate. The terms are used in connection with charts and graphs.

ABSENTEE LANDLORD — A lessor of real property (usually the owner) who does not live in a portion of the property.

ABSENTEE OWNER — An owner of property who does not occupy said property.

ABSORPTION — The filling of space, such as the rental of units or sale of a tract. The time or rate must be estimated and considered as part of the owner's (usually the builder) costs.

ABSTRACT — A summary; an abridgement. Before the use of photostatic copying, public records were kept by abstracts of recorded documents.

ABSTRACT CONTINUATION — (See: Supplemental Abstract).

ABSTRACT EXTENSION — (See: Supplemental Abstract).

ABSTRACTER'S CERTIFICATE — A certificate contained in an abstract which shows the time period and scope of the search of public records done by the abstracter.

ABSTRACT OF JUDGMENT — A summary of the essential provisions of a court judgment, which when recorded in the county recorder's office, creates a lien upon the property of the defendant in that county, both presently owned or after acquired.

ABSTRACT OF TITLE — A compilation of the recorded documents relating to a parcel of land, from which an attorney may give an opinion as to the condition of title. Still in use in some states, but giving way to the use of title insurance.

ABUT — To touch, border on, or be contiguous to.

ABUTMENTS — The verticle members (walls or heavy columns) which bear the load or pressure of the cross member, such as an arch, pier, or similar structure.

ABUTTING OWNER — One whose land is contiguous to (abuts) a public right of way.

ACCELERATED COST RECOVERY SYSTEM(ACRS) — A portion of the Economic Recovery Act of 1981 which allows shorter depreciation of both real and personal property, does not distinguish between new and used property, and disregards salvage value.

ACCELERATED DEPRECIATION — A general term including any method of depreciation greater than straight line depreciation (see which).

ACCELERATION CLAUSE — Clause used in an installment note and mortgage (or deed of trust), which gives the lender the right to demand payment in full upon the happening of a certain event, such as failure to pay an installment by a certain date, change of ownership without the lender's consent, destruction of the property (see Waste), or other event which endangers the security of the loan. (See also: Alienation Clause).

ACCEPTANCE — Voluntarily agreeing to the price and terms of an offer. Offer and acceptance create a contract.

ACCESSIBILITY — The location of a site in terms of how easily it may be reached by customers, employees, carriers, and others necessary to the intended use of the property.

ACCESSION — The right of an owner to an increase in his property by natural means (such as a riparian owner's right to an abandoned river bed, rights of alluvion and reliction, etc.) or artificially, by improvements.

ACCESSORY BUILDINGS — Structures used for the benefit of a central or main building, such as a tool shed, garage, or similar structure.

ACCESS RIGHT — A right to ingress and egress to and from one's property. May be express or implied.

ACCOMMODATION PARTY — Person who lends his name to help secure credit for another, by signing a note or other obligation without receiving consideration.

ACCOMMODATION RECORDING — The recording of documents with the county recorder by a title insurance company, without liability (no insurance) on the part of the company, but merely as a convenience to a customer.

ACCORD — An agreement by which one accepts something different (usually less) from what is owed as full satisfaction. The amount owed may be in dispute or simply accepted as full satisfaction by the creditor or claimant. The agreement and acceptance is called "Accord and Satisfaction".

ACCOUNTS PAYABLE — Money owing. The term is generally used in business rather than personal finances. Usually represents services or materials, such as wood, bricks, payment of subcontractors, etc., to a builder.

ACCOUNTS RECEIVABLE — Money owed to a business for goods or services. Accounts receivable may be sold or borrowed against. Many times the sale of accounts receivable is for less than face value (discounted).

ACCRETION — The gradual addition to the shore or bank of a waterway. The land generally becomes the property of the owner of the shore or bank, except where statutes specify otherwise.

ACCRUAL ACCOUNTING — An accounting method under which income and expenses are charged to the periods for which they are applicable, rather than when payment is received or made. The method calling for income and expenses to be based on payment being received or made is cash accounting.

ACCRUE — To grow or mature.

ACCRUED DEPRECIATION — (1) The amount reserved each year in the accounting system for replacement of a building or other asset. (2) The useful life of a property at any given time.

ACID SOIL — A soil with an acid rather than an alkaline base. This can determine its suitability for farming.

ACKNOWLEDGEMENT — A written declaration by a person executing an instrument, given before an officer authorized to give an oath (usually a notary public), stating that the execution is of his own volition.

ACOUSTICAL MATERIALS — Materials which absorb sound. Usually installed in walls and ceilings and composed of fiberglass, cork, special plaster, or similar materials.

ACOUSTICAL TILE — Tile which absorbs sound.

ACQUISITION APPRAISAL — An appraisal to determine market value of a property to be taken by eminent domain, in order to justly compensate the owner.

ACQUISITION COSTS — Costs of acquiring property other than purchase price: escrow fees, title insurance, lenders fees, etc.

ACRE — A measure, usually of land, equal to 160 sq. rods (43,560 sq. ft.) in any shape.

ACREAGE — Any parcel of land which may be measured in terms of acres. Usually qualified by its zoning or usage, such as residential acreage, industrial acreage, etc.

ACREAGE CONTROL — Federal control setting the number of acres which may be planted with crops which have federal price supports.

ACRE FOOT — A volume of water, sand, coal, etc., equal to an area of one acre with a depth of one foot (43,560 cubic ft.). If a liquid, 325,850 gallons.

ACRE-INCH — A cubic measure of one acre in area with a depth of one inch.

ACTION TO QUIET TITLE — A court action to establish ownership to real property. Although technically not an action to remove a cloud on title, the two actions are usually referred to as "Quiet Title" actions. (See also: Cloud on Title).

ACT OF GOD — Damage caused by nature (floods, winds, etc.) rather than destruction by man.

ACTUAL AGE — The chronological age of a structure as opposed to its effective or economic age.

ACTUAL CASH VALUE — (See: Market Value).

ACTUAL NOTICE — Notice actually and expressly, or by implication, given and received. (See also: Constructive Notice; Statutory Notice).

AD — By, for, relating to, concerning.

ADDENDUM — Something added. A list or other material added to a document, letter, contractual agreement, escrow instructions, etc. (See also: Amendment).

ADDITION — (1) A portion of a building added to the original structure. (2) A synonym for subdivision in certain legal descriptions.

ADDITIONAL DEPOSIT — A buyer of real property will generally give a small deposit with an offer, and a more substantial deposit after the offer has been accepted. The second deposit is the "additional deposit".

ADD-ON INTEREST — A method of charging interest usually used in the financing of automobiles, but not generally used in real estate financing. Interest is computed on the total amount borrowed and added on to the principal. Each payment is then deducted from this total amount. Interest on real estate loans is usually figured based on the balance owing after each payment is made (declining balance).

ADJOINING — Touching or contiguous to.

ADJUDICATION — A judgment or decision by a court.

ADJUSTED GROSS INCOME — Gross income of a building if fully rented, less an allowance for estimated vacancies.

ADJUSTABLE MORTGAGE LOANS(AML'S) — Mortgage loans under which the interest rate is periodically adjusted to more closely coincide with current rates. The amounts and times of adjustment are agreed to at the inception of the loan. Also called: Adjustable Rate Loans, Adjustable Rate Mortgages (ARM's), Flexible Rate Loans, Variable Rate Loans. (See also: Indexing, Rate Index).

ADJUSTABLE RATE LOANS — (See: Adjustable Mortgage Loans).

ADJUSTMENTS — (See: Proration).

AD LITUM — (For the suit). A guardian "Ad Litum" prosecutes or defends a suit for a minor or incompetent.

ADMINISTRATOR — A person given authority by a proper court to manage and distribute the estate of a deceased person when there is no will. (See also: Administrator C.T.A.).

ADMINISTRATOR C.T.A. — Administrator when there is a will but no executor is named or the executor named is unable or unwilling to serve. The C.T.A. stands for Cum Testamento Annexo (with the will attached).

ADMINISTRATRIX — Female administrator.

ADOBE CONSTRUCTION — A structure built of adobe blocks. Adobe blocks are made from adobe mud mixed with straw or a straw-like substance, and then baked. Considered a very good but expensive material.

ADR (THE CLASS LIFE ASSET DEPRECIATION RANGE SYSTEM) — A flexible set of guide lines for depreciation which sets up an "asset depreciation period", rather than using the "useful life" of an asset.

ADULT — One old enough to legally act without the consent of a parent or guardian. One over 18 years old, except in some states for the purchase of alcohol, which is limited to those over 21 years old.

AD VALOREM — "According to value". A method of taxation using the value of the thing taxed to determine the amount of tax. Taxes can be either "Ad Valorem" or "Specific". Example: A tax of $5.00 per $1000.00 of value per house is "Ad Valorem". A tax of $5.00 per house (irrespective of value) is "Specific".

ADVANCE FEE — A fee charged by a broker to a seller to cover all or a portion of the broker's costs of promoting the property. The fee is generally credited against commissions but is not refunded if no commissions are received. Most frequently used in connection with large offerings which require a substantial outlay of funds for promotion.

ADVANCES — Money advanced by a mortgagee (beneficiary under a deed of trust) to pay the mortgagor's (trustor's) obligations of taxes, insurance, or other items necessary to protect the secured property.

ADVERSE LAND USE — A use which causes surrounding property to lose value, such as an industrial development in a residential area.

ADVERSE POSSESSION — A method of acquiring title by possession under certain conditions. Generally, possession must be actual, under claim of right, open, continuous, notorious, exclusive, and hostile (knowingly against the rights of the owner). Exact time (years) of possession and specific requirements (such as payment of property taxes) vary with the statutes of each state.

ADVERTISING — In real estate, mainly confined to newspaper ads and signs on the property, although advertising of the real estate brokerage may extend to radio and television. Recently, newspaper ads have become more binding on the advertiser, especially with regard to the financing advertised.

AEOLIAN SOIL — Soil composed of materials deposited by the wind.

AERATION ZONE — The surface soil to a depth from which plants draw moisture.

AESTHETIC VALUE — The value of a property attributable to the beauty of the improvements or surroundings.

AFFIANT — One who makes an affidavit. Also called a deponent, although technically not the same.

AFFIDAVIT — A written statement or declaration, sworn to before an officer who has authority to administer an oath.

AFFIDAVIT OF ALIMONY AND CHILD SUPPORT — A sworn statement of a separated or divorced person showing the amount (if any) of alimony or child support.

AFFINITY — (1) Relationship not of the blood. Related by marriage. (2) Any group for a specific purpose is called an affinity group, such as clubs, people in the same school, etc.

AFFIRMATION — A substitution for an oath when a person objects to taking an oath (Quakers, atheists, etc.). A lie after an affirmation is still perjury.

AFFORESTATION — The growing of a forest where none previously existed, as opposed to reforestation (the replanting of a harvested or destroyed forest).

A-FRAME — A type of construction usually found in resort areas. The exterior framing of the building is shaped like the letter A.

AFTER ACQUIRED PROPERTY — As applied to a judgment lien, it means that the lien will attach to property of the debtor acquired after the judgment. (See also: After Acquired Title).

AFTER ACQUIRED TITLE — Legal doctrine by which property automatically vests in a grantee when the grantor acquires title to the property after the deed has been executed and delivered.

AGE-LIFE DEPRECIATION — (See: Straight Line Depreciation).

AGENCY — Any relationship in which one party (agent) acts for or represents another (principal) under the authority of the latter. Agency involving real property should be in writing, such as listings, trusts, powers of attorney, etc.

AGENCY AGREEMENT (AGENCY LISTING) — In some states, the term describing a listing under which the broker's commission is protected against a sale by other agents but not by a sale by the principal. Called a "non-exclusive" listing in some states.

AGENCY BY ESTOPPEL — An agency created by operation of law when an agent oversteps his or her authority but the action (or failure to act) by the principal leads one to believe the authority exists. (See also: Apparent Authority).

AGENCY COUPLED WITH INTEREST — A contractual relationship with consideration going from agent to principal; the agency is given as return consideration. Example: A broker agrees to work to obtain property for a builder in return for a listing after the builder has completed the project. The broker would be entitled to (have an interest in) the listing (agency), provided the broker did obtain the property for the builder.

AGENT — One who is authorized to act for or represent another (principal), usually in business matters. Authority may be express or implied.

AGRARIAN — Relating to land, or to a division or distribution of land.

AGREEMENT — A general term usually describing a common view of two or more people regarding the rights and obligations of each with regard to a given subject. Not necessarily a contract, although all contracts are agreements.

AGREEMENT OF SALE — Has two separate meanings, depending on area of the country. In some states it is synonomous with a purchase agreement (See: Purchase Agreement). In other states, it is synonomous with a land contract (See: Land Contract).

AGRICULTURAL LIEN — A lien against crops (only), to secure money or payment for materials used to grow the crop.

AGRICULTURAL PROPERTY — (1) Land which is zoned agricultural, (2) Land used for growing of agricultural products or raising of livestock.

A HORIZON — Surface horizon (layer) of soil, the composition of which is effected by water which percolates through it.

A.I.R. (AMERICAN INDUSTRIAL REAL ESTATE ASSOCIATION) — A specialized association of real estate brokers and salesmen who deal primarily in industrial properties. The goal of the association is to further the knowledge and effectiveness of its members.

AIR RIGHTS — The right to the use of the air space above property without the right to use the surface of the property. However, air rights may restrict surface rights, especially height of improvements.

ALCOVE — A recessed part or addition to a room.

ALIAS — Latin for "otherwise". Commonly meaning that a person is known by more than one name. In some states, indicated by the letters AKA (also known as).

ALIENATION — Transfer of property from one owner to another.

ALIENATION CLAUSE — A type of acceleration clause, calling for a debt under a mortgage or deed of trust to be due in its entirety upon transfer of ownership of the secured property. Also called a "due-on-sale" clause.

ALKALI — The chemical opposite of acid. Heavy concentrations of alkaline salts in soil may damage crops.

ALKALINE SOIL — Soil which has an alkali, rather than an acid base.

ALLEGATION — The assertion or statement of a party to an action, setting forth that which he expects to prove.

ALLEY — A narrow right of way, either public or private, used for access (usually to garages, loading platforms, etc.).

ALLEY INFLUENCE — In appraising, the effect upon value of a property, because of an adjoining side or rear alley.

ALL-INCLUSIVE DEED OF TRUST — (See: Wrap-Around Mortgage).

ALLODIAL TENURE — (See: Allodium).

ALLODIUM — Land owned by individuals, as opposed to the feudal system of ownership of all land by a king or ruler.

ALLOTMENT — A small parcel of land, sold or given to a farm worker for cultivation as a supplementary source of income. Popular in the 1900's before World War II.

ALLUVION (ALLUVIUM, ALLUVIAL) — Deposits formed by accretion.

A.L.T.A. (AMERICAN LAND TITLE ASSOCIATION) — An organization, composed of title insurance companies, which has adopted certain insurance policy forms to standardize coverage on a national basis.

ALTERATIONS — Changes in the interior or exterior of a building, but without changing the exterior dimensions.

AMENDMENT — A change, either to correct an error or to alter a part of an agreement without changing the principal idea or essence.

AMENITIES — Those settings or improvements to property which increase the desirability or enjoyment rather than the necessities of the residents. For example, a pool, a view, etc.

AMERICAN BOND — A process in bricklaying by which every 5th, 6th, or 7th layer of bricks is laid with the wide length facing the wall; the other layers have the narrow length facing the wall.

AMORTIZATION — Payment of a debt in equal installments of principal and interest, rather than interest only payments.

AMORTIZE — To reduce a debt by regular payments of both principal and interest, as opposed to interest only payments.

AMPERE — A measure of electrical current equal to the current produced by the force of one volt through a resistance of one ohm. (See also: Coulomb)

ANCESTOR — Legally, the word may have several meanings. It may imply a lineal descent, such as the parent of a child, or collaterals, such as an older brother being the ancestor of a younger brother. Also means one from whom a person inherits.

ANCILLARY — Subordinate, aiding.

ANNEX — To add or attach. Usually to join a smaller or subordinate thing to a larger or more dominant thing.

ANNEXATION — Permanently affixing to real property, such as a city adding additional land to increase its size.

ANNUAL — By the year.

ANNUAL PERCENTAGE RATE (A.P.R.) — The yearly interest percentage of a loan, as expressed by the actual rate of interest paid. For example: 6% add-on interest would be much more than 6% simple interest, even though both would say 6%. The A.P.R. is disclosed as a requirement of federal truth in lending statutes.

ANNUITY — (1) A payment of money yearly for life or a given period of years. (2) A fixed amount given or left by will, paid periodically, not necessarily yearly.

ANNUITY METHOD — Appraisal method determining present value by future anticipated net income before depreciation, which is then discounted.

ANNUM — Year.

ANTE — Prefix meaning before.

ANTENUPTIAL AGREEMENT — An agreement made by a man and woman in contemplation of marriage, setting forth the property rights of each during the marriage, and in the event of divorce or death.

ANTICIPATION — Appraisal method using the principle that value is created by anticipated future benefits.

APARTMENT — One or more rooms of a building used as a place to live, in a building containing at least one other unit used for the same purpose. Usually has, at least, cooking facilities, a bathroom, and a place to sleep. Those who live in these units pay rent for their use, usually on a monthly basis.

APARTMENT HOTEL — A building combining the features of an apartment building and a hotel. The units are furnished and may offer hotel facilities such as maid service, a restaurant, etc., but whose residents may stay for months or years, paying on a weekly or monthly basis.

APARTMENT HOUSE — A building, containing two or more separate residential units, which is under one ownership. The residents of the units pay rent.

APPARENT AUTHORITY — Action (or failure to act) by a principal which leads one to believe that an agent of said principal has authority which in fact the agent does not have.

APPEL LOAN (ACCELERATING PAYOFF PROGRESSIVE EQUITY LOAN) — A residential property loan which calls for a payment increase over the first 6 years. Level payments are made for the remaining years and the loan paid off during the 15th year. There is no prepayment penalty and P.M.I. is required.

APPOINTMENTS — Furnishings (mostly thought of as decorative) and equipment in a building.

APPORTIONMENT — A proper allocation of income and expenses of property, especially after a division of ownership.

APPRAISAL — An opinion of value based upon a factual analysis. Legally, an estimation of value by two disinterested persons of suitable qualifications.

APPRAISAL METHODS — Generally, three major methods of appraisal: Cost Approach, Income Approach, Market Value (comparables) Approach.

APPRAISAL REPORT — A written report by an appraiser containing his opinion as to the value of a property and the reasoning leading to this opinion. The factual data supporting the opinion, such as comparables, appraisal formulas, and qualifictions of the appraiser, will also be set forth.

APPRAISED VALUE — An opinion of the value of a property at a given time, based on facts regarding the location, improvements, etc., of the property and surroundings.

APPRAISER — One who is trained and educated in the methods of determining the value of property through analysis of various factors which determine said value.

APPRECIATION — An increased value of property due to either a positive improvement of the area or the elimination of negative factors. Commonly, and incorrectly, used to describe an increase in value through inflation.

APPROPRIATION — The private taking and use of public property, such as water from a river or lake. Not to be confused with condemnation or expropriation.

APPROVED ATTORNEY — In states where attorneys examine the chain of title before title insurance is issued, the title company will approve certain attorneys as those whose opinion it will accept for the issuance of a title policy.

APPURTENANCE — Something belonging to something else, either attached or not, such as a barn to a house, or an easement to land. The appurtenance is part of the property and passes with it upon sale or other transfer.

APPURTENANT — Belonging to, accessory to, or incidental to.

APPURTENANT EASEMENT — (See: Easement).

APR — (See: Annual Percentage Rate).

APRON — Any structure resembling the shape of the apron worn as clothing, such as the protruding lower inside part of a window, the portion of a driveway which connects it to the street, the entrance to a loading dock, and similar structures.

AQUATIC RIGHTS — Individual rights to the use of the sea and rivers, for the purpose of fishing or navigation, and to the soil in the sea and rivers.

AQUEDUCT — A large pipe, conduit, or trench to bring water or carry it away.

ARABLE — Land capable of being cultivated for farming.

ARBITRAGE — The buying and selling of money or securities in different markets at a profit. For example: The value of 1 pound sterling is selling in New York for $2.00 and in London for $1.98. If one buys in London for dollars and sells in New York, there is a profit of $.02 per pound sterling. The term has come to be used with regard to the interest rate spread between wrap-around and underlying financing.

ARBITRARY MAP — A map drawn by a title company to be used in locating property in areas where legal descriptions are difficult and complex. Areas are arbitrarily subdivided, usually by ownership at a given time, into lots which are numbered. Recorded documents are then posted to these arbitrary lots by the same "arb" number.

ARBITRATION CLAUSE — A clause in a lease calling for the decision of a third party (arbiter) regarding disputes over future rents based on negotiation. Also used in construction contracts, disputes between brokers, etc.

ARCADE — A seldom used term describing a series of colonnaded arches, covering a walkway with retail stores on one or both sides. A forerunner of the present shopping center.

ARCH — A concave curved span which may be over a doorway or an entire room or building, such as an arched ceiling or roof.

ARCHITECTURAL CONCRETE CONSTRUCTION — Concrete poured into a form to produce a design, giving the affect of stone masonry.

ARCHITECTURE — The design and construction plans for a structure. Recently the design for landscaping has become known as landscape architecture.

ARCHITRAVE — The surrounding molding of a doorway or similar wall opening.

ARCH RIB ROOF — A roof used primarily in industrial buildings, and having the shape of an arch or crescent. It is supported by a bow-string truss which spreads the roof load evenly.

AREA — The surface (plane) space of land or a building. Also describes a neighborhood, or large land section (such as the Southern California area). The term may also indicate a use, such as a work area, living area, play area, etc.

AREAWAY — An old term referring to a cellar or room under the sidewalk.

AREA ZONING — Mainly residential zoning which regulates the ratio of improvements to land, setbacks, etc. Also called bulk zoning.

ARPENT — French land measure of area used in parts of the South, approximately .84625 acre.

ARREARS — (1) Payment made after it is due is in arrears. (2) Interest is said to be paid in arrears since it is paid to the date of payment rather than in advance, as is rent. Example: A rental payment made July 1 pays the rent to August 1. An interest payment made July 1 pays the interest to July 1.

ARTERIAL HIGHWAY — Any major highway or thoroughfare.

ARTESIAN WELL — A well bored into a subterranean body of water, which, being under pressure, rises naturally to the surface without artificial pumping.

ARTICLES OF INCORPORATION — Documentation filed with the state which sets forth general information about a corporation. More specific rules of the corporation would be contained in the by-laws.

ARTIST'S CONCEPTION (RENDERING) — A drawing of a proposed real estate project. Not necessarily to scale and generally used to promote the sale of vacant land or the leasing of proposed buildings.

ASBESTOS — A fire and heat resistant material used in insulation, roofing, etc.

ASHLAR (ASHLER) — A stone which is cut in squares and used both as a facing for masonry walls, and in foundations.

"AS IS" CONDITION — Premises accepted by a buyer or tenant in the condition existing at the time of the sale or lease, including all physical defects.

ASKING PRICE — The price at which the seller is offering property for sale. The eventual selling price may be less after negotiation with a buyer.

ASPECT — The position or direction of the face of a slope or structure, such as a Southern aspect or exposure.

ASSEMBLAGE — The acquisition of contiguous properties into one ownership for a specific use.

ASSEMBLAGE COST — The cost above the value of individual properties because of assemblage, rather than periodic individual sales.

ASSESS — To fix a value; to appraise. Most commonly used in connection with taxes.

ASSESSED VALUE — Value placed upon property for property tax purposes by the tax assessor.

ASSESSMENT — (1) The estimating of value of property for tax purposes. (2) A levy against property in addition to general taxes. Usually for improvements such as streets, sewers, etc.

ASSESSMENT BASE — The total assessed value of all property in a given assessment (tax) district.

ASSESSMENT DISTRICT — An area, the boundaries of which are set for tax assessment purposes only; these boundaries may cross city boundaries.

ASSESSMENT PERIOD — Taxable period. The period during which the tax assessment must be completed.

ASSESSMENT RATIO — The assessed value of a property expressed as a fraction in comparison to market value.

ASSESSMENT ROLL — The list of taxable persons and property in a given area as compiled by the assessor.

ASSESSOR — One who estimates value of property for tax purposes.

ASSETS — Everything owned by a person or corporation which can be used for the payment of debts.

ASSIGN — To transfer property, or an interest in property.

ASSIGNEE — One who receives an assignment. (pl. assigns).

ASSIGNMENT — A transfer to another of any property, real or personal, or of any rights or estates in said property. Common assignments are of leases, mortgages, deeds of trust, but the general term encompasses all transfers of title.

ASSIGNOR — One who makes an assignment.

ASSUMPTION FEE — Lender's charge for paperwork involved in processing records for a new buyer assuming an existing loan.

ASSUMPTION OF DEED OF TRUST — (See: Assumption of Mortgage).

ASSUMPTION OF MORTGAGE — Agreement by a buyer to assume the liability under an existing note secured by a mortgage or deed of trust. The lender usually must approve the new debtor in order to release the existing debtor (usually the seller) from liability.

ATTACHMENT — An act of seizing persons or property by judicial order to bring them within the custody of the court. Most commonly the seizure of property to furnish security for a debt in connection with a pending action.

ATTESTATION CLAUSE — The clause in a document (deed, mortgage, etc.) in which the witnesses certify that the document has been properly executed.

ATTIC — The space under the roof of a structure but before the top story. May be simply an air space or improved and used.

ATTORN — To turn over; to transfer to another. To agree to recognize a new owner of a property and pay rent to him. (See also: Letter of Attornment).

ATTORNEY AT LAW — An advocate, counsel, or official agent employed in preparing, managing, and trying cases in court. Must be licensed by the state.

ATTORNEY-IN-FACT — One who is appointed to act (as agent) for another (principal) under a power of attorney. The scope of the agent's authority is limited to that given by the power of attorney, which may be limited to one specific act or may be broader. (See also: Power of Attorney).

ATTORNMENT AGREEMENT — (See: Letter of Attornment).

ATTRACTIVE NUISANCE — Anything on a property which may attract small children and is dangerous to them. Reasonable care must be used to prevent injury to the children.

AUCTION — A public sale of land or goods to the highest bidder.

AUXILIARY LANE — A paved shoulder of a highway, usually designed for emergency stopping.

AVENUE — Originally, a broad passageway bordered by trees. Now synonomous with street or road, and of no special significance.

AVERAGE DAILY TRAFFIC — The number of vehicles passing a given point in one day. Usually obtained by finding the number for several days and averaging.

AVIGATION EASEMENT — An easement over private property abutting an airport runway, which limits the height of crops, trees, structures, etc., in the aircraft's take off and landing path.

AVULSION — A sudden and substantial tearing away of land by water and the deposit of said land as an addition to the land of another owner. The original boundaries apply and ownership of the land in question remains in the original owner.

AWARD — In condemnation, the amount paid for the property taken.

AWNING — Canvas, metal or other material, which protrudes out over a window or doorway to provide protection from the sun, rain, etc.

AWNING WINDOW — A window which, being hinged at the top, forms an awning when open.

AZIMUTH — Distance in degrees from North to an object, or, in the Southern hemisphere, from South to an object. A surveying term.

AZONAL SOIL — Soil which does not contain distinct horizons (layers).

B

BACKFILL — To replace ground removed by excavation for construction. Used to brace a structure (especially a foundation or footings).

BACK TITLE LETTER — In states where attorneys examine title for title insurance purposes, this letter is given by a title insurance company to an attorney, giving to said attorney the condition of title as of a certain date. The attorney then begins his examination as of that date. Also called a starter or back title certificate. (See also: Starter).

BACKUP OFFER — A secondary offer to buy property, used in case the first (primary) offer fails. A backup offer is especially useful when the primary offer contains difficult contingencies.

BACKWATER — Water in a stream or river which, because of a dam or other obstruction, is stopped in its course or flows back toward its source.

BACKWATER VALVE — A valve set in a lateral sewer line which automatically prevents sewage from flowing back to its source (a building).

BALLOON — (1) The final payment of a balloon note (see which). (2) A landlocked parcel of land.

BALLOON FRAMING — A type of framing for a two story building by which the studs extend from ground to roof, the second floor being supported by nailing the horizonal supports (joists) to the studs and by the use of ribbon or ledger board.

BALLOON NOTE — A note calling for periodic payments which are insufficient to fully amortize the face amount of the note prior to maturity, so that a principal sum known as a "balloon" is due at maturity.

BALTIMORE RULE — An appraisal method for setting a value on a corner lot. The lot is appraised as an inside lot for its front footage on both streets. The two values are then added to find the value of the corner lot. For example: Lot 1 fronts 100' on street A and 100' on street B. The value of a 100' inside lot on street A is added to the value of a 100' inside lot on street B to find the value of lot 1. Also called the Bernard Rule.

BALUSTER — The supporting posts of a handrail in a staircase.

BALUSTRADE — A row of balusters supporting a handrail.

BANK — (1) The elevated land on each side of a river or stream which keeps the water in its natural channel. (2) (See: Commercial Bank).

BANKRUPT — One who is adjudicated a bankrupt by a court having proper jurisdiction. The bankruptcy may be voluntary (petitioned by the bankrupt) or involuntary (petitioned by the creditors of the bankrupt).

BANKRUPTCY — Proceedings under federal bankruptcy statutes to relieve a debtor (bankrupt) from insurmountable debt. The bankrupt's property is distributed by the court to the creditors as full satisfaction of the debts, in accordance with certain priorities and exemptions. Voluntary bankruptcy is petitioned by the debtor; involuntary by the creditors.

BARGE-BOARD — A board (often carved or ornamented) which hangs from the projecting edge of a sloping roof. Also called a vergeboard.

BARGE COUPLE — Either of the two rafters supporting the part of a gable roof which extends beyond the supporting wall.

BARGE COURSE — Tiling on a gable roof projecting beyond the supporting wall.

BARREL — A unit of solid or liquid measure, varying with each trade. For example: A barrel of water is $31\frac{1}{2}$ gallons, oil 42 gallons.

BASE — The lowest part of a construction member. That which bears the load. (See also: Base Title).

BASE AND MERIDIAN — (See: Base Line; Meridian).

BASEBOARD — Generally, any board or molding covering an interior wall where it meets the floor.

BASEBOARD HEATING — A system of perimeter heating in which the baseboard is replaced by the heating units. May also be panels rather than baseboard units.

BASE LINE — (1) A survey line used in the government survey to establish township lines. The base line runs East and West through a principal meridian (line running North and South). (2) A horizontal elevation line used as the centerline in a survey for a highway route.

BASE MAP — A map having background information, such as state, county, or city boundaries, upon which more detailed data is plotted.

BASEMENT — Generally, the story of a building below ground level.

BASE MOLDING — Molding installed along the top of the baseboard.

BASE PROPERTY — Private property owned by a cattle owner, required before a permit will be issued to allow the cattle to graze on public land.

BASE RENT — A specific amount used as a minimum rent in a lease which uses a percentage or overage for additional rent.

BASE SHOE MOLDING — Molding installed along the bottom of a baseboard (junction with floor). Also called carpet molding or carpet strip.

BASE TITLE — The result of an examination of title for the internal use of a title insurance company. Usually covers a large area and is done in anticipation of future sales or subdividing of the area.

BASE YEAR — The year upon which a direct expense escalation of rent is based. [See also: Escalation Clause (3)].

BASIC CAPACITY — In connection with highway use, the greatest number of cars per hour which can pass a given point under ideal driving conditions will give the basic capacity of a lane or road.

BASIC CROPS — Crops usually subject to government price supports and considered the basis of our agricultural economy, such as wheat, corn, oats, rice, and similar crops.

BASIS FOR DEPRECIATION — The value of property for purposes of depreciation. For example: A purchased asset—The basis is cost, whether fully paid for or not. The method for determining the basis is different for gift, inheritance, etc.

BASIS POINT — A finance term meaning a yield of $^1/_{100}$th of 1% annually.

BATHROOM — A room containing a toilet, sink, and bathtub or bathtub-shower combination. In appraisal for federally insured mortgages, a toilet and sink (no bathtub or shower) equal a half bathroom; a toilet, sink, and stall shower equal a three quarter bathroom.

BATT — A strip of insulation fitting closely between the studs of a wall.

BATTEN — A narrow strip (usually of wood), used to cover seams between siding boards.

BATTER — The slope of a structure, such as a wall or bank; expressed in terms of the vertical rise per horizontal distance, such as 3 inches (vertical) per 10 feet (horizontal).

BATTURE LAND — The land between a river bank and the water's edge when the water level is lower than normal.

BAY — (1) The opening between two columns, walls, etc., which forms a room-like space. May be industrial space, parking space, barn space, or other use. (2) A bending or curving of the shoreline so as to form a partially enclosed body of water.

BAY WINDOW — A window which projects in a curve out from a wall, giving a bay-like effect to the interior.

BEACH — That portion of the shore between ordinary low and high water marks. Commonly used to describe any sandy area adjacent to a body of water.

BEAM — A vertical or horizontal member of a structure; may be of wood, steel, concrete, or other strong material, and, unless decorative only, is a load-bearing part of the structure.

BEARING — (1) Relative position or direction of one object to another or to a compass point. (2) Supporting a load, such as a bearing wall.

BEARING VALUE — In construction, the ability of soil to bear the weight of the structure to be built.

BEARING WALL — A wall which supports the weight of a part of a structure in addition to its own weight.

BED A TREE — Preparing a path (bed) on which a tree is to fall so that it will not be damaged.

BEDROCK — Solid rock beneath the soil, as distinguished from rocks or boulders.

BEDROOM COMMUNITY — An area primarily residential. The people living there commute to work.

BEFORE AND AFTER METHOD — An appraisal method used in both condemnation and modernization. In condemnation the method is used in a partial taking. The value of the total land owned by A, for example, is $1.00 per sq. ft. After a partial taking, the remaining land of A is worth $.75 per sq. ft. A should receive $1.00 per sq. ft. for the property taken plus $.25 per sq. ft. for the remaining parcel. In the event the remaining property is worth $1.25 after the taking (increased value), the payment to A could be less than the value of the property taken. In modernization, an appraiser may take the value of property before and after remodeling to determine if the value increased more than modernization costs.

BELT HIGHWAY — A limited access highway carrying traffic around an urban area, with entrances and exits to principal streets. Also called a by-pass.

BELVEDERE — (See: Gazebo).

BENCH MARK — Surveying mark made in some object which is permanently fixed in the ground, showing the height of that point in relation to sea level. Used in topographic surveys and tidal observations.

BENEFICIAL ESTATE — An estate, the right to possession of which has been postponed, such as a devise under a will. More commonly, an estate, the legal ownership of which has not yet vested, as under a land contract. An equitable estate.

BENEFICIAL INTEREST — The equitable, rather than legal ownership of property, such as under a land contract.

BENEFICIAL USE — The doctrine, applicable in some areas, pertains to water rights, giving priority to those who would use the water most beneficially.

BENEFICIARY — (1) One for whose benefit a trust is created. (2) In states in which deeds of trust are commonly used instead of mortgages, the lender (mortgagee) is called the beneficiary.

BENEFICIARY'S DEMAND — Written instructions by a beneficiary under a deed of trust stating and demanding the amount necessary for issuance of a reconveyance, whether a full or partial amount.

BENEFICIARY'S STATEMENT — A statement by a lender under a deed of trust, setting forth the pertinent information necessary to assume said deed of trust, such as the unpaid balance, monthly payment, and interest rate.

BENEFIT OF THE BARGAIN — A rule of damages under which a defrauded purchaser may recover the difference between the actual and misrepresented value of the property purchased, even though greater than the actual loss suffered.

BENEFITS — A term used in eminent domain, referring to the increase in value to land not taken, which is produced by the taking. (See also: General Benefits; Special Benefits).

BENEVOLENT ASSOCIATIONS — Non-profit groups having a philanthropic or charitable purpose.

BEQUEATH — To give personal property by will.

BEQUEST — Personal property left by will.

BERM — (1) A bench, ledge, or other resting place part way up a hill or slope. (2) A mound used to control drainage by diverting all or part of the flow.

BERNARD RULE — (See: Baltimore Rule).

BETTERMENT — An improvement to a structure which is not a repair, restoration, or enlargement. For example: the addition of aluminum siding over a frame wall; paving a street adjoining the structure; adding a fireplace or some similar improvement which increases the value of the property.

B HORIZON — The horizon (layer of soil) beneath the top layer. The composition of the B horizon is changed by the action of percolating water.

BI — A prefix meaning both "every two" or "twice in". Biannual, for example, is twice in one year. Biennial is once every two years.

BIANNUAL — Twice per year. Semiannual.

BID — (1) An offer, usually in competition with others, such as at auction. A builder may bid for the right to do construction (especially for a government contract). (2) Used in some states to describe an offer to purchase real estate.

BIENNIAL — Every two years.

BILATERAL (RECIPROCAL) CONTRACT — Contract under which the parties expressly enter into mutual promises, such as sales contracts.

BI-LEVEL — Two levels. Commonly refers to construction of a house. Also called "split" level.

BILLBOARD — A structure annexed to land for the purpose of posting advertising.

BILL OF SALE — An instrument by which one transfers personal property.

BINDER — (1) A report issued by a title insurance company setting forth the condition of title to certain property as of a certain date, and also setting forth conditions which, if satisfied, will cause a policy of title insurance to be issued. Also called a commitment. (See also: Preliminary Title Report). (2) A policy of title insurance (used primarily by investors) calling for a reduced rate for a future policy if the property is sold within a specified period.

BIRD DOGGING — Obtaining the initial lead regarding property, buyers, investors, potential home improvement customers, etc. The lead is then followed up by one empowered to make the deal.

BIRTH RATE — The number of births in a given area during a given period of time, based on per thousand population.

BLACK ACRE — Fictitious name used by legal writers to describe a specific property without a more complete description.

BLACKTOP — A black paving surface composed of a coal or asphalt material.

BLANKET DEED OF TRUST — (See: Blanket Mortgage).

BLANKET MORTGAGE — (1) A mortgage covering more than one property of the mortgagor, such as a mortgage covering all the lots of a builder in a subdivision. (2) A mortgage covering all real property of the mortgagor, both present and future. When used in this meaning, it is also called a "general mortgage".

BLIGHTED AREA — A term once popular in urban renewal, referring to a run-down area.

BLIND AD — An ad (usually in a newspaper or magazine) which does not identify the party placing the ad. Often used in an ad for a job, asking that a resume be sent to a post office box.

BLIND CORNER — A corner where building or vegetation (trees, shrubs, etc.) extends to the property line and so obstructs the vision of motorists to right angle traffic.

BLIND NAILING — Nailing so that the nails are sunk into the wall and covered with putty so the nail heads do not show.

BLOCK — (1) In a city, a square or rectangular area enclosed by streets. (2) In some states, a part of a subdivision legal description, such as Lot 1, Block 1, Tract 1. (3) A pulley in a frame. (4) An auctioneer's platform.

BLOCK BUSTING — An illegal method of obtaining houses at below fair market value by telling the inhabitants that people of a different race or religion, moving into the area, will cause property values to fall.

BLUE LAWS — Actually, laws adopted in some New England colonies regarding religious and personal conduct. Later came to mean any laws regarding the conducting of business on Sunday. Do not confuse with Blue Sky Laws.

BLUEPRINT — A plan of a building in such detail as to enable workmen to construct it from the print. The name comes from the photographic process which produces the plan in white on a blue background.

BLUE SKY LAWS — Laws to regulate the sale of securities to avoid investment in fraudulent companies or high risk investments without disclosure of the risks to the investor.

BOARD — (1) A term which, in the lumber trade, refers to a piece of lumber less that 2 inches thick, and 8 or more inches wide. (2) A group of persons authorized by law to exercise management and control, either of a public function, such as a board of supervisors, board of health, etc., or a private corporation, as a board of directors.

BOARD AND BATTEN — A siding constructed of wide boards (usually one foot wide) placed $1/2$ inch apart; the seams are covered by 3 inch wide battens.

BOARDFOOT — A unit of measurement for lumber. One boardfoot equals 144 cubic inches or 12" × 12" × 1".

BOARDING HOUSE — A house where one can rent a room and receive board (meals), the cost of which is included in the rent. Not common today.

BOARD OF ALDERMEN — The governing body of a municipal corporation. Equivalent to a city council.

BOARD OF EQUALIZATION — State board charged with the duty to bring equitable uniformity to the various local property tax assessments.

BOILER PLATE — The form language (generally printed) which is contained in deeds, deeds of trust, CC&R's, and other documents and contracts. The specifics for each instance are then filled in.

BOILER PLATING — Using form language for a contract, CC&R's (restrictions), etc.

BOLE — A tree trunk.

BONA FIDE PURCHASER — A purchaser in good faith, for valuable consideration, without notice or knowledge of adverse claims of others. Sometimes abbreviated to B.F.P.

BOND — (1) An insurance agreement by which one is insured against loss by acts or defaults of a third party. In construction, a performance bond insures that the builder will finish his project. The insured could be a lender, purchaser, or other interested party. (2) A method of financing long term debt, issued by a government or private corporation, which bears interest and has priority over stock in terms of security.

BONUS CLAUSE — (See: "No Bonus" Clause).

BOOK COST — The actual cost as carried in the account ledger.

BOOK DEPRECIATION — Depreciation reserved (on the books) by an owner for future replacement or retirement of an asset.

BOOK VALUE — The value of a property as a capital asset (cost plus additions to value, less depreciation).

BOOM — (1) A barrier forming an enclosure for logs or timber. (2) A beam of a crane or derrick, used for guiding whatever it lifts.

BOOT — Something given in addition to. Generally used in exchange to refer to something given other than the major properties to be exchanged, in order to equalize value.

BORING TEST — Study of soil by boring holes and removing samples.

BOROUGH — A part of a city, having authority over certain local matters. The best known boroughs are the five boroughs of New York City.

BORROW — Material such as sand or gravel used for grading, which is brought from another location.

BORROW BANK — The place from which borrow material is taken.

BORROW PIT — The pit left after the removal of borrow material. The pit is sometimes filled as a lake and even stocked by some states for fishing.

BOTEL — A name given to a hotel or motel adjacent to a marina and catering to boat travelers.

BOTTOM LAND — Low land along a river formed by alluvial deposits. Also low lying ground such as a valley or dale.

BOULEVARD — A wide street, usually having a median or promenade, and lined with trees.

BOUNDARY — A separation, natural or artificial, which marks the division of two contiguous properties.

BOUNDS — Boundaries.

BRACED FRAMING — Framing reinforced with posts and braces, forming a frame more rigid than balloon framing.

BRADLEY FOUNTAIN — (See: Bradley Sink).

BRADLEY SINK — A circular lavatory, usually found in industrial buildings, capable of use by several persons at the same time by utilization of a center column containing multiple water jets operated by foot pedals. Also called a Bradley Fountain.

BREACH OF CONTRACT — Failure to perform a contract, in whole or part, without legal excuse.

BREACH OF COVENANT — The failure to do or to refrain from doing that which was covenanted. (See also: Covenant; Condition; Restriction).

BREACH OF WARRANTY — In real property, the failure of the seller to pass title as either expressed or implied (by law) in the conveyancing document. (See also: Warranty Deed; Grant Deed; Quitclaim Deed).

BREAK EVEN POINT — In income property, when there is neither a positive nor a negative cash flow.

BREAST-HEIGHT — The height at which the diameter of a tree is measured. A height of $4\frac{1}{2}$ feet above the ground level. The abbreviation D.B.H. (diameter-breast-height) is usually used.

BREATHER ROOF — A storage tank roof which rises and lowers depending on the level of the stored gas or liquid.

BREEZEWAY — (1) In construction of a house with no garage, a canopy which extends from the house over the driveway as a protection from the weather for an automobile and for those people going between the house and the automobile. (2) A covering over a porch or patio, connecting two sections of a house or a house and garage. Open on two sides, allowing air circulation (breeze).

BRICK — A building material made from clay, which is molded and heated. The effect of the heat on the iron in the clay gives a red color. Addition of lime or magnesia produces a yellow color.

BRIDGE — A structure over a waterway, highway, or other obstruction, to facilitate passage and for the benefit of travelers.

BRIDGE FINANCING — A form of interim loan, generally made between a short term loan and a permanent (long term) loan, when the borrower needs to have more time before taking the long term financing.

BRIDGING — Floor joist bracing, usually of wood or metal.

BRIDLE PATH (ROAD) — Technically a private road designated as a bridle road without specific use. More modernly, a road designated for equestrian use.

BRITISH THERMAL UNIT (B.T.U.) — Unit of heat required to raise one pound of water one degree Fahrenheit. Used to express the capacity of heating and cooling systems.

BROKERAGE — The act of bringing together principals (buyer-seller; landlord-tenant; etc.) for a fee or commission, rather than acting as a principal.

BROKERAGE COMMISSION — (See: Commission).

BROKER, REAL ESTATE — One who is licensed by the state to carry on the business of dealing in real estate. A broker may receive a commission for his or her part in bringing together a buyer and seller, landlord and tenant, or parties to an exchange.

BROOM CLEAN — A term used to describe the condition of a building, delivered to a buyer or tenant. As the term indicates, the floors are swept and free of debris.

BUCKED — A tree, cut into logs.

BUDGET — As the word is applied to condominiums and planned developments, the common expenses shared by the unit owners. This will determine the amount each unit will be charged (usually monthly) for expenses of the common area (taxes, insurance, maintenance, etc.).

BUFFER STRIP (BUFFER ZONE) — A parcel of land separating two other parcels or areas, such as a strip of land between an industrial and residential area.

BUILDER — One whose occupation is the construction of structures (buildings).

BUILDER BOND — (See: Performance Bond).

BUILDING — A structure built to shelter people, animals, or goods. May be a residence, business, or meeting place, such as a church.

BUILDING AND LOAN ASSOCIATION — An organization for the purpose of accumulating a fund by subscription and savings of its members, to assist them with loans for building or purchasing real estate.

BUILDING CODE — A comprehensive set of laws which control the construction of buildings, including design, materials used, construction, use, repair, remodeling, and other similar factors.

BUILDING CONTRACT — A contract setting forth the terms under which construction is to be undertaken. Price may be set, or based on the builder's cost plus a profit.

BUILDING LINE — A line beyond which there can be no construction. Set by law, the purpose of such a line is to keep buildings from being built too close to the street, both for safety and aesthetic reasons.

BUILDING PAPER — An insulation. A waterproof, heavy paper used in the construction of a roof or wall.

BUILDING PERMIT — A permit given by a local government to construct a building, or make improvements.

BUILDING RESIDUAL TECHNIQUE — An appraisal method by which building and land are appraised separately, based on potential income. Used to determine if the building is adequate for the land value.

BUILDING RESTRICTIONS — Prohibition by a governmental body (zoning restriction) or a private party (a former owner) against construction of certain structures on a property.

BUILD TO SUIT — A method of leasing property whereby the lessor builds to suit the tenant (according to the tenant's specifications). The cost of construction is figured into the rental amount of the lease, which is usually for a long term.

BUILT-IN'S — Commonly stoves, ovens, dishwashers, and other appliances, framed into the building construction and not movable.

BUILT-UP ROOF — A level roof composed of layers of roofing materials (tars and waterproof paper), covered with fine gravel.

BULKHEAD — (1) A partition in a ship. (2) A retaining wall to hold back water and thereby extend the shoreline.

BULKHEAD LINE — A line established in navigable waters beyond which no solid fill can be used. The Army Corps of Engineers establishes the bulkhead line and also the pier line, beyond which no pier can be constructed.

BULK SALE — A transfer in bulk, not in the ordinary course of business, of all or substantially all of the inventory and fixtures of a business.

BULK SALES ACT — Laws to protect creditors against secret sale of all or substantially all of a merchant's goods. Requires certain notice before sale, and sets forth methods of voiding improper sales. (See also: Uniform Commercial Code).

BULK ZONING — (See: Area Zoning).

BUS — A copper bar through which electrical current flows.

BUS DUCT — A metal clad enclosure containing a bus.

BUSINESS — Unqualified, the word has no definite meaning, but has come to be understood to be any activity by which people earn money.

BUSINESS CYCLE — The economic cycle of prosperity, followed by a decline, and then a return to prosperity.

BUSINESS OPPORTUNITY — The sale of a business (may or may not include the sale of real estate). Some states require a real estate license for these sales even when real estate is not involved. The Uniform Commercial Code, state statutes, and special laws for alcoholic beverage licenses (when applicable) should be studied by the business opportunities broker.

BUTTE — A steep hill, usually standing alone.

BUTTERFLY ROOF — A roof formed by two gable roofs concave to a center ridge. The roof resembles the shape of a butterfly's wings.

BUTT JOINT — The meeting end to end (butting) of two members to form a connection (joint).

BUTT LOG — The log immediately above the stump of a tree.

BUTTRESS — A support for a wall. A prop. If the buttress projects from the wall and supports by lateral pressure, it is called a "flying buttress".

BUTTS AND BOUNDS — (See: Metes and Bounds).

BUYDOWN — A payment to the lender from the seller, buyer, third party, or some combination of these, causing the lender to reduce the interest rate during the early years of a loan. The buydown is usually for the first 1 to 5 years of the loan. (See also: Certificate Backed Mortgage).

BUYER'S MARKET — A market condition favoring the buyer. In real estate, when more homes are for sale than there are interested buyers.

BUY-SELL OFFER — An offer by one owner of a business or real estate to buy out the interest of another owner of the same business or real estate (a partner or other shareholder), or to sell the offeror's interest at the same price or proportionate price if unequal ownership. Example: A and B each own a $1/2$ interest in lot 1. A offers to buy B's interest for $10,000, or to sell A's interest to B for $10,000. Theoretically very fair, since B has the option to buy or sell. However, B's interest may be worth $12,000, but B is financially unable to buy A's interest (also worth $12,000).

BX CABLE — The main conduits coming into a home. Electrical wiring run through metal conduits.

BY-LAWS — Rules and regulations, adopted by an association or corporation, which govern its activities.

BY-PASS — A road designed to avoid or pass by a high density area, such as a business section of a city, in order to ease traffic congestion. Also called a belt highway.

C

CABINET WORK — Any interior carpentry which will be seen and must be finished with skill and care. One who does this work is called a cabinet maker or, more commonly, a finish carpenter.

C.A.E. (CERTIFIED ASSESSMENT EVALUATOR) — An assessor who, through the completion of required courses, experience, and examinations, has earned this designation by the International Association of Assessing Officers.

CAISSON — A watertight chamber in which men work underwater, or in an open excavation where loose soil or sand could cave in on the workers. It may also be filled with concrete after it is used, and become a support.

CALIFORNIA RANCH ARCHITECTURE — A sprawling, one story, ranch-style building, lending itself to interior flexibility in floor plan design.

CALL — In a metes and bounds description, the angle and distance of a given line or arc. Each call is usually preceeded by the word then or thence. Example: N 22° E 100' (1st. call), thence N 80° E 100' (2nd. call).

CAL-VET LOANS — Real estate loans available to armed forces veterans from California, at low interest rates.

CAMBER — A slight bending or arching to a convex angle. Used to prevent beams, girders, flooring, ship decks, timbers, and similar load-bearing members, from taking a concave shape.

CAMINO — A Spanish word meaning highway.

CAMPANILE — A free standing bell tower.

CANAL — (1) A man made waterway used to connect bodies of water for navigation. (2) An irrigation waterway.

CANCELLATION CLAUSE — A clause in a lease or other contract, setting forth the conditions under which each party may cancel or terminate the agreement. The conditions may be as simple as giving notice or complex and require payment by the party desiring to cancel.

CANDLE — A measure of light, being the luminous intensity of a $\frac{7}{8}$ inch sperm candle burning at 120 grains per hour. An international candle is based on the burning of platinum.

CANDLE HOUR — A measure of light, equal to one candle burning for one hour.

CANDLE POWER — The intensity of a light, expressed in candles.

CANTILEVER — A structural support which itself is supported at one end only and bears its load through its material strength and rigidity.

CANTILEVER BRIDGE — A bridge formed by two cantilevered members extending toward each other and connecting each other or a suspended span.

CAP — (1) A fitting used by a plumber to seal (cap) a pipe end. (2) A cornice, lintel, or top of a structural member such as a column.

CAPACITY — One's ability to carry on normal business transactions. Lack of capacity may be natural (unsound mind) or simply by law (a minor). Restrictions may be full or partial.

CAPE COD HOUSE — An adaptation of the New England cottage. May be one or two stories with sloping roof, usually with dormer windows, cornices, and of frame painted white.

CAPITA — Literally, heads. Commonly, persons individually. (See also: Per Capita).

CAPITAL — Money used to create income, either as investment in a business or income property.

CAPITAL ASSETS — Assets of a permanent nature used to produce income, such as machinery, buildings, equipment, land, etc. Must be distinguished from inventory. A machine which makes pencils, for example, would be a capital asset to a pencil manufacturer, but inventory to the company whose business is to sell such machines.

CAPITAL EXPENDITURES — Money spent on improvements such as land, buildings, machinery, and similar major expenditures which are not inventory.

CAPITAL GAINS — Gains realized from the sale of capital assets. Generally, the difference between cost and selling price, less certain deductible expenses. Used mainly for income tax purposes.

CAPITALIZATION — Determining a present value of income property by taking the annual net income (either known or estimated) and discounting by using a rate of return commonly acceptable to buyers of similar properties. For example: Net income of a property is $10,000 per year. Capitalizing at a rate of 10%, the property would be worth $100,000.

CAPITALIZATION APPROACH — (See: Income Approach).

CAPITALIZATION RATE — The percentage (acceptable to an average buyer) used to determine the value of income property through capitalization.

CAPITALIZE — To determine the present money value of future income, whether estimated or fixed.

CAPITALIZED VALUE — The value of the property after use of the capitalization approach of appraisal.

CAPITAL STOCK — A general term referring to the stock a corporation may issue, the amount actually subscribed by shareholders, the value of the company, liability to the shareholders, etc.

CAP RATE (APPRAISAL) — (See: Capitalization Rate).

CAPRICIOUS VALUE — In appraisal, a value based on whim or emotion and not reflective of the fair market value.

CAR — California Association of Realtors.

CARAVAN — An inspection of newly listed properties, either by the entire sales staff of an office or by sales personnel from more than one office in conjunction with a multiple listing group. Generally conducted on a regular basis.

CAR FLOAT BRIDGE — The connection (bridge) used to transfer railroad cars to or from land and a barge. The bridge must be vertically mobil to adjust to changing water levels.

CARPORT — A roof supported by pillars or cantilevered which shelters a car. May either extend from a structure (usually a house) or be constructed separately (often to accommodate several cars).

CARRYING CHARGES — The costs involved in keeping a property which is intended to produce income (either by sale or rent) but has not yet done so.

CASE — (1) An external framework of a structure. (2) A court action.

CASE LAW — (See: Common Law).

CASEMENT WINDOW — A window hinged at its sides, allowing it to swing open vertically.

CASH — Money or its equivalent (checks, bank notes, etc.). Ready money.

CASH ACCOUNTING — (See: Accrual Accounting).

CASH ASSETS — Money which is available to meet the requirements of operating a business.

CASH DISCOUNT — A discount from a billed amount if paid within a certain period.

CASH FLOW — In investment property, the actual cash the investor will receive after deduction of operating expenses and debt service (loan payment) from his gross income.

CASHIER'S CHECK — A check drawn by a bank on itself rather than on an account of a depositor. A cashier's check is generally acceptable to close a sale without waiting for the check to clear.

CASH ON HAND STATEMENT — A statement of cash on hand which the buyer intends to apply to closing costs, impounds, and down payment. Also shows the source of the money (savings, gift, etc.).

CASH OUT — To take the entire amount of a seller's equity in cash rather than to retain some interest in the property, such as a purchase money mortgage or deed of trust. Also loosely used when paying off anyone having an interest in property, thereby ending the interest.

CASH RENT — A term used in farm rental to distinguish between money rent and rent paid by giving a portion of the crop to the owner (share crop).

CASH SALE — A sale for full payment in cash, as opposed to a credit sale. A payment by check is considered cash. May be qualified, as "cash to new loan", "cash to existing loan", etc.

CASING — The exterior surface or covering of a building such as aluminum siding, a roof, etc.

CATTLE GUARD — A grill or grating placed in the ground over which cattle will not cross.

CATWALK — A narrow, elevated walkway along a wall, girders, or over a stage or other area where it may be necessary for a person to go for operation or repair.

CAUSEWAY — A raised roadbed over lowlands. (See also: Levee).

CAVEAT EMPTOR — "Let the buyer beware". Legal maxim stating that the buyer takes the risk regarding quality or condition of the item purchased, unless protected by warranty or there is misrepresentation. Modernly, consumer protection laws have placed more responsibility for disclosure on the seller and broker.

CAVITY WALL — Refers to a brick or stone wall which is actually built as two separate walls, joined only at the top and ends, and so "hollow". Also called a hollow wall.

CC&R'S (COVENANTS, CONDITIONS, AND RESTRICTIONS) — A term used in some areas to describe the restrictive limitations which may be placed on property. In other areas, simply called restrictions.

CELLAR — A storage room or group of rooms, usually under a building, which are used for storage.

CEMENT — A mineral powder which, when mixed with water and allowed to set will dry hard and can be used in construction as floors, walls, etc.

CEMENT BLOCK — A building block, composed of cement, and usually hollow. (See also: Cinder Block).

CEMETERY — Large parcels of land used for burying deceased persons. May be public or private, the private usually being of a specific religious denomination.

CENTRAL ASSESSMENT — An assessment of property under one ownership but located in more than one assessment district. Used for railroads and public utilities to stabilize the assessment value.

CENTRAL BUSINESS DISTRICT — An area of a city where most of the major businesses are located. The "downtown" area.

CENTRAL CITY — (1) The downtown area of a major city. (2) A city which is central to a metropolitan area containing many cities. The name of the central city is used for the whole area. For example: Los Angeles metropolitan area.

CERTIFICATE — A writing, either from a court or other public body, giving assurances of existing conditions or facts, and giving rights or creating obligations.

CERTIFICATE BACKED MORTGAGE — A variation of the buydown. The seller purchases a savings certificate (usually with the proceeds of the sale) from the lender. The lender sets the buyer's interest rate below market (generally 2 percent above the certificate rate). Should the seller withdraw the certificate funds, the buyer's rate goes to market rate.

CERTIFICATE OF DEPOSIT (C.D.) — A specific sum of money deposited into a savings institution for a specified time period, and bearing a higher rate of interest than a passbook account if left to maturity. Does not have withdrawal privileges as does a passbook account. Also called a time certificate of deposit (T.C.D.).

CERTIFICATE OF ELIGIBILITY — A certificate obtained by a veteran from a Veteran's Administration office which states that the veteran is eligible for a V.A. insured loan. There is a list of requirements (when and how long the veteran served, type of discharge, etc.) which also may be obtained from the V.A. office.

CERTIFICATE OF OCCUPANCY — A certificate issued by a local building department to a builder or renovator, stating that the building is in proper condition to be occupied.

CERTIFICATE OF PURCHASE — (See: Certificate of Sale).

CERTIFICATE OF REDEMPTION — Evidence of redeeming (buying back) a property by the owner after losing it through a judicial sale. The time limit for redemption is set by statute.

CERTIFICATE OF SALE — Certificate issued to the buyer at a judicial sale (such as a tax sale), which will entitle the buyer to a deed upon confirmation of the sale by the court or if the land is not redeemed within a specified time.

CERTIFICATE OF TITLE — In areas where attorneys examine abstracts or chains of title, a written opinion, executed by the examining attorney, stating that title is vested as stated in the abstract.

CERTIFIED CHECK — A personal check drawn by an individual which is certified (guaranteed) to be good. The bank holds the funds to pay the certified check and will not pay any other checks drawn on the account if such payment would impede payment of the certified check. The bank also will not honor a stop payment of a certified check.

CERTIFIED COPY — A true copy, attested to be true by the officer holding the original.

CERTIORARI — An appellate review of the complete record of a lower court action, rather then simply a review of an appeal for judicial error.

CESSPOOL — A pit or pool which holds raw sewage.

CESTUI QUE TRUST — One having an equitable interest in property, legal title being vested in a trustee.

CESTUI QUE VIE — The person whose life is used to determine the length of an estate based on a life in being.

CHAIN OF TITLE — The chronological order of conveyancing of a parcel of land, from the original owner (usually the government) to the present owner.

CHAINS AND LINKS — Measurements. In real estate measurements (surveying) a chain is 66' long or 100 links, each link being 7.92". The measurement may change when used in fields other than surveying.

CHAIN STORE — A store belonging to a series of similar stores under central ownership and management, and striving for uniformity in design, inventory, and service.

CHANGE OF NAME — When there is a name change of a party appearing on a document (deed, etc.), it may be reflected in several ways, such as: (1)Mary Smith, a married woman, W.A.T.A. (who acquired title as) Mary Jones, an unmarried woman. (2) Mary Smith, AKA (also known as) Mary Jones. (3) Mary Smith, formerly Mary Jones. (4) Mary Smith, alias Mary Jones. Each may be applicable in different circumstances (how and why the name was changed).

CHANNEL — (1) An open or closed duct or conduit. (2) A gutter, furrow, or groove. (3) The deepest part of a natural waterway through which the main current flows, and which affords the best passageway for ships.

CHANNELIZATION — The term used to describe traffic direction. Traffic is "channeled" by use of one way streets, signs directing turns, island barriers, etc.

CHAPEL — (1) A place of worship apart from a church, such as a hospital chapel, college chapel, etc. Generally for a small group. (2) A portion of a church secondary and subordinate to the main altar.

CHATTEL — Personal property.

CHATTEL MORTGAGE — A lien on personal property. Also called a security interest or financing statement.

CHATTEL REAL — All estates in real property less than fee estates, such as a lease.

CHECK ROW — A method of planting rows of plants on intersecting lines, forming a "checkerboard" effect. Used for corn, tomatoes, and other vegetables.

CHECK VALVE — A valve to prevent backup of material being carried through a pipe or other conduit.

CHILD CARE STATEMENT — A statement by a working husband and wife showing the amount paid for child care and to whom paid.

CHIMNEY — Any passage through which smoke from a fire passes. Most commonly the passage, constructed of brick, from a fireplace to above the roof of a building.

CHIMNEY BACK — The back wall or lining of a fireplace or furnace chimney.

C HORIZON — The horizon (layer) of the Earth below the A and B horizons. Called the substratum, it is usually not affected by rain, change of temperature, or other surface conditions.

CHOSE IN ACTION — A right to an action for recovery of a debt or to possession of anything held by another. The right to possession rather than possession.

CHOSE IN POSSESSION — Something in possession, rather than the right to possession.

CHURCH — A public place of worship, usually Christian worship. (See also: Synagogue; Temple).

CIENAGA — A Spanish word meaning a swamp or marsh, formed by hillside springs.

CINDER BLOCK — A building block composed of cinders (ashes) and cement, which does not have the weight or strength of a cement block.

CIRCLEHEAD WINDOW — A semicircular window, usually above a door, which has no moving parts and is used as a decoration as well as to admit light.

CIRCUIT BREAKER — An electrical device which has taken the place of the fuse in most homes. The circuit is broken (electricity shut-off) when there is an overload. The circuit breaker can be reset rather than replaced as a fuse must be.

CIRCULATION PATTERN — The regular traffic pattern, as from a residential area to a business district and back.

CIRCUMFERENTIAL HIGHWAY — A highway which arcs around the central business district of a city. Also called a belt highway or by-pass.

CISTERN — A tank used for storing rain water for use in areas where there is no water brought to the property by plumbing.

CITY — Technically, a municipal corporation having voting by representatives to operate its functions, rather than direct voting, as in a town. Commonly, any large incorporated town is called a city.

CITY PLAN — (See: Master Plan).

CIVIL ACTION — Any action which is not a criminal action.

CIVIL LAW — (1) Roman Law. The legal system derived from the Romans which is prevalent in most of the non-English speaking countries, and, to some degree, in Louisiana. Differs from Common Law of England, from which United States Law is derived. (2) Any laws which are not criminal laws.

CLAIM — An assertion of some right or demand.

CLAPBOARD — Narrow boards used as siding for frame houses, and having one edge thicker than the other. The boards run horizontally with the thicker edge overlapping the thinner edge.

CLARIFIER — Underground system of tanks with filters or chemical agents designed to remove or neutralize harmful wastes from water before emptying said water into a sewer or septic tank.

CLASS ACTION — An action brought on behalf of a group of people having a similar claim. Has become increasingly popular in the consumer movement, and is a strong weapon against unfair pricing when the price of overcharging in one instance would be too minor to bring suit.

CLASSIFIED PROPERTY TAX — Property tax which varies in rate depending on the use (zoning classification) of the property.

CLEAN ROOM — A room specially designed to have a controlled atmosphere, for health reasons or experimentation accuracy, such as a germ free room or a dust free room.

CLEARANCE — (1) The removal of structures from an area for urban renewal. (2) The maximum height of a vehicle which may safely pass under a bridge or through a tunnel.

CLEAR HEADWAY — The height of the lowest overhead framing member (usually the top of a door frame) as measured from the floor.

CLEAR LUMBER — High quality lumber "clear" of most defects, particularly knots.

CLEAR SPAN — An interior area which does not use columns or posts to hold up the roof, thereby creating a large, open area with maximum visibility and use of the floor space.

CLEAR TITLE — (See: Free and Clear).

CLERESTORY — A wall or portion of a wall to which the roof attaches at a higher level than the other walls or portions of a wall of a building. Generally found in church construction and contains windows.

CLERESTORY WINDOW — Window in a clerestory.

CLIENT — Traditionally one who employs an attorney. Has loosely been used to refer to the principal of a real estate agent, insurance agent, stock broker, etc.

CLOSING — (1) In real estate sales, the final procedure in which documents are executed and/or recorded, and the sale (or loan) is completed. (2) A selling term meaning the point at which the client or customer is asked to agree to the sale or purchase and sign the contract. (3) The final call in a metes and bounds legal description which "closes" the boundaries of the property.

CLOSING COSTS — Expenses incidental to a sale of real estate, such as loan fees, title fees, appraisal fees, etc.

CLOSING STATEMENT — The statement which lists the financial settlement between buyer and seller, and also the costs each must pay. A separate statement for buyer and seller is sometimes prepared.

CLOUD — (See: Cloud on Title).

CLOUD ON TITLE — An invalid encumbrance on real property, which, if valid, would affect the rights of the owner. For example: A sells lot 1, tract 1, to B. The deed is mistakenly drawn to read lot 2, tract 1. A cloud is created on lot 2 by the recording of the erroneous deed. The cloud may be removed by quitclaim deed, or, if necessary, by court action.

CLOVERLEAF — An intersection using loop shaped ramps and grade separation to accomplish the intersecting of traffic without signal lights or stop signs. When viewed from above, the shape of the intersection resembles a cloverleaf.

CLOVERLEAFING — A method of real estate canvassing by looping around a specific property (one listed or sold) in the shape of a cloverleaf, in order to obtain listings or buyers.

CLUSTER HOUSING — Building houses close together with little yard space and a large common area, rather than each house having a large yard. The density is usually greater in the cluster project.

CO-ADMINISTRATOR — One who shares the duties of administrator with one or more other administrators.

COAST — The seashore or land near it.

COASTAL COMMISSION — A commission set up to control construction in coastal areas.

CODE — A comprehensive set of laws drawn up to cover completely a given subject. Covers diverse subjects, such as the criminal code, and the building code.

CODE OF ETHICS — (See: Ethics).

CODICIL — An addition to a will, which modifies the will by adding to it, subtracting from it, or clarifying it.

CO-EXECUTOR — One who shares the duties of executor with one or more other executors.

COFFERDAM — (See: Caisson).

COINSURANCE — A sharing of the risk of an insurance policy by more than one insurer. Usually one insurer is liable up to a certain amount; the other liable over that amount.

COLD CANVASS — Soliciting door to door without any previous contact, such as a phone canvass. A good method for a salesperson to begin to establish a farm area. [See: Farm (3)].

COLLAPSIBLE CORPORATION — A corporation which is sold instead of its product, in order to create a capital gain rather than ordinary income for tax purposes. For example: A and B (persons) are real estate developers who want to build an office building to sell. They form a corporation which builds the building. Then, rather than selling the building, A and B sell the corporation, claiming capital gain on the stock profit. Federal tax laws regulate such transactions.

COLLAR TIE — (See: Tie Beam).

COLLATERAL — By or at the side, additional or auxiliary. Mistakenly used to mean collateral security.

COLLATERAL ASSIGNMENT — An assignment of property as collateral security, and not with the intent to transfer ownership from assignor to assignee.

COLLATERAL SECURITY — Most commonly used to mean some security in addition to the personal obligation of the borrower.

COLLUSION — An agreement of two or more people to do something unlawful. Generally, an agreement between people who represent different interests and "sell out" these interests for personal gain.

COLONIAL ARCHITECTURE — Two story houses with windows divided into small panes, usually with shutters. The main facade is detailed and symmetrical, generally with a center entrance. Architecture following the style of New England colonial houses.

COLONNADE — Columns, regularly spaced, which support an architrave. (See also: Peristyle; Portico).

COLOR OF TITLE — That which gives the appearance of good title, but actually contains some defect. For example: A conveyance given without the grantor having good title.

COLUMN — A large vertical support member of a structure. A pillar, usually cylindrical.

COLUMN FOOTINGS — The support bases for load-bearing columns. Generally composed of reinforced concrete.

COLUMN LOTS — Small lots for the placement of columns to support a structure, such as a billboard or other structure which has its largest parts not touching the ground.

COLUMN STEEL — Steel used inside of a column for reinforcement.

CO-MAKER — A surety (see which) under a loan. The co-maker is equally responsible for repayment as the borrower (maker).

COMBED PLYWOOD — An interior paneling, grooved as if by a comb.

COMBINATION DOOR — An outer door using interchangeable panels of glass and screen, depending on the weather.

COMBINATION SEWER — A sewer that is both a sanitary and storm sewer.

COMBINATION WINDOW — A window using interchangeable panels of glass and screen, depending on the weather.

COMMENSURATE PROPERTY — (See: Base Property).

COMMERCIAL ACRE — (See: Net Acre).

COMMERCIAL BANK — An institution for savings, loans, checking accounts, and other services not all of which are found in savings and loan institutions. Banks are generally more active in construction loans rather than long term real estate financing.

COMMERCIAL PAPER — Negotiable instruments used in the course of business, such as promissory notes, which are bought and sold (usually at a discount).

COMMERCIAL PROPERTY — Property which is zoned "commercial" (for business use). Property such as stores, restaurants, etc., falling between residential and industrial.

COMMINGLING — To mix funds held in trust with other funds. For example: A broker or builder mixes deposits (should be in a trust account) with his funds by putting the deposits in his general account. Although commingling is in itself a violation for which a broker may lose his license, it does not mean that, by commingling, the broker or builder intended to misappropriate the funds. [See also: Conversion (2)].

COMMISSION — An amount, usually as a percentage, paid to an agent (real estate broker) as compensaton for his services. The amount to a real estate broker is generally a percentage of the sale price or total rental.

COMMITMENT — (1) Title insurance term for the preliminary report issued before the actual policy. Said report shows the condition of title and the steps necessary to complete the transfer of title as contemplated by buyer and seller. (2) A written promise to make or insure a loan for a specified amount and on specified terms.

COMMON AREA — The area owned in common by the owners of condominiums or planned unit development homes in a subdivision.

COMMON BRICK — A brick having no special surface treatment, making each brick different in color. Used to describe a surface of bricks which are artificially treated so that each is different in color.

COMMON LAW — The body of laws, originated and developed in England, which was adopted by most states and still prevails if not superseded by statute. Also referred to as case law.

COMMON LAW MORTGAGE — Any mortgage which contains the elements of a mortgage according to the Common Law.

COMMON OF ESTOVERS — (See: Estovers).

COMMON STOCK — A share of ownership in a corporation.

COMMON WALL — (See: Party Wall).

COMMUNITY PROPERTY — Property owned in common by a husband and wife, which was not acquired as separate property. A classification of property peculiar to certain states.

COMMUNITY SHOPPING CENTER — An intermediate size shopping center. May contain a small department store and coordinated small shops. Larger than a neighborhood center and smaller than a regional center.

COMPACTION — The pressing together and joining of sedimentary layers of ground by the pressure of the weight of overlying layers. A report showing the density of the soil and its make-up is required in some areas before permits for construction will be issued.

COMPARABLES — Properties used as comparisons to determine the value of a specific property.

COMPARATIVE ANALYSIS — (See: Market Value Approach).

COMPARATIVE METHOD — A method of estimating replacement construction cost by comparing the property to be built with the cost per square foot or cost per cubic foot of a similar building.

COMPARISON METHOD — (See: Market Value Approach).

COMPENSATING BALANCE — Funds deposited into a bank, saving and loan association, or other lending institution, to induce the lender to make a specific loan or establish a line of credit. The deposit may be made by the party desiring the loan, or a third party.

COMPENSATION — A payment to make amends for the abridgement of rights or an injury. In condemnation, the payment for the taking of a person's property without the owner's consent.

COMPENSATORY DAMAGES —. Damages to cover a loss or injury and nothing more. (See also: Exemplary Damages).

COMPETENT — Legally fit. Having the necessary age, ability, and authority to accomplish any given acts or duties.

COMPONENT CONSTRUCTION — Also called modular construction or prefabrication. (See also: Prefabrication).

COMPONENT PANEL — A modular (prefabricated) wall, fully finished, which is installed as a part of a building.

COMPOSITE RATE — A rate reflecting both the income flow of a building (or other depreciating asset) and the recapture of invested capital.

COMPOSITION — (1) A mixture of gravel or stones embedded in a heavy tar roof shingle, and called a "composition" roof. (2) A creditor's composition, (see which).

COMPOUND AMOUNT OF AN ANNUITY — The total amount at the end of a given period, including investment and reinvestment of the annuity payments.

COMPOUND AMOUNT OF AN INVESTED SUM — The total amount at the end of a given period, including the reinvestment of all interest plus the original amount invested.

COMPOUND INTEREST — Interest paid on accumulated interest as well as on the principal.

COMPOUND SLOPE — A slope composed of two or more separate slopes with different grade angles.

COMPREHENSIVE COMMUNITY PLAN — (See: Master Plan).

COMPUTER LISTING — A system of processing listings through a computer so that anyone belonging to the service may learn of the listing through a telephone call directly into the computer. The listings are coded by area, number of bedrooms, and other features of the property. The largest of these services is Realtron of Detroit, Michigan, which operates throughout the country.

CONCAVE — Having an angle or curvature less than 180 degrees.

CONCEALED HEATING — (See: Radiant Heating).

CONCESSION — A granting of a right, by government or privately, usually to use of land or area in a building to carry on a business.

CONCRETE — A cement mixture containing sand and gravel which is combined by mixing with water, poured to a desired shape, and hardens as it dries. (See also: Poststressed Concrete; Prestressed Concrete; Reinforced Concrete).

CONCRETE (PLAIN) — A concrete which has not been prestressed, poststressed, or reinforced in any way except possibly to hinder shrinkage or expansion caused by temperature changes.

CONCRETE CONSTRUCTION — (See: Architectural Concrete Construction; Reinforced Concrete Construction).

CONCRETE TILT-UP — An inexpensive method of constructing walls by pouring concrete into forms flat on the ground, allowing to harden, then raising the forms by a crane or block and tackle to a vertical position, thereby forming the wall.

CONCRETION — A mineral mixture which forms, generally in rock of a different composition, various size grains or modules.

CONDEMNATION — The taking of private property for public use without the consent of the owner, but only upon payment of just compensation.

CONDEMNATION VALUE — Market value paid upon condemnation.

CONDEMNEE — The owner of property taken by condemnation (eminent domain).

CONDEMNER — The party taking property by condemnation (eminent domain).

CONDENSATION — The forming of water on a barrier from warm air meeting cooler air, as in air conditioning units.

CONDENSATION DUCT — A duct which carries away the water given off by condensation from an air conditioning unit.

CONDITION — In real property law, some limiting restriction to a grant or conveyance of property, stating that upon the happening or not happening of a stated event, the estate shall be changed in some manner.

CONDITIONAL COMMITMENT — A loan commitment given before a borrower (buyer) is obtained, and subject to approval of the buyer by the lender.

CONDITIONAL SALE OF REAL PROPERTY — (See: Land Contract).

CONDITIONAL SALES CONTRACT — A sale in which the title to property or goods remains with the seller until the purchaser has fulfilled the terms of the contract, usually payment in full. (See also: Land Contract).

CONDITION PRECEDENT — A condition to be performed before an agreement becomes effective or some right vests or accrues.

CONDITION SUBSEQUENT — A condition following an agreement, the happening of which changes the estate.

CONDOMINIUM — A structure of two or more units, the interior space of which are individually owned; the balance of the property (both land and building) is owned in common by the owners of the individual units. The size of each unit is measured from the interior surfaces (exclusive of paint or other finishes) of the exterior walls, floors, and ceiling. The balance of the property is called the common area.

CONDOMINIUM MAP (PLAN) — A recorded map showing the condominium units and common area. The map includes both horizontal and vertical measurements of the units. It is important that the map agree with the declaration of restrictions (recorded at the same time).

CONDOMINIUM OWNER'S ASSOCIATION — [See: Home Owner's Association (2)].

CONDUCTION — Transmission of electricity or heat through a conductor.

CONDUCTOR — A material (usually metal) which can transmit electrical current or heat.

CONDUIT — A natural channel for the flow of water, or artificial channel, such as a pipe, used for conveying and protecting water, wires, or other materials.

CONDUIT, ELECTRICAL — A metal pipe, usually flexible, through which electrical wiring is installed.

CONDUIT SYSTEM — A system of metal casings (conduits) containing wiring and conductors.

CONFESSION OF JUDGMENT — The written, voluntary, submission of a debtor to a judgment by a creditor for a specified amount.

CONFIGURATION — Outline of a shape.

CONFIRMATION DEED — (See: Rerecording).

CONFIRMATION OF SALE — (See: Order Confirming Sale).

CONFORMITY, PRINCIPLE OF — An appraisal term stating that general uniformity of structures in an area produces highest value.

CONGRUOUS — Suitable or appropriate. In appraisal, a property which conforms to the area.

CONSANGUINITY — Blood relationship, rather than legal relationship (through marriage). (See also: Affinity).

CONSENT JUDGMENT — A written agreement between plaintiff and defendant to have a judgment entered and recorded. Although the court does no actual finding for one party or the other, the judgment, once approved by the court, is binding on both parties.

CONSEQUENTIAL DAMAGES — Damages created by a change in other property. An owner's right to compensation varies with state statutes. (See also: Lateral Support: Inverse Condemnation).

CONSERVATION — (1) Care and preservation of natural resources. (2) Preservation, through zoning, of improved areas to maintain the quality of the area.

CONSERVATOR — A guardian, court appointed.

CONSIDERATION — Anything which is, legally, of value, and induces one to enter into a contract.

CONSOLIDATION — (1) The coming together, either through merger or partial ownership, of two or more companies. (2) The solidification of loose material or liquid, usually under pressure.

CONSTANT — (See: Loan Constant).

CONSTRUCTION COST — The total cost of building, including overhead and profits as well as land, labor, and materials.

CONSTRUCTION LOAN — Short term financing of real estate construction. Generally followed by long term financing called a "take out" loan, issued upon completion of improvements.

CONSTRUCTIVE EVICTION — (1) Regarding a landlord and tenant relationship, constructive eviction is any act by the landlord which substantially interferes with the tenant's use and enjoyment of the leased property, but is not actual eviction. (2) The inability of the buyer to obtain possession because of a superior title of a third party. This constitutes a breach of the covenant of quiet enjoyment warranted by the seller.

CONSTRUCTIVE MORTGAGE — (See: Equitable Mortgage).

CONSTRUCTIVE NOTICE — Notice given by publishing in a newspaper, recording, or other method which legally notifies the parties involved, but may not actually notify them.

CONSTRUCTIVE TRUST — A trust created by operation of law to change an inequitable situation. If one acquires title to property through fraud, the court will hold that the legal owner holds in trust for those who really should have ownership. Also called an involuntary trust.

CONSUMER LENDING — Loans made for personal property, such as automobiles, appliances, etc.

CONTEMPORARY ARCHITECTURE — A general term encompassing any number of modern designs which do not conform to any traditional architectural styles.

CONTIGUOUS — Near or close to, whether actually touching or not. Generally refers to actual touching or bordering on.

CONTINGENCY — Commonly, the dependence upon a stated event which must occur before a contract is binding. For example: The sale of a house, contingent upon the buyer obtaining financing.

CONTINGENT BENEFICIARY — One who, under the terms of a will or trust, may or may not share in the estate upon the happening of an uncertain event. Example: A leaves property to B when B reaches 30, stipulating that if B dies before 30, property goes to C. C is the contingent beneficiary.

CONTINGENT FEES — Fees to be paid only in the event of a future occurrence. A broker's commission is paid only if the property is sold or leased (unless otherwise agreed upon). Attorneys (especially in negligence cases) may be paid based on winning the suit and collecting damages.

CONTINGENT INTEREST — An interest subject to the occurrence of a specified but uncertain event.

CONTOUR FURROWS — Furrows plowed laterally across a slope to control water running down the slope.

CONTOUR LINE — (1) A line showing the shape (outline) of a parcel of land or body of water. (2) A line on a topographical map connecting all portions of the property which have the same elevation.

CONTOUR MAP — A map which uses lines (most always curved) to outline the configuration and elevation of surface areas.

CONTRACT — An agreement between two or more persons or entities which creates or modifies a legal relationship. Generally based upon offer and acceptance.

CONTRACT OF SALE — In some areas of the country, synonymous with land contract. In other areas synonymous with purchase agreement.

CONTRACTOR — (See: General Contractor; Subcontractor).

CONTRACTOR'S OVERHEAD — Expenses over and above labor and materials, such as return on money invested, carrying costs of land, office expense, interest on loans, etc.

CONTRACTOR'S PROFIT — Price at which property is sold, less costs of land, labor and materials, and overhead.

CONTRACT RENT — Rent paid under a lease. The actual rent as opposed to the market rental value of the property.

CONTRACTUAL LIEN — A voluntary lien such as a mortgage or deed of trust.

CONTRIBUTION — The right of one who pays a common liability to recover all but his or her share from the others who are liable. For example: A, B, and C own a property. A pays the taxes. A may recover that portion from B and C which B and C should have paid.

CONTROL — Referring to traffic, the term is used to indicate a traffic light or stop sign at an intersection, which slows (controls) traffic. A retail site, such as a gas station or fast food restaurant, prefers a corner location with control.

CONTROLLED ACCESS HIGHWAY — (See: Limited Access Highway).

CONTROLS — In government projects such as urban renewal, the limits on use, density, and other limits which would be contained in zoning laws in a private venture.

CONVECTION — In heating, the motion created by the gravitational pull on air or water at different temperatures, and therefore, different densities.

CONVENTIONAL LOAN — A mortgage or deed of trust not obtained under a government insured program, (such as F. H. A. or V. A.).

CONVENTIONAL MORTGAGE — (See: Conventional Loan).

CONVERSION — (1) A legal term referring to the "legal" changing from real to personal property (or vice versa), although there is no actual change in the property. (2) A taking of something for one's own use which was originally in his possession only to hold for the owner. (3) The changing of an apartment to a condominium.

CONVEX — Having an angle or curvature greater than 180 degrees.

CONVEYANCE — Transfer of title to land. Includes most instruments by which an interest in real estate is created, mortgaged, or assigned.

CONVEYANCE TAX — (See: Transfer Tax).

COOP — A structure to shelter chickens.

COOPERATING BROKER — The broker who finds the buyer and so shares in the commission with the listing broker.

COOPERATIVE APARTMENT — Also called a stock cooperative or a co-op. A structure of two or more units in which the right to occupy a unit is obtained by the purchase of stock in the corporation which owns the building. Difficult to obtain financing because there is not individual ownership of each unit. A forerunner of the condominium.

CO-ORDINATES — A general term encompassing a number of methods to determine the position of intersecting lines, planes, points, etc.

COPING — The top or "cap" of a wall, usually convex to permit the run-off of water.

CORBEL — A timber or stone, set in and projecting from a wall, and used to support a load.

CORD — A measure, usually associated with cut wood. 128 cubic feet of cut wood, or a pile 4' high, 4' wide, and 8' long.

CORNER — Most commonly, the acute angle formed by intersecting streets or walls.

CORNER BEAD — A reinforcement placed in corners before plastering. Commonly a strip of iron with metal lath.

CORNER BOARDS — The boards (trim) covering the outside corners of a frame building.

CORNER BRACES — Braces nailed diagonally to the studs as a reinforcement at corners.

CORNER INFLUENCE — In appraisal, the effect on the value of a property because it is on a corner or near a corner.

CORNER LOT — A lot contiguous to two intersecting streets, and, for purposes of value, having access to both streets.

CORNICE — The "crowning" member of a wall. The top molding or facade, generally of a decorative nature.

CORPORATE RESOLUTION — An action taken by vote of the directors of a corporation. A title insurance company may require a corporate resolution before insuring a sale or loan made by a corporation.

CORPORATION — A general term encompassing any group of people "incorporating" by following certain statutory procedures. Most common type of corporation is a private one formed to carry on a business.

CORPOREAL — Concerning material objects or property, rather than non-material things, such as ideas. A machine would be corporeal; the patent for it would be incorporeal.

CORPOREAL PROPERTY — That property which can be touched. For example: A window (glass) is corporeal. The view through the window is incorporeal.

CORPUS — A body; of people, laws, etc.

CORRECTION DEED — (See: Rerecording).

CORRECTION LINES — (See: Standard Parallels).

CORRELATION — The use of different appraisal methods to reach an estimate of value of a property. The methods must be weighed as to relative value in each specific appraisal.

CO-SIGNATORY — (See: Co-maker).

COST — Technically, the original amount paid for anything. The term is generally used as a synonym for value or the total amount invested, including expenses after the original purchase.

COST APPROACH — An appraisal method, estimating the replacement cost of a structure, less depreciation, plus land value.

COST ESTIMATING — (1) In construction, the expenditure of building based on a detailed cost of materials to be used. (2) In appraisal the term is general, referring to replacement cost, but not limited to a specific method of arriving at said cost.

COST OF LIVING ESCALATION — [See: Escalation Clause (2)].

COST OF LIVING INDEX — A government indicator of the increase or decrease of living costs for the average person on a monthly basis. [See also: Escalation Clause (2)].

COST OF REMODELING — Expense of alterations to raise the value of a property, rather than to make repairs.

COST OF REPAIRS — Expenses to maintain the value of a property by restoring the worn-out or broken parts of the structure.

COST-PLUS CONTRACT — A building contract setting the builder's profit at a set percentage of actual cost of labor and materials.

COTENANCY — A general term covering both joint tenancy and tenancy in common.

CO-TRUSTEE — One who shares the duties of trustee with one or more other trustees.

COTTAGE — Originally, a house with no surrounding land belonging to it. Modernly, a small house, perhaps used as a summer home.

COULOMB — A measure of electricity equal to a one second electrical charge in a current having a constant flow of one ampere.

COUNSELOR (COUNSELLOR) — (1) A lawyer. (2) One designated as a real estate counselor by the American Society of Real Estate Counselors. The designation indicates an extremely high standard of knowledge and experience on the part of the conferee.

COUNTER FLASHING — Flashing (tar substance) used on chimneys at the roofline to prevent entry of moisture, and cover the metal sheet flashing.

COUNTER-LETTER — In civil law (Louisiana), when a deed is given to a lender as security, an agreement to reconvey (counter-letter) upon payment of a certain amount is given by the lender.

COUNTER OFFER — An offer (instead of acceptance) in response to an offer. For example: A offers to buy B's house for X dollars. B, in response, offers to sell to A at a higher price. B's offer to A is a counter offer.

COUNTY — A political division within a state, usually encompassing one or more cities or towns. There are exceptions such as New York City which contains more than one county. Louisiana uses the word parrish instead of county; New York uses both borough and county, as in Kings County (the borough of Brooklyn).

COUNTY MORTGAGE — A mortgage placed on property by the county to secure aid given to indigent persons. Generally paid upon sale of the property. Also called an indigent mortgage.

COUNTY RECORDS — Public recorded documents by which notice is given of changes of title, liens, and other matters affecting real estate.

COUNTY ROAD — (1) A road lying entirely in one county. (2) Any road or portion of a road under the jurisdiction and maintenance of the county. (3) Loosely, any road not a federal or state road.

COURSE — (1) The path or direction of a river. (2) Something designed so that it must be used by following a certain direction, such as a golf course or race course. (3) A continuous row or layer of wood, bricks, masonry, etc.

COURSES AND DISTANCES — Terminology used in surveying, meaning metes and bounds. (See also: Metes and Bounds.)

COURT — (1) A totally uncovered space, wholly or partly surrounded by walls or buildings. (2) A blind alley, short street, or short cul de sac. (3) A courtroom.

COURTESY TO BROKERS — Willingness of a seller to pay a commission to any broker supplying a suitable buyer; or the willingness of a listing broker to share the commission with any broker supplying a suitable buyer.

COVE — (1) An arched, rather than square angle, meeting of a ceiling and wall. (2) An inlet or small bay.

COVE MOLDING — A small, concave faced molding, used to cover a narrow gap or angle.

COVENANT — Generally, almost any written agreement. Most commonly in real estate, assurances set forth (expressed) in a deed by the grantor or implied by law. Example: Covenant against encumbrances, covenant of right to convey, etc.

COVENANT OF QUIET ENJOYMENT — Usually inserted in leases or conveyances whereby lessor or grantor promises that the tenant or grantee shall enjoy possession of the premises in peace and without disturbance caused by defective title.

COVENANTS RUNNING WITH THE LAND — (See: Running With The Land).

C.P.M. (CERTIFIED PROPERTY MANAGER) — A designation conferred by the Institute of Real Property Management upon one who has completed certain required courses and has been active in property management.

CRADLE — (1) A framework or support, built to shield or protect its contents. (2) The path prepared to catch a falling tree to prevent damage to the tree.

CRAWL SPACE — A space between the ground and the first floor of a structure (usually a house). Repair of utilities under the house may be made by a person crawling through the shallow space.

CREATIVE FINANCING — A general term which encompasses any method of financing property going beyond traditional real estate lending.

CREDIT — (1) The financial worthiness of a borrower. The history of whether this borrower has met financial obligations on time in the past. (2) An accounting term designating money received or receivable, as opposed to debit which is money payed or payable.

CREDITOR'S COMPOSITION — An agreement by creditors to take a portion of a debt as satisfaction for the total due. Generally done to avoid a debtor having to declare bankruptcy.

CREDITOR'S POSITION — (1) The portion of the value of property which is mortgaged, rather than the equity. (2) The portion of the value of property upon which a first mortgage could be obtained.

CREDIT REPORT — A report on the past ability of a loan applicant to pay installment payments. Several national and local companies make such reports.

CREEK — (1) An inlet, going deeper into land than a cove. (2) A stream which empties into a river or bay.

CRICKET — A small, convex roof, placed on a larger roof or surface, to promote drainage in areas of the surface which have barriers to said drainage.

CROFT — An obsolete term referring to a small farm or area to be farmed.

CROP — A specific harvest in a single growing season, such as the corn crop, apple crop, etc.

CROPLAND — (1) Any land suited for farming (the growing of crops). (2) Land upon which crops are actually grown or growing.

CROP ROTATION — The planting of crops such as peas and beans (leguminous plants), which add nitrogen to the soil, on an alternating basis with crops such as corn, wheat, etc., which take nitrogen from the soil.

CROSS-BRIDGING — Strengthening a structure by bracing cross members between the joists, thereby spreading the weight over a larger area.

CROSS CONNECTING ROAD — A road connecting two parallel roads, usually at a right angle.

CROSS SECTION — The surface exposed by cutting at a right angle to an axis (usually the longer axis) of an object.

CROWN MOLDING — A large molding used on a cornice or to cover a wide gap or angle.

CRUISE — A surveying report showing the amount and type of timber in a given area or stand.

CRV (CERTIFICATE OF REASONABLE VALUE) — An appraisal of property for the purpose of insurance by the Veteran's Administration.

CUBIC CONTENT — The number of cubic feet in a building, measured from the exterior surfaces of the exterior walls and roof, and the interior surface of an unfinished floor or six inches below the finished surface of the floor.

CUBIC FOOT COST — The cost of construction of a structure, divided by the number of cubic feet of the structure. (See also: Cubic Content).

CUBIC FOOT METHOD — (See: Comparative Method).

CUBIC FOOT PER SECOND — A flow of water of one cubic foot per second. Used as a measurement term in determining the flow of a river or stream.

CUL DE SAC — A street or alley open at one end only. Modernly, a street in a subdivision, open at one end, and having a large, rounded, closed end to facilitate U turns.

CULTURA — A parcel of land which can be cultivated.

CULTURAL FEATURES — A term denoting man made changes to land.

CULVERT — A waterway or drainage ditch which crosses under a road.

CURABLE DEPRECIATION — Repairs which an owner of real estate should make to retain a high value, but which have not been made.

CURB CUTS — The part of a curb which lowers to street level to form the apron of a driveway.

CURB LINE — The line between the right of way for automobiles (road) and the right of way for pedestrians (sidewalk).

CURRENT ASSETS — An accounting term meaning cash or those things which can be readily converted to cash, such as short term accounts receivable.

CURRENT LIABILITIES — Short term debts.

CURTAIL SCHEDULE — The schedule of partial principal payments (both amounts and due dates) to reduce and retire an indebtedness.

CURTAIN WALL — An outside wall which lends no structural support to a building, but acts merely to enclose.

CURTESY — A common law interest of a husband in the property of his deceased wife. Abolished in most states.

CURTILAGE — The grounds and secondary buildings surrounding a house which are commonly used in connection with the everyday use of the house. Usually fenced.

CURVILINEAR — Having boundaries of curved lines; may refer to architecture, streets, etc.

CUSTODIAN — (1) One who is entrusted with the care and keeping of real or personal property. (See also: Custody). (2) A janitor.

CUSTODY — The care and keeping of property (real or personal). For example: An escrow agent has custody of documents and funds until closing.

CUSTOM BUILDER — One who builds for a specific owner, designing the building to suit said owner's need, rather than building and then looking for a buyer.

CUSTOMER — A buyer of goods or services.

CUT-OVER LAND — Land from which the original growth has been cut away by logging.

CUTS — In construction, the excavation of land into a terrace or terraces, to control flooding, locate a highway, building, or affect the grade for some other purpose.

CYCLICAL MOVEMENT — A term in economics describing the business cycle of the national economy, from good to bad to good again.

D

DADO — (1) To secure by setting in a groove. (2) To make a rectangular groove in a board or plank.

DALE — A valley between hills or other high ground.

DAM — An earthen, metal, masonry, or wooden wall or barrier across a flow of water, which is used to restrict or prevent the water from flowing.

DAMAGES — (1) Money recoverable by one suffering a loss or injury. (2) The loss of value to property adjoining a property taken in condemnation proceedings, rather than the value of the property taken.

DAMPER — An adjustable plate in the flue of a fireplace or furnace, which is used to control the draft from the flames.

DATA PLANT — Information on real property, filed and held by an appraiser, lender, etc.

DATED DATE — Indicates the date a document was executed (signed), rather than the date of recording (recording date).

DATUM — A position from which distances are measured.

DATUM LINE — A horizontal line from which heights and depths are measured. Varies with the area but is usually set forth in the local building code.

DBA (DOING BUSINESS AS) — An identification of the owner or owners of a business and the business name. Not a partnership or corporation.

DE — Latin for of; by; from; concerning.

DEAD-END STREET — A street having ingress and egress at one end only. Differs from a cul de sac in that the dead-end street does not have an enlarged area at the closed end for U turns.

DEAD LOAD — (1) Most commonly, the weight of a truck, exclusive of cargo. (2) The weight of a building or other structure, including furnaces, air conditioning units, elevators, and other permanent machinery, but not furniture, people, or inventory of a business in the structure.

DEAD RENT — A term used in mining to indicate the fixed annual rent, exclusive of royalties. In commercial percentage leases, usually called minimum rent or base rent.

DEALER — One who buys and sells real estate as a business, as opposed to an investor. The importance of the term is for tax purposes. If IRS determines that a taxpayer is a dealer, said taxpayer will not be allowed the capital gains benefits of an investor, but will be taxed at ordinary income rates. The term applies to the transactions more than

43

the person. One may be a dealer in certain transactions and an investor in others.

DEATH RATE — Number of deaths in a given area in a given time. Based on a per 100 or per 1000 population.

DEBIT — An accounting term used to designate a payment or owing, as opposed to a credit which is a receiving or being owed.

DEBT — Money owing from one person to another.

DEBTOR — One who owes a debt.

DEBTOR'S POSITION — Value of property over the amount of mortgages. Commonly called the equity.

DEBT SERVICE — The amount of financing (mortgages or trust deeds) on a property.

DECEDENT — Originally, one who was dying. Modernly, one who is dead.

DECENTRALIZATION — The movement of people and businesses from a central area (a city or downtown area) to more scattered positions (surrounding suburbs).

DECIBEL — A unit of measurement for sound or noise levels. Some states require a builder to make a purchaser aware of the noise level in given areas (usually near airports).

DECIDUOUS TREES — Those which shed their leaves or fruit at seasonal intervals.

DECK — Any flat surface which resembles the deck of a ship, and is not enclosed. A flat area on a roof, roof of a porch, etc.

DECK PAINT — An exterior paint having a high resistance to wear, and used in areas of heavy use, such as a porch.

DECK ROOF — A flat roof without parapets.

DECLARATION — (See: Declaration of Restrictions; Restriction; Condominium Map).

DECLARATION OF HOMESTEAD — (See: Homestead).

DECLARATION OF RESTRICTIONS — A set of restrictions filed by a subdivider to cover an entire tract or subdivision.

DECLARATION OF TRUST — A written acknowledgement by one holding legal title to property that the property is held in trust for the benefit of another.

DECLINING BALANCE METHOD OF DEPRECIATION — Depreciation by a fixed annual percentage of the balance after deducting each yearly depreciation amount.

DECORATE — To adorn or add to the beauty of something. Connotes only superficial changes, but, in some areas, is used to indicate major repair.

DECREE — The judgment of a court.

DECREE OF DISTRIBUTION — The final determination of the rights of heirs to receive the property of an estate.

DEDICATED — Property given by an owner for public use.

DEDICATION — The giving by an owner of private property for public use, and the acceptance by the proper public authority. Most commonly the dedication by a builder of the streets in a subdivision.

DEED — Actually, any one of many conveyancing or financing instruments, but generally a conveyancing instrument, given to pass fee title to property upon sale.

DEED OF RECONVEYANCE — (See: Reconveyance).

DEED OF TRUST — An instrument used in many states in place of a mortgage. Property is transferred to a trustee by the borrower (trustor), in favor of the lender (beneficiary), and reconveyed upon payment in full.

DEED POLL — The common form of deed executed by the grantor(s) only. When the grantee(s) also execute the deed (perhaps to accept certain restrictions or liens), it is an indenture deed (see which).

DEED RESTRICTIONS — Limitations on the use of property placed in the conveyancing deed by the grantor, which bind all future owners.

DEFAULT — An omission or failure to perform a legal duty.

DEFAULT JUDGMENT — A judgment entered against a party who fails to appear in court at the scheduled time.

DEFEASANCE — A deed, made collaterally with a conveyancing deed, which imposes conditions which, if met, will defeat the conveyance.

DEFEASIBLE TITLE — Title which is not absolute but possibly may be annulled or voided at a later date. For example: Title conveyed to A with condition that if A marries before age 30, title will go to B. A's title may be good (doesn't marry) or may be defeated (marries before 30).

DEFECTIVE TITLE — (1) Title to a negotiable instrument obtained by fraud. (2) Title to real property which lacks some of the elements necessary to transfer good title.

DEFENDANT — The person against whom a civil or criminal action is brought.

DEFERRED MAINTENANCE — Repairs necessary to put a property in good condition. A concern of a purchaser. An owner may have an account for such maintenance.

DEFERRED PAYMENTS — (1) Payments to begin at a future time. (2) Installment payments.

DEFICIENCY JUDGMENT — Commonly, the amount for which the borrower is personally liable on a note and mortgage if the foreclosure sale does not bring enough to cover the debt. Actually the judgment is for the total amount and not for the deficiency, the recovery from the foreclosure sale being deducted from this amount.

DEFLATION — A decrease in the supply of money and credit. The value of money is increased in relation to what it will buy (price drop). Opposite of inflation.

DEGREE — (1) A geometric measure. 360° makes a circle; 180° a straight line; 90° a right angle, etc. Used in metes and bounds descriptions to show the direction the boundaries follow. A degree is itself divided by minutes and seconds, 60 minutes making 1 degree, and 60 seconds making 1 minute. (2) A term used in inheritance to show the closeness of blood relationships. (3) Extent, such as 1st. degree murder. (4) That which is received upon graduation from school, such as a law degree.

DELAYED RECONVEYANCE — A reconveyance of a deed of trust which is issued and recorded after transfer of title and issuance of title insurance (not showing the deed of trust). Usually occurs when the lender is in another state and will not issue the reconveyance until paid in full.

DELIVERY — In conveyancing, the placing of the property in the actual or constructive possession of the grantee. Usually accomplished by delivery of a deed to the buyer or agent of the buyer, or by recording said deed.

DEMAND — (1) The quantity of goods which can be sold at a specified price, in a given market, at a particular time. (2) A letter from a lender showing the amount due in order to pay off a mortgage or trust deed.

DEMAND NOTE — A note having no date for repayment, but due on demand of the lender.

DEMISE — A lease or conveyance for life or years. Loosely used to describe any conveyance, whether in fee, for life, or for years.

DEMOGRAPHICS — Statistics. Commonly refers to statistical information required by certain businesses (especially chain stores) regarding a possible new location.

DENSITY — (1) The degree of crowding together of people or buildings. (2) Weight or thickness.

DEPARTMENT OF REAL ESTATE — That department of the state government responsible for the licensing and regulation of persons engaged in the real estate business. The person heading the department is usually called The Real Estate Commissioner. Other names for the department are The Division of Real Estate and The Real Estate Commission.

DEPLETION — The reduction or exhaustion of an asset, such as a wasting asset, and its corresponding loss of value.

DEPLETION RATE — Percentage of the total amount of a wasting asset (oil, minerals, etc.) to be mined, drilled, or otherwise used yearly.

DEPONENT — One who makes a sworn written statement (deposition). If the statement is an affidavit, the maker is called an affiant.

DEPOSIT — (1) Money given by the buyer with an offer to purchase. Shows good faith. Also called earnest money. (2) A natural accumulation of resources (oil, gold, etc.) which may be commercially recovered and marketed.

DEPOSITION — Written testimony taken under oath.

DEPOSIT RECEIPT — (See: Purchase Agreement).

DEPOT — (1) A railroad or bus station. (2) Any place used for the storage and protection of goods.

DEPRECIABLE LIFE — A tax term meaning the number of years used to determine depreciation of an asset (generally a building). The time used is determined by the local IRS office under general guide lines.

DEPRECIABLE PROPERTY — Property on which a useful life can be determined for depreciation. For example: A building is depreciable (has a lifetime) but the land under it is not (lasts forever).

DEPRECIATION — (1) Decrease in value to real property improvements caused by deterioration or obsolescence. (2) A loss in value as an accounting procedure to use as a deduction for income tax purposes. (See specific types of depreciation).

DEPRECIATION METHODS — Accounting methods to compute the decrease in value of an improvement.

DEPRECIATION RESERVE — An account for the amount needed for depreciation caused by time and use of equipment, buildings, etc. Common in accounting of public utilities.

DEPRESSION — The bottom of a business cycle, when production, prices, and purchasing, are usually low, and unemployment is high.

DEPTH CURVE — An appraisal graph showing the increase or decrease in value of lots of equal front footage, as the depth increases or decreases (depth factor).

DEPTH FACTOR — The increase or decrease of the value of a lot as the depth increases or decreases; the frontage remains the same.

DERAIGN — To displace, as by proving something to be false.

DEROG — A slang shortening of the word derogatory. Used in reference to information on a credit report.

DESCENT — Technically, to pass by succession (operation of law). Modernly, the term includes passing by will.

DESCRIPTION — (See: Legal Description).

DESIGN — A plan of a structure, encompassing all phases of its appearance and function.

DESIST AND REFRAIN — To stop doing what one is doing, and not to start doing it again in the future. The real estate commissioner in some states has the power to issue a desist and refrain order when real estate laws are violated.

DETERIORATION — A gradual wearing away of a structure through use or exposure to the elements, rather than a sudden destruction. Also called physical depreciation.

DEVELOPER — (1) A builder. (2) One who prepares the raw land for construction and then sells lots to a builder.

DEVELOPMENT — A planned construction project, rather than simply the building of unrelated buildings.

DEVELOPMENT COST — (See: Off-Site Improvements).

DEVELOPMENT LOAN — A loan for the purchase of land or off-site improvements, rather than building costs. The land involved is used to secure the loan.

DEVEST — (See: Divest).

DEVISE — Real estate left by will.

DEVISEE — One to whom real estate is given by will.

DEVISOR — A testator who leaves real estate.

D HORIZON — Limestone deposits under the C horizon.

DIAGRAM RULES — A method of determining the boards to be produced from a log by drawing a cross section of the log, and cross sections on it of the boards to be produced, leaving between each board the width of a saw kerf.

DIKE — (1) A ditch or channel for water. (2) A barrier erected to restrain the flow of water. A levee.

DILUVIUM — A deposit of land produced by a flood.

DIMENSION LUMBER — Lumber cut to commonly used sizes or cut to a custom order.

DIMINISHING ASSETS — (See: Wasting Assets).

DIMINISHING RETURNS — (See: Increasing and Diminishing Returns).

DIRECT COMPENSATION — (See: Compensation).

DIRECT COSTS — Construction costs not including overhead.

DIRECT EXPENSE ESCALATION — [See: Escalation Clause (3)].

DIRECTIONAL GROWTH — The path of growth of an urban area. Used to determine where future development will be most profitable.

DIRECT REDUCTION MORTGAGE — An amortized mortgage. One on which principal and interest payments are paid at the same time (usually monthly) with interest being computed on the remaining balance.

DIRECT STEAM SYSTEM — A radiator system fed from a steam boiler.

DISCHARGE — (See: Release).

DISCLAIMER — (1) Statement on a publication attempting to limit liability in the event the information is inaccurate. (2) Renunciation of a claim or right of another. (3) Refusal to accept an estate, either as trustee or as owner.

DISCOUNT — The difference between face value of an installment note and mortgage or deed of trust, and the present cash value.

DISCOUNTED CASH FLOW — The present value of future cash flow, determined by a given discount rate.

DISINTERESTED APPRAISAL — An estimate of value of real estate by one having no personal interest in the property.

DISPOSABLE INCOME — (See: Spendable Income).

DISPOSAL FIELD — A system of clay tiles and gravel used to dispose of the waste draining from a septic tank. The percolating qualities of the soil determine the extent of the field needed. (Also called a tile field).

DISPOSITION — The giving up or alienating of property.

DISPOSITION OF REAL ESTATE STATEMENT — A statement that the buyer will occupy the property being purchased even though the buyer owns other property. The buyer states that the other property will be sold or rented. Particulars must be given as to any loan on the property and the equity or rent to payment amounts.

DISPOSSESS PROCEEDINGS — Eviction proceedings by a landlord to remove a tenant from possession because of nonpayment of rent or other breach of the rental agreement. The term is not widely used.

DISBURSEMENTS — Payments made during the course of an escrow or at closing.

DISSEISIN — A wrongful dispossession of someone seised (in rightful possession) of real property.

DISSOLUTION — A cancellation or annulment of a contract or business association, such as a partnership or corporation.

DISTEMPER — A mixing of paint with egg whites or size, to use as background decoration for a painting on a wall or ceiling.

DISTRESS SALE — A sale of property when the seller is under extreme pressure to sell. Generally the property is sold for less than market value.

DISTRIBUTED LOAD — Weight distributed over a surface, such as a floor, or along a beam or other support member, and measured in pounds or tons per square foot of area.

DISTRIBUTION BOX — (1) (See: Fuse Box). (2) An underground box which receives the waste from a septic tank and distributes it laterally to a disposal field.

DISTRIBUTION PANEL — A board containing electrical circuits which distribute the main load to branch circuits.

DISTRIBUTION TILE — Tile, usually clay or cement, used in a disposal field.

DISTRICT — An area geographically set apart for a specific purpose, such as a congressional district or drainage district. The boundaries of one may overlap the other.

DITCH — A trench, natural or man made, especially when used for drainage or irrigation.

DIVEST — To take away. The opposite of invest.

DIVIDED INTEREST — Different estates in the same property, such as the interest of owner, lessee, mortgagee, etc.

DIVIDED RATE — (See: Split Rate).

DIVIDEND — A dividing into shares of a fund of money or property for distribution, as among shareholders of a corporation. The money or property distributed is the dividend.

DIVIDEND YIELD — Ratio of cash flow to cash invested, expressed as a percentage.

DIVISA — A boundary, commonly of a farm. Seldom used.

DIVISION FENCE — A term used in ranching to describe the fence separating pastures.

DIVISION OF REAL ESTATE — (See: Department of Real Estate).

DIVISION WALL — (1) A wall between two buildings, but not a part of either. (2) A wall which divides a building into rooms. Differs from a partition in that it is load-bearing.

DIVORCE — The legal dissolution of a marriage, leaving the parties with the results of the marriage (includes alimony, child support, property settlements, etc.) rather than an annulment which puts the parties in the position they were before the marriage.

DOCK — (1) A platform used for loading and unloading ships, trucks, or railroad cars. (2) A landing pier for boats. (3) The part of a courtroom where a prisoner is kept.

DOCUMENT — (See: Instrument).

DOCUMENTARY TAX STAMPS — Stamps, similar to postage stamps, affixed to a deed, showing the amount of transfer tax paid. Most states now "stamp" the deed rather than actually affixing a stamp.

DOCUMENTARY TRANSFER TAX — A state tax on the sale of real property, based on the sale price or equity transferred, being $.55 for each $500 of the taxable amount in most states. Some states use $1.10 per $1000; $.50 per $500; $1.00 per $1000.

DOG — A mechanical device for holding logs together in a logging operation; usually has some type of claw which penetrates the wood.

DOLPHIN — (1) A bumper around a boat to prevent damage. (2) A buoy with a ring for mooring.

DOMESTIC CORPORATION — (1) Refers to a state rather than a country. For example: In Delaware, a corporation organized under Delaware law would be a domestic corporation. In New York, a corporation organized under Delaware law would be a foreign corporation (foreign to New York). (See also: Corporation). (2) In international terms, refers to the country in which the corporation is based. In the U.S., for example, U.S. based corporations are domestic.

DOMICILE — (1) A legal term signifying a place where a person has his permanent home. The most accurate meaning is the layman's understanding of the place where a person "lives", since this takes into consideration the intent of the person to make a particular property his "home". (2) The state or country in which a corporation is chartered (organized), such as a corporation "domiciled" in the U.S.

DOMINANT TENEMENT — A parcel of land which benefits from an easement. For example: An easement exists over parcel A for access

49

to parcel B. Parcel B is the dominant tenement; parcel A is the servient tenement.

DONEE — One who receives a gift.

DONOR — One who gives a gift.

DOOR — A sliding or hinged structure, covering an opening to a cupboard, closet, room, building, etc. May be used as an entrance or exit. Usually constructed of wood, glass, or metal, depending on its service.

DOOR BUCK — (See: Door Jamb).

DOOR JAMB — The members surrounding a door or door opening.

DORMER WINDOW — (1) A window which rises vertically above the roof line of a sloping roof. (2) Originally any bedroom window.

DOUBLE DECLINING BALANCE METHOD OF DEPRECIATION — A use of the declining balance method, but with double the depreciation allowable by straight line. An accelerated method.

DOUBLE ESCROW — Two concurrent escrows on the same property, having the same party as buyer and seller of the property. Example: Escrow 1- A buys from B. Escrow 2- A sells the same property to C. A is using C's money to buy B's property. The process is illegal in many states unless full disclosure is made.

DOUBLE FLOOR — A floor and subfloor, both of wood.

DOUBLE FRAMING — A method of adding strength to framing by doubling the amount of structural supports.

DOUBLE GABLED ROOF — (See: M Roof).

DOUBLE GLAZING — (See: Thermal Window).

DOUBLE HOUSE — (See: Duplex).

DOUBLE-HUNG WINDOW — A window which opens vertically from the top and bottom, containing two separate sashes with a locking device, usually at the center where the top of the lower sash meets the bottom of the upper sash.

DOUBLE PITCH — The most common roof for houses, coming to a crest at the center and sloping away in two directions.

DOVETAIL JOINT — A joint which interlocks in a zigzag pattern, similar to the tail of a dove.

DOWEL — A cylindrical piece of wood used to join members together by fitting the ends into corresponding holes of the members.

DOWER — A common law interest of a wife in the property of her deceased husband. Being changed in many states by statute to give more equality between men and women in property rights.

DOWN PAYMENT — Cash portion paid by a buyer from his own funds, as opposed to that portion of the purchase price which is financed.

DOWNSPOUT — A pipe leading from the gutters of a roof to the ground and into a sewer or away from the building.

DOWNSTROKE — Slang for down payment.

DOWNTOWN — (1) In a small city or town, the business area. (2) In a larger city, a business section reference to distinguish the area from midtown or uptown.

DRAFT CURTAINS — Fire retardant partitions (usually of sheet metal or dry wall) which attach to the interior of a roof, to divide a building in order to prevent the spread of fire within the building.

DRAGNET CLAUSE — A clause in a mortgage or deed of trust which places the real estate as security for existing debts between the parties.

DRAINAGE — (1) The gradual flowing of liquid off a surface. (2) Any system to remove liquid waste or rainwater by having it flow to a designated area.

DRAINAGE DISTRICT — (1) A geographical area under the authority of a single unit of local government which controls the construction and operation of the drainage systems of the area. (2) The governmental body having control over the area drainage systems.

DRAINAGE DITCH — Any open water channel, natural or man made, used for drainage.

DRAW — (1) Portions of a construction loan, given after certain stages of completion. (2) An advance against future income.

DREDGE — (1) A machine which drags over the bottom of a waterway, to excavate or gather. (2) To excavate or gather by using a dredge.

DRESS — To finish or ornament, such as lumber, masonry, a facing of a building, etc.

DRESSER DRAWER TITLE — The failure to record evidence of title; instead, placing it in a "dresser drawer". Also called: Trunk Title.

DRIFT — The stress or thrust of an arch in a horizontal direction.

DRIFT FENCE — A barrier to prevent cattle from "drifting" into an area as they graze. The fence does not form an enclosure.

DRIP — (1) A small pipe, used to drain larger pipes of condensation. (2) A projection from a roof edge or sill to throw off rainwater. (See also: Drip Cap.)

DRIP CAP — A molding which projects from over the exterior of a door or window, forcing rainwater to drip away from the building.

DRIVEWAY — (1) Commonly, a private roadway, paved or unpaved, leading from a public street to a garage or other shelter for an automobile. (2) An entrance to private land for any purpose, to be used by a motor vehicle.

DROP SIDING — A siding applied to the exterior of a frame structure by tongue and groove method.

DROUGHT — Lack of water due to insufficient rainfall over an extended period of time.

DRUMLIN — A long narrow hill of glacial deposit, sometimes trapping water and so forming a swamp at its foot.

DRY MORTGAGE — A lien which places no personal liability on the mortgagor, looking only to the property for security.

DRY-WALL CONSTRUCTION — Type of construction by which the interior wall is attached in a dry condition, generally as sheet materials, as contrasted to wet plaster application.

DUAL AGENCY — The representation of opposing principals (buyer and seller) at the same time. In brokerage many states get around this by saying that the agent aids the buyer but is the agent of the seller only. A problem arises if both buyer and seller pay the broker. Then full disclosure must be made. An escrow agent is the agent of buyer and seller and usually paid by both. This is why an escrow agent must be neutral.

DUCTS — Any conduit holding gas, water, electrical wiring, etc., as a means of carrying said gas, water, or electricity from one place to another.

DUE-ON-SALE CLAUSE — (See: Alienation Clause).

DUFF — Organic matter, mostly leaves, in various stages of decomposition on the floor of a forest.

DUPLEX — Any building containing exactly two dwelling units. Most commonly refers to the units which are side by side, with a common wall and roof.

DURESS — Forcing one to do that which he would not voluntarily do.

DUTCH DOOR — A door divided horizontally into halves, each opening and closing independent of the other, or latched together to act as one door.

DWELLING UNIT (DWELLING HOUSE) — The apartment, building, or group of buildings, occupied by a person as a residence.

E

EARNEST MONEY — [See: Deposit (1)].

EARNINGS — Money received for labor or personal services rather than a return on capital, although corporate income from all sources is described as "earnings".

EASEMENT — A right created by grant, reservation, agreement, prescription, or necessary implication, which one has in the land of another. It is either for the benefit of land (appurtenant), such as right to cross A to get to B, or "in gross", such as a public utility easement.

EASEMENT APPURTENANT — An easement for the benefit of another parcel of land, such as the right to cross parcel A to reach B. The easement will pass with the transfer of property to a new owner. (See also: Dominant Tenement; Servient Tenement).

EASEMENT BY PRESCRIPTION — (See: Prescriptive Easement).

EASEMENT IN GROSS — An easement for the benefit of a person or company, rather than for the benefit of another parcel of land. Commonly, such easements as for public utilities.

EASEMENT OF NECESSITY — An easement granted by a court when it is determined that said easement is absolutely necessary for the use and enjoyment of the land. Commonly given to landlocked parcels.

EAVES — The margin or lower part of a roof projecting beyond an exterior wall.

EBB TIDE — The tide at its low, or the period from high to low.

ECONOMIC LIFE — The "profitable" life of an improvement. Generally shorter than the physical life (before it is worn out).

ECONOMIC OBSOLESCENCE — Loss of desirability and useful life of a property through economic forces, such as zoning changes, traffic pattern changes, etc., rather than deterioration (functional obsolescence).

ECONOMIC RECOVERY ACT OF 1981(ERTA) — Laws designed to stimulate the economy, including stimulation of the real estate market. (See: Accelerated Cost Recovery System).

ECONOMIC RENT — The market rental value of a property at any given time, even though the actual rent may be different.

ECONOMICS — The study of the laws and theories pertaining to the creation and distribution of wealth, either of the private sector or of governments.

EFFECTIVE AGE — Age of a structure as estimated by its condition rather than actual age. Takes into account rehabilitation and maintenance.

EFFECTIVE DEMAND — A qualifying term meaning the ability to pay as well as desire to buy.

EFFECTIVE GROSS INCOME — (See: Adjusted Gross Income).

EFFICIENCY — An apartment consisting of one room, sectioned into areas for a kitchen, bedroom, etc.

EFFLUENT — (1) The flowing of a branch of a stream out from the main stream. (2) The flow of sewage, either from a storm sewer or sanitary sewer, after some stage of treatment.

EGRESS — A term concerning a right to come and go across the land (public or private) of another. Usually part of the term ingress and egress.

EJECTMENT — Most commonly, a court action to recover real property, usually by eviction of a tenant. In some states, an action to enforce specific performance.

ELECTRICAL CURRENT — Any flow of electricity.

ELECTRIC HEATING — Any heating system using electricity as its power source. May be a water or air system.

ELEEMOSYNARY CORPORATION — A corporation created for charitable purposes. There are tax advantages accorded to such corporations. The corporation may operate the same as a profit making corporation. Commonly called a nonprofit corporation.

ELEVATION — (1) Height above sea level. (2) The exterior design of a structure, usually but not necessarily, viewed from the front. Called a horizontal elevation. (3) Height measured from any point, such as elevation from a floor. Called vertical elevation.

ELUVIATION — The movement of soil materials, either in a downward or horizontal direction, caused by excessive water in the soil.

EMBLEMENTS — Growing crops. Considered chattels which may be removed by a tenant at the expiration of his lease.

EMINENT DOMAIN — A governmental right to acquire private property for public use by condemnation, and the payment of just compensation.

EMPLOYMENT LETTER — A letter from an employer stating the time a person has been employed and income from said employment.

ENCROACHMENT — Generally, construction onto the property of another, as of a wall, fence, building, etc.

ENCUMBRANCE, INCUMBRANCE — A claim, lien, charge, or liability attached to and binding real property. Any right to, or interest in, land which may exist in one other than the owner, but which will not prevent the transfer of fee title.

END LOAN — (See: Take Out Loan).

ENDORSEMENT, INDORSEMENT — The act of the holder of a note, bill, check, or other negotiable instrument, of assigning said instrument by signing the back of the instrument, with or without qualifications.

ENGLISH ARCHITECTURE — A general term, encompassing the styles of various English design, but which have common elements. The exterior being either of large stones, or exposed timbers with large stones or brick placed between the timbers, in a decorative manner. The roof is most often of slate and windows are hinged vertically.

ENTITY — A separate existence or being, most commonly referring to a corporation or other form of business, rather than an individual.

ENTRANCE — (1) The opening used to go into an enclosed area, such as a door, gate, etc. (2) To go upon land, such as to gain entrance to, the point of entrance not necessarily being through a door, gate, or other opening.

ENTREPRENEUR — A businessman, taking the risk of loss and gaining profit, rather than a salaried employee.

ENVIRONMENT — Surroundings. As an appraisal term, the characteristics of the area around a property which bear on the value of the property.

ENVIRONMENTAL DEFICIENCY — Deficiency of the area surrounding a property, (environment), which decreases its value, such as poorly designed streets and traffic patterns, a high crime rate, no major sewer lines, etc.

ENVIRONMENTAL IMPACT REPORT — A report of the probable effect of a development on the surrounding area (environment). The report is prepared by an independant company to federal, state, or local guide lines.

ENVIRONMENTAL PROTECTION AGENCY (EPA) — The federal agency concerned with the protection of our resources of land, water, and air.

EQUAL CREDIT OPPORTUNITY ACT — Federal law granting women certain independant status, and preventing lenders from considering such negative credit aspects as the possibility of a woman having children and dropping out of the labor market.

EQUALIZATION — (See: Board of Equalization).

EQUATOR — The imaginary circle separating the Northern and Southern Hemispheres of the Earth, and used as the starting point for measurements of latitude, its own latitude being zero degrees.

EQUIPMENT — As an industrial term, everything necessary to produce a product, such as land, improvements, machinery, etc.

EQUITABLE CONVERSION — A legal fiction applied to a land contract which treats the vendee's (buyer's) interest as a real property interest even though the seller holds legal title, and the seller's interest as a security interest (personal property). This enables the buyer to act as the "owner" of the property without having "legal" title.

EQUITABLE LIEN — A lien enforceable in a court of equity, based on evidence of an intent between debtor and creditor to create a lien on specific property of the debtor, but a failure to legally create said lien.

EQUITABLE MORTGAGE — (1) A lien against real property (mortgage) which is enforceable in a court of equity, but does not legally constitute a mortgage. (2) A deed given as security for a debt will be held to be a mortgage rather than a transfer of title. Also called a constructive mortgage.

EQUITABLE OWNERSHIP — Ownership by one who does not have legal title, such as a vendee under a land contract or, technically, a trustor under a deed of trust (legal title being in the trustee). Also called equitable title.

EQUITABLE TITLE — (See: Equitable Ownership).

EQUITY — (1) A legal doctrine based on fairness, rather than strict interpretation of the letter of the law. (2) The market value of real property, less the amount of existing liens.

EQUITY BUILD-UP — The reduction of principal on a mortgage or deed of trust by periodic payments, which increases (builds-up) the difference (equity) between the property value and amount of the lien.

EQUITY LINE OF CREDIT — A combination of a line of credit and equity loan. A maximum loan amount is established based on credit and equity. A mortgage (deed of trust) is recorded against the potential borrower's property for said maximum loan amount. The potential borrower has the right to borrow, as needed, up to the amount of the mortgage.

EQUITY LOAN — A loan based upon the equity in a property. The credit of the borrower is not a major factor. (See also: Personal Property Loan).

EQUITY OF REDEMPTION — Properly, the right to pay off the lien of a mortgage which is in default by payment of the principal, interest, and costs which are due. Often confused with the redemption period after the foreclosure sale, which is a right established by statute.

EQUITY PARTICIPATION — (See: Participation).

EQUITY PURCHASER — One who purchases the equity of another in real property, either assuming or taking subject to existing mortgages or deeds of trust.

EROSION — The wearing away, over a prolonged period, of rock, earth, or other portions of land.

ESCALATION CLAUSE — A clause in a lease providing for an increased rental at a future time. May be accomplished by several types of clauses, such as (1) Fixed increase - A clause which calls for a definite, periodic rental increase. (2) Cost of living - A clause which ties the rent to a government cost of living index, with periodic adjustments as the index changes. (3) Direct expense - The rent is adjusted according to changes in the expenses of the property paid by the lessor, such as tax increases, increased maintenance costs, etc.

ESCALATOR CLAUSE — (See: Escalation Clause).

ESCARPMENT — A cliff.

ESCHEAT — A reversion of property to the state in the absence of an individual owner. Usually occurs when a property owner dies intestate, and without heirs.

ESCROW — Delivery of a deed by a grantor to a third party for delivery to the grantee upon the happening of a contingent event. Modernly, in some states, all instruments necessary to the sale (including funds) are delivered to a third (neutral) party, with instructions as to their use.

ESCROW ACCOUNT — (See: Impound Account).

ESCROW INSTRUCTIONS — Instructions which are signed by both buyer and seller, and which enable an escrow agent to carry out the procedures necessary to transfer real property, a business, or other assignable interest.

ESCROW OFFICER — An escrow agent. In some states, one who has, through experience and education, gained a certain degree of expertise in escrow matters.

ESTATE — (1) The interest or nature of the interest which one has in property, such as a life estate, the estate of a deceased, real estate, etc. (2) A large house with substantial grounds surrounding it, giving the connotation of belonging to a wealthy person.

ESTATE FOR LIFE — (See: Life Estate).

ESTATE FOR YEARS — Any estate for a definite period of time. Commonly, a lease.

ESTATE OF INHERITANCE — An estate which may descend to heirs. For example: A fee estate is an estate of inheritance, whereas a life estate is not.

ESTATE TAX — A tax against the property of a deceased, based on the value of the estate.

ESTOPPEL — The prevention of one from asserting a legal right because of prior actions inconsistent with the assertion.

ESTOVERS — Old doctrine allowing use, primarily of timber, by a tenant for fuel and repair of his shelter. Not much application in the U.S. today.

ET AL — And others.

ET CON — And husband.

ETHICS — With regard to professions, a code of professional standards, containing aspects of fairness and duty to the profession and the general public.

ET UX — And wife.

ET VIR — Latin: meaning "and husband".

EVICTION — A court action to remove one from possession of real property. Most commonly, the removal of a tenant.

EVIDENCE OF TITLE — A document establishing ownership to property. Most commonly, a deed.

EXCAVATE — To dig and then remove, leaving a pit or hollow. Used to describe the removal of earth in construction; or coal, copper, etc., in mining.

EXCAVATION — (1) A pit or other opening which remains after the removal of dirt, minerals, etc., from the surface of the Earth. (2) The process of digging and removal of dirt, minerals, etc., from land.

EXCEPTION — (1) Specific items set forth in an insurance policy which are not covered by said policy. (2) Any item specifically excluded.

EXCESS CONDEMNATION — Taking, by right of eminent domain, more property than actually necessary for the intended purpose. This happens frequently, the excess property being sold at auction after completion of the project.

EXCESS INCOME — (See: Excess Rent).

EXCESS RENT — Rental income (usually under a lease) which exceeds the fair rental value of the property.

EXCHANGE — A reciprocal transfer of real property which has certain tax advantages over a sale. Definite procedures must be followed in order to qualify the transfer as an exchange.

EXCHANGE AGREEMENT — Instrument (contract) used in an exchange. (See also: Exchange).

EXCLUSIVE AGENCY AGREEMENT — (See: Agency Agreement).

EXCLUSIVE LISTING — A written contract between a property owner and a real estate broker, whereby the owner promises to pay a fee or commission to the broker if certain real property of the owner is sold during a stated period, regardless of whether the broker is or is not the cause of the sale. The broker promises to put forth his or her best efforts to sell the property, and may make specific promises as to advertising or other promotion in certain instances.

EXCLUSIVE RIGHT TO SELL — (See: Exclusive Listing).

EXECUTE — To complete; to fulfill a purpose, such as to execute an instrument, meaning to sign, seal (modernly, to notarize), and deliver.

EXECUTED SALE — One which is final and completed.

EXECUTION SALE — Sale of real property under a writ of execution by a court. A judicial mortgage foreclosure sale is in this category.

EXECUTOR — One who is appointed under a will to carry out (execute) the terms of the will.

EXECUTOR'S DEED — A deed, court approved, under which the grantor is an executor.

EXECUTORY CONTRACT — A contract under which there is still to be performance. (See also: Executory Sale).

EXECUTORY SALE — A sale not fully completed, such as (at least in theory) a land contract sale. (See also: Executed Sale).

EXECUTRIX — A female executor.

EXEMPLARY DAMAGES — Damages to punish (make an example of) the offender. This is done when the wrong is deliberate or grossly negligent and compensatory damages do not appear to be sufficient.

EXIT — (1) The leaving or departing, usually of a person. (2) The place through which one leaves, as a door, gate, etc.

EXPANSIBLE HOUSE — A house specifically designed for later additions or expansion.

EXPANSION JOINT — Any connection of two members which allows for movement of the members when effected by pressure toward or away from the connecting area (joint). A joint in a bridge, building, or similar structure, allowing for expansion or contraction of the parts of the structure from temperature changes.

EXPENSES — (See: Operating Expenses).

EXPERT TESTIMONY — Testimony by one acknowledged to have special training and knowledge in a particular subject. Only testimony on the subject in which the witness is "expert" is considered expert testimony.

EXPERT WITNESS — One acknowledged to have special training and knowledge of a particular subject, and testifying on that subject.

EXPOSURE — (1) The degree to which a property for sale, lease, etc., is made noticeable (exposed) to potential buyers, tenants, etc., through advertising, multiple listing groups, etc. (2) The direction in which a property faces. For example: Does a store depending on walk-in trade face the sun in the morning when people walk in the sun to get warm (eastern exposure), or face the sun in the afternoon when people walk in the shade to keep cool (western exposure).

EXPRESS — Clear and definite; set forth, as opposed to implied.

EXPRESSWAY (FREEWAY) — A highway (usually divided) with control of access, and with major streets crossing it at a different grade level. Distinguished from "toll roads" in that no fee is charged to those using the expressway.

EXPROPRIATION — A taking, as under eminent domain. The word has come to be used in connection with a foreign location, such as a foreign government taking an American industry located in the foreign country. The word is used instead of eminent domain in Louisiana.

EXTENDED COVERAGE — With reference to insurance, coverage beyond the normal (standard) policy.

EXTENSION — A continuing under the same conditions, as opposed to a renewal, which implies new terms or conditions.

EXTERIOR — The outside surface of any structure.

EXTERIOR FINISH — The outside covering of a structure, such as wood, brick, stucco, etc.

EXTERIOR WALL — The outer vertical surface of a structure, which encloses the entire structure, and the dimensions of which are used to find the gross area of the enclosure for appraisal purposes.

F

FACADE — The main face or front elevation of a building.

FACE — (1) The front or facade of a structure (See also: Facade). (2) The positioning of a structure, [as to front (face) the ocean]. (3) To surface or cover the front or outer surface of an object. (4) The outside or main appearance of the surface of an object.

FACE BRICK — A treated brick, usually glossy and of even quality, made for use as an exterior finish.

FACED WALL — A masonry wall, using different materials as a facing and backing, but with facing and backing bonded as one unit for load-bearing.

FACE VALUE — The value of notes, mortgages, etc., as stated on the face of the instrument, and not considering any discounting.

FACTOR — (1) One who buys or sells goods in his own name, but acting as an agent for another. (2) One who buys accounts receivable at a discount.

FACTORING — Purchasing accounts receivable from a business at a discount.

FAIR CASH VALUE — (See: Market Value).

FAIR CREDIT REPORTING ACT — A federal law giving one the right to see his or her credit report so that errors may be corrected. A lender refusing credit based on a credit report must inform the buyer which company issued the report. The buyer may see the report without charge if refused credit, or for a charge if just curious.

FAIR MARKET VALUE — Price that probably would be negotiated between a willing seller and willing buyer in a reasonable time. Usually arrived at by comparable sales in the area.

FAIR RENTAL — (See: Economic Rent).

FAIR VALUE — The setting of a reasonable value by a court or board, for the establishment of public utility rates.

FAIRWAY — (1) The deepest part of a river or bay, through which boats travel. (2) A passageway kept open in a harbor or bay for boats to enter or exit. (3) A portion of a golf course, bounded on its width by the rough and on its length by the tee and the green.

FALLOW — (1) Land tilled and prepared for planting, but not planted. A method of soil conservation. (2) Land left idle which would ordinarily be planted.

FALSE ADVERTISING — In most instances when in connection with real estate, newspaper classified advertising which misrepresents the property, price, or terms. A broker may have his or her license suspended or revoked if the offense is prolonged or deliberately fraudulent.

FAMILY ROOM — A room used informally for recreation, usually built off the kitchen.

FANNIE MAE — (See: FNMA).

FAN WINDOW — (See: Circlehead Window).

FARM — (1) A large parcel of land devoted to raising crops. (2) Land used for producing dairy products (dairy farm) or raising certain fish or animals, such as a lobster farm, oyster farm, etc. (3) A geographical area in which a real estate salesperson concentrates his or her business efforts (farms).

FASCIA — A flat, long finishing band or board, used at the outer edge of a cornice, or to conceal rafter ends.

FAST FOOD RESTAURANT — A limited menu restaurant, offering quick service, low prices, and usually over-the-counter service rather than table service.

FATHOM — A measure of depths, used at sea, being six feet.

FEASIBILITY SURVEY — A study of an area before construction of a project, to determine the probable financial success of the project.

FEDERAL DEPOSIT INSURANCE CORPORATION (F.D.I.C.) — The federal corporation which insures against loss of deposits in banks, up to a maximum amount (currently $40,000.00).

FEDERAL FAIR HOUSING LAW — Title VIII of the Civil Rights Act which forbids discrimination in the sale or rental of residential property because of race, color, sex, religion or national origin.

FEDERAL HOME LOAN BANK BOARD — The board which charters and regulates federal savings and loan associations, as well as controlling the system of Federal Home Loan Banks.

FEDERAL HOME LOAN BANKS — Banks created under the Federal Home Loan Bank Act of 1932, in order to keep a permanent supply of money available for home financing. The banks are controlled by the Federal Home Loan Bank Board. Savings and loans, insurance companies, and other similar companies making long term mortgage loans may become members of the Federal Home Loan Bank System, and thus may borrow from one of the regional banks throughout the country.

FEDERAL HOME LOAN BANK SYSTEM — (See: Federal Home Loan Banks).

FEDERAL HOME LOAN MORTGAGE CORPORATION (THE MORT-GAGE CORPORATION) — A semi-governmental purchaser of mortgages in the secondary market. The trading of mortgage securities (Participation Certificates) for mortgages in its guarantor program has been highly successful.

FEDERAL REVENUE STAMPS — Also called IRS stamps. A transfer of tax of $.55 per $500, based on the sale price of real estate (less remaining loans). The tax ended as a federal tax and was taken up by most states with slight modifications in some areas. (See also: Documentary Transfer Tax).

FEDERAL ROAD — (See: Interstate Highway System).

FEDERAL SAVINGS AND LOAN ASSOCIATION — A federally chartered institution for savings and home mortgages, under the regulation of the Federal Home Loan Bank Board.

FEDERAL SAVINGS AND LOAN INSURANCE CORPORATION — A federal corporation insuring against loss by depositors·in a savings and loan association, in much the same way the Federal Deposit Insurance Corporation insures against loss by depositors in banks.

FEDERAL TAX LIEN — A lien attaching to property for nonpayment of a federal tax (estate, income, etc.). A federal tax lien differs from other liens in that it is not automatically wiped out by foreclosing on a mortgage or trust deed recorded before the tax lien (except by judicial foreclosure).

FEE — (1) Modernly, and not in strict legal terms, synonymous with fee simple or "ownership". (2) A charge made by a landlord to a tenant, which is not refundable. For example: A cleaning deposit would be refunded if the tenant left the rented property reasonably clean. A cleaning fee would be a charge by the landlord for cleaning the rented property and would not be refunded regardless of the condition of the property.

FEE SIMPLE — An estate under which the owner is entitled to unrestricted powers to dispose of the property, and which can be left by will or inherited. Commonly, a synonym for ownership.

FEE SIMPLE DEFEASIBLE — (See: Defeasible Title).

FEE TAIL — An estate of inheritance which specifies the descendants or classes or heirs of the devisee who may succeed to the said estate.

FELT — A fabric composed mainly of wool mixed with fur, hair, or synthetics, under heat and pressure.

FELT PAPER — A highly absorbent, porous paper, used with tar or asphalt as a roofing paper, or over studs as an insulation.

FENCE — A barrier, usually to enclose one's property; may be made of wood, brick, wire, etc.

FENESTRATION — The decorative manner or plan of placing doors or windows in a structure.

F.H.A. (FEDERAL HOUSING ADMINISTRATION) — A federal agency which insures first mortgages, enabling lenders to loan a very high percentage of the sale price.

FHA ESCAPE CLAUSE — A clause stating that the buyer (borrower) shall not be obligated to buy nor shall any deposit be lost if the appraisal is less than the agreed upon amount.

FHLMC (FREDDIE MAC) — Federal Home Loan Mortgage Corporation. A federal agency purchasing first mortgages, both conventional and federally insured, from members of the Federal Reserve System, and the Federal Home Loan Bank System.

FIBERBOARD — (See: Insulation Board).

FIBER GLASS — Particles of glass spun into a form of insulation, or materials such as used in drapes.

FICTITIOUS DEED OF TRUST — (See: Fictitious Instrument).

FICTITIOUS DOCUMENT — A document containing general provisions but not regarding specific property. The fictitious document is recorded in all counties of a state. Whenever the same type of document is recorded regarding specific property, the provisions of the fictitious document are incorporated by reference, saving both the costs of printing, and recording extra pages.

FICTITIOUS INSTRUMENT — An instrument (usually a mortgage or deed of trust) which is recorded not on specific property but to be incorporated by reference into future mortgages or deeds of trust. This is done by reference to the recording information of the fictitious instrument in the instrument recorded against specific property. This shortens the latter instrument and thereby cuts costs of printing, paper, recording, etc. The fictitious instrument contains general language applicable to any specific property.

FICTITIOUS MORTGAGE — (See: Fictitious Instrument).

FICTITIOUS NAME — Commonly refers to a company name in a business not incorporated. The owner files a certificate of fictitious name. For example: Joe Smith (real name); Joe's Garage, (fictitious name). Also called a D.B.A. (doing business as).

FIDUCIARY — One acting in a relationship of trust, regarding financial transactions.

FIELD TILE — A series of tiles placed at the base of the superstructure to retard seepage of ground waters through the foundation. (See also: Disposal Field).

FILL — (1) To supply an area with additional material (fill) to raise or obtain a uniform grade level. (2) The materials used for fill such as dirt, gravel, etc.

FINAL DECREE — A decree completely deciding all pending matters before a court, and obviating the need for further litigation.

FINANCIAL CORPORATION — A general term encompassing companies dealing in finance, such as banks, savings and loan associations, insurance companies, and similar companies.

FINANCIAL STATEMENT — An accounting statement showing assets and liabilities of a person or company. Used generally for large loans or other instances when the credit report (history of payment of debts) in itself is not sufficient.

FINANCING COSTS — The cost of interest and other charges involved in borrowing money to build or purchase real estate.

FINANCING STATEMENT — A recorded instrument, taking the place of personal property liens in some states. Used instead of chattel mortgages, inventory liens, pledges, etc.

FINDER'S FEE — A fee paid to someone who finds a buyer or property for a broker, buyer, etc. The term is sometimes used to attempt to pay a commission to an unlicensed person. Generally, a finder's fee is considered a commission and may only be paid to one who holds a real estate license.

FINISH FLOOR — The flooring over the subfloor, usually of hardwood, tile, or other finish on which one may walk. In some modern construction where carpeting is installed by the builder, plywood is used as a finish floor.

FINISH HARDWARE — (See: Hardware).

FIREBACK — (See: Chimney Back).

FIREBRICK — A brick specially made of clay which can be exposed to extremely high temperatures without damage. Used in furnaces, fireplaces, and similar high temperature areas.

FIRE INSURANCE — Insurance against loss or damage by fire to specific property. May also include other coverage.

FIREPLACE — A square, rectangular, or arched opening usually in a wall at the base of a chimney, lined with stone or masonry, and used for an open fire within a structure. Modernly, a decorative, more than necessary, part of a home.

FIREPROOF CONSTRUCTION — Having all exposed and load-bearing members of a noncombustible material, and structural members which can be injured by fire (such as iron or steel) protected by noncombustible materials.

FIRE-RESISTIVE — Able to withstand specified temperatures for a certain time, such as a one hour wall. Not fireproof.

FIRE ROCK — (See: Igneous Rock).

FIRE SPRINKLER SYSTEM — (See: Sprinkler System).

FIRE STOP — A means of preventing fire or smoke from traveling through a structure by filling concealed air spaces with fire-resistive materials.

FIRE WALL — A wall to divide parts of a building, and prevent the spread of fire. Should rise from basement level to a minimum of three feet above roof level, and all openings through the wall should be protected by fireproof doors.

FIRM COMMITMENT — [See: Commitment (2); Conditional Commitment].

FIRST BOTTOM — The flood plain of a river or stream.

FIRST MORTGAGE — A mortgage having priority over all other voluntary liens against certain property.

FIRST REFUSAL RIGHT — A right, usually given by an owner to a lessee, which gives the lessee a first chance to buy the property if the owner decides to sell. The owner must have a legitimate offer which the lessee can match or refuse. If the lessee refuses, the property can then be sold to the offeror.

FIRST USER — A tax term signifying the one who builds or buys property and is the first one to put the buildings to use. Certain tax (depreciation) advantages are given to a first user. The term concerns only depreciable property (improvements) and prior use of the land only (farming) would not be considered.

FISCAL YEAR — An accounting year, which may be the calendar year, or any other one year period. The United States budget is based on a fiscal year from July 1, to June 30.

FIXED ASSETS — Permanent assets, necessary for the operation of a business, such as buildings, heavy machinery, etc.

FIXED RATE MORTGAGE — A mortgage having a rate of interest which remains the same for the life of the mortgage.

FIXED WINDOW — A window which has no moveable parts, such as a picture window.

FIXTURES — Personal property which is attached to real property, and is legally treated as real property while it is so attached. Fixtures, not specifically excepted from an accepted offer to purchase, pass with the real estate.

FLAGSTONE — A decorative, flat, slate-like stone, used in walkways and patios, and processed in a variety of colors.

FLANGE — A projecting border, edge, rim, etc., used as a means of attachment to another object, as a method of adding strength, stability, etc.

FLANK — The side of any structure, hill, etc.

FLASHING — Sheet metal or similar material, used at different points in a structure to prevent water seepage, such as around vent pipes, chimneys, etc.

FLAT — A building containing a single living unit on each floor, and sometimes referred to by the number of units, such as two flat, four flat. Flats are no longer built, having given way to duplexes, fourplexes, etc.

FLAT COST — The direct cost of labor and materials used in construction of a project.

FLAT LEASE — (See: Straight Lease).

FLAT ROOF — A roof having an almost level surface, except for either being slightly convex, to allow drainage towards its edges, or slightly concave, allowing water to drain at the center of the roof.

FLEXIBLE CONDUIT — A conduit that can flex (bend) to reach from another line (gas, electric, etc.) to the point of intended use.

FLEXIBLE INTEREST RATE — (See: Variable Interest Rate).

FLEXIBLE RATE MORTGAGE — (See: Adjustable Mortgage Loans).

FLIGHT PATTERN — The path (pattern of flights) used by airplanes for approaching and departing from an airport.

FLITCH BEAM — A beam formed by two or more timbers, cut lengthwise, called flitches, between any two of which is placed a metal plate for additional strength, and all pieces are bolted together.

FLOATING RATE — (See: Variable Interest Rate).

FLOOD — An overflowing of a body of water from its normal boundaries, so that land usually dry is covered with water. May be a regular occurrence (sometimes even desirable for farming) or a disaster, if severe.

FLOOD INSURANCE — Insurance indemnifying against loss by flood damage. Required by lenders (usually banks) in areas designated (federally) as potential flood areas. The insurance is private but federally subsidized.

FLOODPLANE — The extent of the land adjoining a river, which, because of its level topography, would flood if the river overflowed its banks.

FLOOR — (1) The inside bottom or lowest horizontal surface of a room, on which one walks or stands. (2) The different levels (stories) in a building, such as main floor, second floor, etc.

FLOOR DRAINS — Sewer drains in the floor of a building, used where there may be a heavy accumulation of water, such as in a basement of a house, or where floors may be cleaned with a hose, such as in an industrial building.

FLOOR FURNACE — A furnace placed directly below a floor, which has no ducts and heats only through a grill in the floor.

FLOOR HANGER — An iron, stirrup-like brace, used to support a floor joist.

FLOOR JOIST — A joist used to support flooring placed over it.

FLOOR LOAD — The live load in pounds per square foot, which a floor is capable of holding safely.

FLOOR LOAN — The lower of two amounts of a single take out loan. For example: A lender agrees to loan on an office building being constructed, in the amount of eighty percent of appraised value if the building is seventy-five percent occupied, but only seventy percent of appraised value if the building is less than seventy-five percent occupied. The lower amount is the floor loan.

FLOOR OF FOREST — The covering of the ground of a forest, composed of partially decomposed vegetation, twigs, etc. Also called duff.

FLOOR PLAN — The layout of a building or portion of a building (apartment, office, etc.), showing the size of the rooms and the purpose of each (bath, bedroom, etc.). A good floor plan should be very important to a builder, since it will be important to a buyer or tenant.

FLOOR TIME — A period during the working day when a specific salesperson is responsible for general inquiries (walk-in or telephone) regarding property in a brokerage office. This is generally established as a set, rotating number of hours per week for each salesperson. When a salesperson is "on the floor" he or she must be in the office or make arrangements with another salesperson to cover the floor during those hours.

FLOWAGE EASEMENT — Not an easement by agreement, but the common law servitude of land of a lower grade level to allow water from land of a higher level to flow across it.

FLOW TIDE — High tide. The highest tide under normal weather conditions, as determined by the phases of the moon.

FLUE — (1) The opening or passageway in a chimney through which smoke, gases, etc., pass from a building. (2) Any opening or passageway for the elimination of gases, fumes, etc.

FLUME — (1) A natural gorge or ravine, through which a stream flows. (2) An artificial channel, inclined as a chute, and used to hold running water on which logs are floated from one place to another.

FLUORESCENT LIGHTING — Tubular glass lights, the interior of which has a fluorescent coating. Light is produced by the action of a stream of electrons upon the coating.

FNMA (FANNIE MAE) — A private corporation dealing in the purchase of first mortgages, at discounts.

FNMA BUYDOWN — FNMA (Federal National Mortgage Association) accepts loans containing a buy down provision on single family residential, owner occupied properties. A prepayment (points) will buy a lower rate of interest during the first one to five years of the loan. Restrictions apply as to the amount of the buydown and rise in payment amount as the loan progresses.

FOOTING — A foot-like projection at the base of a foundation wall, column, pier, etc., used to secure, support, and help eliminate settling or shifting.

FORCED-AIR FURNACE — A furnace having a fan or blower which forces the warm air through the ducts, rather than having the air circulated by the action of gravity.

FORCED PRICE — The price paid at a forced sale.

FORCED SALE — A sale which is not the voluntary act of the owner, such as to satisfy a debt, whether of a mortgage, judgment, etc. The selling price under such a sale would not be considered market value.

FORCED VALUE — (See: Forced Sale).

FORCE MAJEURE (FRENCH) — A force which cannot be resisted. In other words, something beyond the control of the parties involved. Includes Acts of God (see which) and acts of man (riots, strikes, arson, etc.). Used primarily in insurance but may be extended to any type of performance contract, such as construction.

FORECLOSURE — A proceeding in or out of court, to extinguish all rights, title, and interest, of the owner(s) of property in order to sell the property to satisfy a lien against it.

FORECLOSURE SALE — A sale of property used as security for a debt, to satisfy said debt.

FOREIGN CORPORATION — A corporation incorporated in another state. In New York, for example, a Delaware corporation would be a foreign corporation. (See also: Corporation; Domestic Corporation).

FORESHORE — The shore between the average line of the flow tide and the average line of the ebb tide.

FOREST — A large area of land, covered with a heavy growth of trees and underbrush.

FORFEITURE — The taking of an individual's property by a government, because the individual has committed a crime. In the United States, private property cannot be taken, except by eminent domain upon payment of just compensation, or for nonpayment of taxes.

FORGERY — A false signature or material alteration with intent to defraud. The forged signature of the grantor will not pass title regardless of recording or lack of knowledge by the grantee or future grantees. Title insurance will insure against forgery. The word may extend beyond signatures (forged paintings, documents, etc.)

FORMICA — A synthetic material under a trade name. Mainly used for counter-tops in kitchens, bathrooms, etc. Other uses include paneling, facing of wallboards, etc., as a durable interior finish.

FORMS — (1) Restraints, such as plywood sheets, to control the shape of poured concrete until it hardens. (2) A general term meaning instruments which are not unique, but printed in quantity, usually with blank spaces to be filled in to identify specific facts.

FOUNDATION — The part of a building which supports the superstructure, usually below ground level.

FOYER — The open area or hallway upon entering a building, such as in a theater or hotel; also found in many homes. (See also: Lobby).

FRACTIONAL APPRAISAL — An appraisal of a portion of a property, such as the value of a leasehold interest, value of an improvement without land, etc.

FRACTIONAL INTEREST — (See: Divided Interest).

FRACTIONAL PROPERTY — A part of a property considered separately from the whole property (usually for appraisal or insurance purposes).

FRACTIONAL RATE — (See: Split Rate).

FRAME CONSTRUCTION — Type of construction in which the structural parts are of wood or are dependent on a wooden frame for support.

FRAME HOUSE — Commonly used to describe a wood sided house. (See also: Wood Frame Construction).

FRAMING — The outer structural member of a building or part of a building, such as window framing, or the skeletal support of members of a building.

FRANCHISE — (1) A statutory right which could not be exercised in the absence of the statute, such as the statutes enabling persons to form a corporation. Since a corporation is created by the statute, it could not be formed except by the grant of the legislature. (2) A combination of individual ownership and central control. One may own a fast food restaurant, hotel, hardware store, etc., yet use the name of a national company. Each individual owner pays for the name use, advertising, and may be required to make certain purchases (napkins, buns, etc.) from the national company. The individual benefits from the name and advertising. The real estate brokerage business was slow to use the franchise method, but now has many companies operating in this manner.

FRAUD — A deception, intended to wrongfully obtain money or property from the reliance of another on the deceptive statements or acts, believing them to be true.

FREE AND CLEAR — Real property against which there are no liens, especially voluntary liens (mortgages).

FREEHOLD — An estate, at least of duration of a lifetime, or of fee.

FREE STANDING BUILDING — A building containing one business, rather than a row of stores or businesses with a common roof and side walls.

FREEWAY — A highway with ramp entrances and exits only, all crossroads at a different grade level, and charging no tolls or fees.

FRENCH CURVE — A draftsman's tool used in drawing noncircular curves. Also called an irregular curve.

FREON — The gas added to a refrigerator or air conditioner, which produces cold.

FRESCO — A method of painting on a wall on wet plaster. The paint becomes part of the wall and remains much longer than if simply painted on a dry plaster wall.

FRIABLE — Easily reduced to powder or crumbled. Nonpliable.

FRONT — (1) The external portion (face) of a building, which usually contains the main entrance. (See also: Facade). (2) That portion of land bordering on a river, ocean, street, etc.

FRONTAGE ROAD — (See: Service Road).

FRONT ELEVATION — [See: Elevation (2)].

FRONT FOOTAGE — Linear measurement along the front of a parcel, that is, the portion fronting on the major street or walkway.

FRONT FOOT COST — A determination of the value of real property based on a value per foot as measured along the frontage of a parcel. Usually used with commercial property.

FROSTLINE — The depth to which the soil freezes.

FRUCTUS INDUSTRIALES — Those things created by the labor (industry) of man rather than by nature alone. For example: A planted crop rather than an iron ore deposit. Important because Fructus Industriales is treated as personal property. (See also: Emblements; Fructus Naturales).

FRUCTUS NATURALES — Produced by nature alone, such as trees (not planted by man), or minerals in the ground. Considered real property. (See also: Emblements; Fructus Industriales).

FULL DISCLOSURE — In real estate, revealing all the known facts which may affect the decision of a buyer or tenant. A broker must disclose known defects in the property for sale or lease. A builder must give to a potential buyer the facts of his new development (are there adequate school facilities?; sewer facilities?; an airport nearby?; etc.). A broker cannot charge a commission to buyer and seller unless both know (disclosure) and agree.

FUNCTIONAL — The ability of anything to perform its intended use or purpose.

FUNCTIONAL OBSOLESCENCE — The need for replacement because a structure or equipment has become inefficient because of improvements discovered or invented since its construction.

FUNDS — Money available for a qualified purpose, such as loan funds for F.H.A. insured loans, conventional loan funds, etc.

FURLONG — A linear measure, one eighth of a mile, used in horse racing.

FURNACE — An enclosed heating device. Modernly, a box-shaped unit containing a burner, which is fed oil or gas through a pipe. The heat from the burning gas or oil is circulated, usually with the aid of a fan, through ducts to areas to be heated.

FURNITURE AND FIXTURES — An entry in an accounting statement, referring to those items considered depreciable, as business fixtures and furniture, rather than real property.

FURRING — Narrow strips of wood or metal which are applied to walls, floors, ceilings, etc., as a means of leveling the area before applying the surface boards or laths.

FUSE — A device to prevent the overloading of an electrical circuit, by containing a strip of metal which melts at relatively low heat and breaks the circuit. In modern construction, the fuse has been replaced by circuit breakers.

FUSE BOX — A metal box containing the main wiring and all electrical circuit connections, protected by fuses.

FUTURE ACQUIRED PROPERTY — Property acquired after a loan or sale. For example: A loan agreement may state that the loan is a lien on all property presently owned or which the borrower may acquire in the future. (See also: After Acquired Property; After Acquired Title).

FUTURE ADVANCE CLAUSE — Also called an additional advance clause. A clause in a mortgage or deed of trust which allows the borrower to borrow additional sums at a future time, secured under the same instrument and by the same real property security. Contained in an open-end mortgage or deed of trust.

FUTURE INTEREST — A present interest, but only a future right to possession and enjoyment of the land, such as a remainder interest, reversionary interest, etc.

G

GABLE — The exterior wall surface, triangular in shape, formed by the inclined edges of a ridged roof (gable roof).

GABLE ROOF — A ridged roof, having two sloping edges which, at the ends of the ridge, form a gable.

GAIN — Profit. Important for tax purposes when realized from the sale of a capital asset. (See also: Capital Gain).

GALLERY — (1) A covered walkway, open on one side, running along an upper story of a building, either inside or outside. (2) The highest theater balcony, having the cheapest seats. (3) A building or portion of a building used for exhibits, such as an art gallery.

GALLON — A liquid measure of 231 cubic inches or 4 quarts. (See also: Imperial Gallon).

GAMBREL ROOF — A ridged roof, each side having two slopes, the lower of which is more inclined.

GAP COMMITMENT — A commitment to loan the difference between the floor amount of a take out loan and the full amount. The commitment is issued to enable a construction lender to loan the full amount of a take out commitment, rather than only the floor amount. (See also: Floor Loan; Take Out Loan).

GARAGE — A place to keep or repair motor vehicles; either a building adjacent or attached to a residence, or as a commercial enterprise.

GARBAGE DISPOSAL — A small tank with metal grinders, which is usually installed under the drain in a kitchen sink. The grinders pulverize discarded food into particles which may be washed into the sanitary sewer.

GARDEN — A small parcel of land used for growing fruits, vegetables, or flowers, which are usually not sold, but used by the grower.

GARDEN APARTMENTS — An apartment development consisting of two or more structures, surrounded by an abundance of lawns, plants, flowers, etc., giving a garden-like atmosphere.

GARNISH — To bring garnishment proceedings.

GARNISHEE — The person against whom a garnishment is issued. The party holding funds of the debtor and not the debtor.

GARNISHMENT — A legal proceeding under which a person's money in control of another (such as salary) is taken for payment of a debt. The amount which may be taken is set by statute (usually as a percentage), and, in most states, a judgement is necessary before garnishment.

GARRET — (See: Attic).

GAS STATION — (See: Service Station).

GAZEBO — An open structure, usually in the garden of a "summer house" where one may sit and enjoy the view. Also called a belvedere.

GEM — (See: Growing Equity Mortgage).

GENERAL BENEFITS — In condemnation, benefits accruing to property not taken, but which benefits are caused by the taking.

GENERAL CONTRACTOR — One who contracts for the construction of an entire building or project, rather than for a portion of the work. The general contractor hires subcontractors, such as plumbing contractors, electrical contractors, etc., coordinates all work, and is responsible for payment to the said subcontractors.

GENERAL INDEX (G.I.) — A title insurance company term for the books used to find liens against individuals which may effect real property, but which are not recorded against the property being insured, such as liens against a buyer.

GENERAL LIEN — (1) A lien such as a tax lien or judgment lien which attaches to all property of the debtor rather than the lien of, for example, a trust deed, which attaches only to specific property. (2) The right of a creditor to hold personal property of a debtor for payment of a debt not associated with the property being held. Must be done under an agreement since against general precepts of law.

GENERAL OVERHEAD COSTS — (See: Indirect Construction Costs).

GENERAL PARTNER — A member of a partnership who has authority to beind the partnership and shares in the profits and losses. A partnership must have at least one general partner and may have more, as well as limited partners.

GENERAL PARTNERSHIP — A partnership made up of general partners, without special (limited) partners. (See also: Limited Partnership; Partnership).

GENERAL PLAN — (See: Master Plan).

GENERAL PLAN RESTRICTIONS — Restrictions imposed on an entire subdivision, usually by the developer. Also called a declaration of restrictions.

GENERAL POWER — [See: Power of Attorney (1)].

GEODETIC SYSTEM (THE UNITED STATES COAST AND GEODETIC SURVEY SYSTEM) — A network of bench marks (surveyor's marks), located by longitude and latitude, covering the entire country. Originally, this system was used to locate federally owned land, and has since been extended nation-wide.

GEORGIAN ARCHITECTURE — A colonial style of architecture dating back to the eighteenth century. Characterized by first floor windows extending to the ground, its exterior placements (windows, doors, etc.) are simple and well balanced, yet formal in appearance.

GEORGIAN COLONIAL ARCHITECTURE — A more formal and elaborate form of Georgian Architecture.

GERRYMANDER — To divide an area into districts, against the obvious natural divisions, in order to accomplish an unlawful purpose. For example: To divide a school district to keep out certain people for reasons of race or religion; to divide a political voting district so as to give power to a political party.

GIFT — A voluntary transfer of property without valuable consideration.

GIFT CAUSA MORTIS — A gift made in contemplation of death. The gift is conditioned upon the death of the donor and may be revoked before the donor's death.

GIFT DEED — A deed for nominal consideration.

GIFT LETTER — A letter to HUD from the donor (giver) stating that a gift of money has been made to the buyer in order to purchase specific property. The relationship of the donor and donee is stated, as well as the amount of the gift.

GIFT TAX — A federal and sometimes a state tax on inter vivos transfers without consideration.

G.I. LOAN — [See: Veteran's Administration (V.A.) Loan].

GINGERBREAD WORK — Use of ornamentation in architecture, especially residential, which adds to emotional appeal, rather than functional value.

GIRDER — (1) One of the heavy beams supporting flooring joists, (2) A metal framing member of a series of heavy supports for a building, bridge, etc.

GIRT — A horizontal bracing member, running between columns or other vertical members to stiffen the framing.

GLASS — A usually transparent or translucent substance, formed by the fusion of some silica, such as sand. Glass is colored by the addition of metallic oxides, and comes in a great variety of shapes and sizes.

GLASS BLOCK — A building block of hollow glass, used as a decorative wall, but not usually a bearing wall.

GLASS-WOOL INSULATION — Insulation made in sheets from glass fibers, covered with water resistant or asphalt treated paper.

GLAZE — To finish with a glossy surface.

GLAZED BRICK — A brick having a glazed (glossy) surface.

GLUE LAMINATED BEAMS — Beams composed of layers of wood, pressed and glued together, and used to support roof rafters.

GNMA (GINNIE MAE) — Government National Mortgage Association. A federal association, working with F.H.A., which offers special assistance in obtaining mortgages, and purchases mortgages in a secondary capacity.

GNMA (GOVERNMENT NATIONAL MORTGAGE ASSOCIATION) OPTIONS — A method of purchasing GNMA securities through "puts" and "calls". A GNMA Call Option is the right to buy GNMA securities at a specific yield for a specified time. A Put Option is the right to sell GNMA securities at a specific yield for a specified time. The buyer pays for the option and may exercise it, not exercise it, or sell it.

GOOD FAITH — Something done with good intentions, without knowledge of fraudulent circumstances, or reason to inquire further.

GOOD WILL — A salable asset of a business, based on its reputation rather than its physical assets.

GORE — A small parcel of land, usually triangular in shape, resulting from the failure of a legal description to join 2 tracts. (Also called: Hiatus).

GOVERNMENT LOTS — Irregularly shaped parcels of land, usually fronting on water, which could not practically be divided into sections under government survey.

GOVERNMENT NATIONAL MORTGAGE ASSOCIATION — (See: GNMA).

GOVERNMENT SURVEY — The survey from which our present system of townships, sections, etc., was developed.

GPM — (See: Graduated Payment Mortgage).

GRACE PERIOD — A period of time past the due date for a payment (mortgage, insurance, etc.), during which time a payment may be made and not considered delinquent.

GRADE — The degree of the slope of land.

GRADED LEASE — (See: Step-Up Lease).

GRADED TAX — A property tax designed to promote local development by increasing the tax rate on land and decreasing it on improvements.

GRADE SEPARATION — A structure, such as a cloverleaf of a highway, enabling roads to intersect one over the other, obviating the need for a traffic light or stop sign.

GRADIENT — The degree of the slope of land.

GRADUATED LEASE — A lease calling for a varying rental, usually based on periodic appraisal or simply the passage of time.

GRADUATED PAYMENT MORTGAGE — A mortgage or deed or trust calling for increasingly higher payments over the term of the loan. This allows the buyer low beginning payments. The payments then increase as (theoretically) the buyer's earnings increase. (See also: G.E.M.)

GRAIN — (1) The direction, size, and arrangement of the fibers of wood, leather, etc. (2) Seeds from cereal plants, such as wheat, oats, corn, etc. (3) A small particle, such as a grain of sand. (4) A unit of weight equal to $\frac{1}{7000}$ th of a pound.

GRAIN ELEVATOR — (1) A structure for the processing and storage of grain. (2) Modern farm machinery used for loading and unloading grain.

GRANDFATHER CLAUSE — The clause in a law permitting the continuation of a use, business, etc., which, when established, was permissible but, because of a change in the law, is now not permissible. (See also: Nonconforming Use).

GRAND LIST — The term used for the tax roll or assessment list in the New England states.

GRANT — To transfer an interest in real property; either the fee or a lesser interest, such as an easement.

GRANT DEED — One of the many types of deeds used to transfer real property. Contains warranties against prior conveyances or encumbrances. When title insurance is purchased, warranties in a deed are of little practical significance.

GRANTEE — One to whom a grant is made. Generally, the buyer.

GRANTOR — One who grants property or property rights.

GRANTOR-GRANTEE INDEX — The record of the passing of title to all the properties in a county as kept by the county recorder's office. Property is checked by tracing the names of the sellers and buyers (chain of title). Title companies usually have more efficient methods by keeping records according to property description, rather than people's names.

GRAPH — A diagram representing statistical data by the use of dots and lines to show a relationship among things.

GRAVEL — Loose rock about two millimeters in diameter, found in great quantity, and used for roadbeds, as a surface or under paving.

GRAVEL PIT — An excavation from which gravel is removed. (See also: Borrow Pit).

GRAVEYARD — (See: Cemetery).

GRAVITY FURNACE — A hot air furnace which circulates by the different weights of hot and cold air, rather than by a fan.

GREEN LUMBER — Unseasoned lumber, having a higher content of moisture than that of seasoned or air-dried lumber.

GRID — (1) A network of pipes (as for the distribution of water or gas). (2) A network of uniformly spaced horizontal lines, as on a map or chart, used for locating points by coordinates. (3) A chart used by insurance companies and lenders for rating property, risk of the borrower, neighborhood, etc.

GRIDIRON PATTERN (GRIDIRON PLAN) — A layout of streets in a subdivision or city which resembles a gridiron.

GROIN — (1) In architecture, the curved point at which arched ceilings or roofs meet or intersect each other. (2) A structure, usually of pilings, used to resist shifting of coastal sands.

GROSS — Total, with no allowances or deductions, such as gross acre, gross lease, gross income, gross sales, etc.

GROSS ACRE — An acre (43,560 sq. ft.). Distinguished from a net (usable) acre.

GROSS AREA — In building measurement, the outside dimensions determine the gross area, irrespective of the area inside actually usable or rentable.

GROSS EFFECTIVE INCOME — (See: Adjusted Gross Income).

GROSS INCOME — The scheduled (total) income, either actual or estimated, derived from a business or property.

GROSS INCOME MULTIPLIER — A figure which, when multiplied by the annual gross income, will theoretically determine the market value. A general rule of thumb which varies with specific properties and areas.

GROSS LEASE — A lease which obligates the lessor to pay all or part of the expenses of the leased property, such as taxes, insurance, maintenance, utilities, etc.

GROSS NATIONAL PRODUCT (GNP) — The money value of all goods and services produced by a nation's economy for a given period of time.

GROSS PROFIT — The total profit before deductions. A general term which varies, depending upon accounting procedures.

GROSS SALES — The total sales for a given time, before deductions for refunds, allowances, etc.

GROUND BEAM — A horizontal beam, very heavy and strong, installed at ground level to support and distribute the weight of that part of the building above the foundation.

GROUND LEASE — A lease of vacant land, or land exclusive of any buildings on it. Usually a net lease.

GROUND LEVEL — Being at the level of the surrounding land, such as the ground floor of a building.

GROUND RENT — Rent paid for vacant land. If the property is improved, ground rent is that portion attributable to the land only.

GROUNDS — (1) The area surrounding a building which goes with and is of the same ownership as the building. The word would be used if the area were substantial, as opposed to a yard. (2) Strips of wood placed over the lath, to which molding is nailed.

GROUND WATER — Water in the subsoil or of a spring or shallow well.

GROUT — (1) Thin mortar used in masonry work to fill joints between bricks, blocks, tiles, etc. (2) A variety of plaster used to finish ceilings of superior quality.

GROWING CROP — A crop is considered "growing" from the time the seed is planted. It then stops being personal property and becomes part of the land passing with the fee unless specifically excepted.

GROWING EQUITY MORTGAGE (G.E.M.) — A fixed rate, graduated payment loan allowing low beginning payments and a shorter term because of higher payments as the loan progresses. Based on the theory of increasing income by the buyer and, therefore, ability to make higher future payments. When state law applies, usury laws in some states may not presently allow such loans when less than interest only payments create interest on interest.

GROYNE — (See: Groin).

GUARANTEED MORTGAGE — (See: Insured Mortgage).

GUARANTOR — One who makes a guaranty.

GUARANTY — Agreement to pay the debt or perform the obligation of another in the event the debt is not paid or obligation not performed. Differs from a surety agreement in that there must be a failure to pay or perform before the guaranty can be in effect.

GUARDIAN — One who is court appointed to manage the affairs of a minor or incompetent.

GUIDE MERIDIAN — (See: Meridian).

GULLY EROSION — The formation of a gully by continued erosion through the soft topsoil (rill erosion) into the subsoil, where a more permanent channel is cut, separating areas and preventing the movement of animals, machinery, etc.

GUTTER — (1) A channel along the eaves to direct rainwater to a downspout. (2) The channel formed by the meeting of the street and curb, where rainwater runs to a sewer.

GYPSUM — An ingredient of plaster or cement; it is hydrated calcium sulphate.

GYPSUM BLOCKS — Building material used in non load-bearing walls and partitions, composed of a plaster type material.

GYPSUM PLASTER — A coarse plaster used as a basecoat, or for some exterior uses.

GYPSUM SHEATHING BOARDS — (See: Gypsuum Wallboard).

GYPSUM WALLBOARD — Commonly known as dry wall. A wallboard or gypsum (plaster) covered with a paper which can be painted or wallpapered.

H

HABENDUM — The clause in a deed, following the granting clause, which defines the extent of the estate of the grantee.

HABITABLE ROOM — A room used for living area, such as a kitchen, bedroom, dining room, etc., as opposed to bathrooms, closets, hallways, and similar spaces. Generally, habitable rooms are the only ones counted in the number of rooms in a house; bathrooms are counted separately.

HABITANCY — A legal term meaning the place which a person inhabits (lives). The layman's meaning of a place where someone "lives" is probably the closest definition.

HACIENDA — An estate, farm, or, commonly, even a house. Originally, the royal estate.

HACK STAND — An area where taxicabs may park to solicit fares.

HALF SECTION — One half of a section of land, divided either North and South, or East and West. (See also: Section).

HALF-TIMBERED — Residential construction exposing the timber frame of the interior walls, the space between being lath and plaster. In simulated half-timbering, the attaching of boards (or a plastic which is treated to resemble a timber surface) to the surface of an interior wall. In simulated half-timbering, the boards are strictly decorative, and not load-bearing.

HALL — Originally, a large building used as a meeting place, such as a town hall. The term has also become synonymous with "hallway", the latter being a relatively narrow passageway between rooms.

HAMLET — A small village or town.

HAND — A lineal measure equal to four inches, the approximate width of a man's hand. Most commonly used to measure the height of a horse.

HARBOR — A natural or man made sheltered area for ships to anchor. May or may not have docks and other port facilities.

HARD FINISH — A smooth outer coat of varnish, plaster, or similar finish material.

HARD MONEY MORTGAGE — A mortgage given in return for cash, rather than to secure a portion of the purchase price, as with a purchase money mortgage.

HARDPAN — A compacted layer of soil, usually containing clay, through which it is difficult to drain or dig.

HARDWARE — In construction, the metal accessories, such as door-knobs, hinges, locks, etc.

HARDWOOD — Wood used for interior finish, such as oak, maple, and walnut. Although the term originally referred to the type of tree and not the hardness of the wood, modern usage usually refers to the hardness of the wood.

HARMONIOUS — Blending compatibly, as parts of buildings, buildings in a neighborhood or subdivision, etc.

HATCHWAY — Usually describes a door in the deck of a boat. A door in the ceiling or floor of a building, giving access to the attic or cellar.

H-BEAM — A beam, the cross-section of which is the shape of a capital H.

HEAD — (1) The upper framing member of a door or window. Also called a header. (2) The beginning of a river or stream.

HEADER (LINTEL) — A horizontal beam over a wall opening, such as a doorway, fireplace, etc. The header is attached to vertical framing members, and spreads the weight from above to these members.

HEAD OF A FAMILY (HEAD OF HOUSEHOLD) — A term used in homestead exemptions to designate the person in charge of managing and supporting a family. It need not be a parent.

HEARTH — (1) The fireside. (2) The fireplace floor, of stone, brick, tile, etc.

HEARTWOOD — A dead portion of a tree, no longer producing sap. The wood from the center of the tree (pith) to the wood which produces sap (sapwood).

HEATER — Connotes a device working by itself to heat a small area (space heater), rather than a heating system, composed of a central source of heat (furnace) and pipes and ducts which heat several spaces.

HEATING SYSTEM — A general term encompassing any system designed to heat a structure in its entirety, as opposed to a space heater.

HEAT PUMP — A pump used in either heating or cooling.

HEAVY INDUSTRY — Any industry designated "heavy industry" under a zoning ordinance. Usually connected with some type of pollution, such as air, water, or noise pollution.

HEAVY STEEL FRAME — A building having heavy steel beams, girders, or other framing members, which carry heavy floor loads.

HECTARE — A French unit of measurement, equaling 10,000 square meters (2.471 acres).

HEEL — That part of a vertical framing member which rests closest to the floor.

HEIGHT DENSITY — A zoning term referring to the regulation of maximum building heights for structures in given areas.

HEIR — One who by law, rather than by will, receives the estate of a deceased person.

HEIRS AND ASSIGNS — Words usually found in a deed, showing the interest the grantee is receiving. A deed to "A, his heirs and assigns", would grant the property to A, with the right to assign said property or have it descend to A's heirs upon A's death. This would be considered a fee interest (estate). This would differ from, for example, a life estate granted to A, which would terminate upon A's death and could not be inherited by A's heirs.

HEREDITAMENTS — (1) Anything which could be considered real property. (2) Anything which may be inherited.

HETEROGENEOUS — An appraisal term describing an area composed of buildings of varied styles or uses. Not as desirable as homogeneous property.

HIATUS — (See: Gore).

HIGHEST AND BEST USE — The use of land which will bring the greatest economic return over a given time.

HIGH-RISE APARTMENT BUILDING — An apartment building considered "high" in the area where it is built. There is no national height standard.

HIGH WATER LINE — The line on the shore to which high tide rises under normal weather conditions.

HIGHWAY — Technically, any public road, regardless of size. Most commonly, a paved road which carries traffic at high speeds.

HIGHWAY CAPACITY — The number of vehicles which may move along a highway at the same time. The number may vary as the type (size) of the vehicles vary, speed limit changes, access changes, etc.

HIGHWAY FRONTAGE — Technically, land which fronts on a highway. For purposes of determining value, land which fronts on and has access to a highway.

HIP — The convex angle at the exterior meeting of the sides of a hip roof.

HIP RAFTER — The rafter which forms the intersection of a convex roof angle.

HIP ROOF — A roof with four sloping sides which rise to a ridge. Usually found on garages or church steeples. Also called a pyramid roof.

HISTORICAL COST — The cost of a building when first constructed, as opposed to the original cost (cost to the present owner), although they may be the same.

HOGWALLOWS — Small depressions formed by heavy rains, resembling the depressions left after the wallowing of hogs.

HOLDBACK — Portion of a loan held back by the lender until a contingency is met. In the sale of a home insured by V.A. or F.H.A., funds may be held back to make necessary improvements to bring the property to V.A. or F.H.A. standards. The money to make "these" repairs may not be available until closing. One and one half to double the estimated amount necessary is held back. If repairs are not made in the time allowed, these funds are used to make the repairs. In construction financing, funds are held back until, for example, a certain percentage of a subdivision has been sold, or a certain portion of a building has been completed.

HOLDER IN DUE COURSE — A holder of a check or note who takes, for value and in good faith, the note before it is overdue or the check without knowledge that it has bounced, if, in fact, it has.

HOLD HARMLESS AGREEMENT — (See: Indemnity Agreement).

HOLDING ESCROW — An open escrow for the life of a land contract, under which the escrow holder may be empowered to collect the payments due under the contract and pay underlying encumbrances, and record a deed and purchase money mortgage, which are executed at the time of the inception of the land contract and held in the escrow, in the event of default by the vendee. A cumbersome and costly method not used in all states, and in states where used, rapidly being replaced by the security (installment) land contract.

HOLDING PERIOD — The time period used by the IRS to determine a long or short term capital gain. The period during which the taxpayer owns the capital asset.

HOLD OVER TENANT — A tenant who retains possession after the expiration of a lease.

HOLLOW-NEWEL STAIR — A circular stairway having a hollow center. Usually the curve of the circle is severe.

HOLLOW WALL — (See: Cavity Wall).

HOLOGRAPH OR HOLOGRAPHIC WILL — A will written and executed entirely in the handwriting of the testator.

HOME OWNERS' ASSOCIATION — (1) An association of people who own homes in a given area, formed for the purpose of improving or maintaining the quality of the area. (2) An association formed by the builder of condominiums or planned developments, and required by statute in some states. The builder's participation as well as the duties of the association are controlled by statute.

HOME OWNERSHIP — Ownership as opposed to a rental status. (See also: Ownership).

HOMESTEAD — The dwelling (house and contiguous land) of the head of a family. Some states grant statutory exemptions, protecting homestead property (usually to a set maximum amount) against the rights of creditors. Property tax exemptions (for all or part of the tax) are also available in some states. Statutory requirements to establish a homestead may include a formal declaration to be recorded.

HOMESTEAD EXEMPTION — (See: Homestead).

HOME WARRANTY INSURANCE — Private insurance insuring a buyer against defects (usually in plumbing, heating, and electrical) in the home he has purchased. The period of insurance varies and both new and used homes may be insured.

HOMOGENEOUS — Similar or the same. In appraisal, an area having similar style properties or properties of similar use is considered more valuable than a heterogeneous area.

HOOD — A projecting canopy, as over a door or window. Any covering serving the protective purpose of a clothing hood.

HOPPER — A device used on the sides of hospital windows to prevent drafts.

HOPPER WINDOW — (See: Hospital Window).

HORIZON — (1) The line where the sky and ground appear to meet, when viewed from a distance. (2) A layer of soil. (See specific horizons, A, B, C, & D).

HORIZONTAL — Parallel to the horizon. From side to side, rather than up or down.

HOSPITAL — An institution where care, nursing, and surgery are performed for the sick and injured. May be government, or privately owned.

HOSPITAL WINDOW — A window that opens inwardly from bottom hinges and has hoppers (draft preventers) on its sides.

HOT AIR HEATING SYSTEM — (See: Warm Air Heating System).

HOTEL — Originally, any place for travelers to spend the night. Any hotel built today would be a multi-storied structure having sleeping rooms with private bathrooms, suites, telephones in each rentable room, at least one restaurant, and many other amenities.

HOT WATER HEATER — A tank, usually glass lined, in which water is heated for household, commercial, or industrial use.

HOT WATER HEATING SYSTEM — A heating system using circulating hot water from a boiler through a series of pipes to the areas to be heated, and back to the boiler.

HOUR-INCH — A flow of one miner's inch for one hour. The value of a miner's inch is not standard, being 1/40th of a cubic foot per second in some areas, and 1/50th of a cubic foot per second in others.

HOUSE — Any building used as a residence. When in the phrase "the house of", it is usually used to describe a commercial business (from the French "chez").

HOUSE SEWER — The sewage system from the public sewer in the street to and in the house it serves.

HOUSING AND HOME FINANCE AGENCY — A federal agency created in 1947. A forerunner of HUD, having many of the same powers and duties.

HOUSING AND URBAN DEVELOPMENT (HUD), DEPARTMENT OF — The federal department responsible for the major housing programs in the United States, such as F.H.A.

HOUSING STARTS — Number of houses on which construction has begun. The figures are used to determine the availability of housing, need for real estate loans, need for labor and materials, etc.

HUMIDIFIER — A unit, usually part of a heating system, which raises the relative humidity in a room or building by the emission of water vapor into the air.

HUMMOCKS — Low mounds or conical knolls rising above the ground.

HUMUS — The organic portion of soil, formed by partially decomposed animal and vegetable matter.

HUNDRED PERCENT LOCATION — An appraisal term referring either to land of the highest value in an area, or land best suited to a specific use.

HUSBAND — A man legally married to a living woman.

HUTCH — (1) A hut or hovel used as a shelter by a person. (2) A house for rabbits.

HYDRAULIC CEMENT — A cement which resists moisture.

HYDROELECTRIC PLANT — A plant which generates electricity from flowing water, usually at a waterfall.

HYDROGRAPH — A device which records or charts the depth of water, as in a well, or flow, as in a stream.

HYPOTHECATE — To mortgage or pledge without delivery of the security to the lender.

I

I-BEAM — An iron or steel structural framing member, in cross-section forming the letter I.

IDEM SONANS — Sounding the same. Legally, names improperly spelled need not void an instrument, provided the written name sounds the same as the correctly spelled name, and there is no evidence of any intent to deceive by incorrect spelling.

I-GIRDER — (See: I-Beam).

IGNEOUS ROCK — Rock produced by the cooling of magma within the earth (plutonic rock) or on the surface (volcanic rock).

ILLUVIATION — The deposit of soil material by eluviation.

IMPERIAL GALLON — A measure of 277 cubic inches, as opposed to the 231 cubic inch standard gallon.

IMPLIED — Something apparent from the circumstances, rather than from direct action or communication.

IMPLIED AGENCY — An agency which is not expressly set out but must be deduced from the circumstances and other facts. It is an actual agency as opposed to an ostensible agency or agency by estoppel (see which).

IMPLIED CONTRACT — A binding contract created by the actions of the principals, rather than by written or oral agreement of the parties.

IMPLIED LISTING — An implied contract (see which) which would be governed by contract law, including the statute of frauds.

IMPLIED NOTICE — A form of actual notice not expressly given. For example: "A" purchases property from "B". "C" is in possession. "A" will have implied notice that "C" may have an interest in the property if reasonable observation and inquiry on the part of "A" would have disclosed the interest of "C".

IMPOUND ACCOUNT — Account held by a lender for payment of taxes, insurance, or other periodic debts against real property. The mortgagor or trustor pays a portion of, for example, the yearly taxes, with each monthly payment. The lender pays the tax bill from the accumulated funds.

IMPROVED LAND — Land having either on-site improvements, off-site improvements, or both.

IMPROVED VALUE — An appraisal term encompassing the total value of land and improvements (buildings) rather than the separate values of each.

IMPROVEMENTS — Generally, buildings, but may include any permanent structure or other development, such as a street, utilities, etc. (See also: On-Site Improvements; Off-Site Improvements).

IMPROVEMENTS-ON-LAND — (See: On-Site Improvements).

IMPROVEMENTS-TO-LAND — (See: Off-Site Improvements).

INADEQUATE IMPROVEMENT — (See: Underimprovement).

INCHOATE — Incomplete; begun but not completed; contingent.

INCHOATE DOWER — The dower interest of a wife during the life of her husband. May vest at his death.

INCHOATE INSTRUMENT — An unrecorded instrument (such as a deed) which is valid only between the parties and those having actual notice; but not against "the world" as it would be after recording.

INCINERATOR — A heavily insulated, furnace-like device for burning rubbish, giving off a minimum of heat and smoke, and burning the rubbish more completely than an open fire.

INCOME — Generally, any increase in the assets of a person or corporation caused by labor, sales, or return on invested funds. May be different for tax purposes.

INCOME APPROACH — An appraisal method to determine the value of rental property by use of the estimated net income over the life of the structure, discounted to determine its present value.

INCOME AVERAGING — A method of figuring income tax by paying tax on the average income per year for the past five years. For example: A, a real estate salesperson, earns $10,000 taxable income for 4 years. In the fifth year, A sells a shopping center and earns $100,000 taxable income. A could take the total income for 5 years ($140,000), divide by 5 ($28,000), and pay tax on $28,000 for the past 5 years, less what A has already paid.

INCOME PROPERTY — Property which produces income, usually from rental. May also include any property not entirely owner occupied.

INCOME TAX LIEN — [See: Tax Lien (2)].

INCOMPETENT — One who is mentally or physically unable to handle his property without help. A court will appoint someone to handle the financial affairs of such a person.

INCORPORATE — To create a corporation.

INCORPOREAL RIGHTS — Rights to intangibles, such as legal actions, rather than rights to property (rights to possession or use of land).

INCREASE CLAUSE — (See: Escalation Clause).

INCREASING AND DIMINISHING RETURNS — An economic theory that an increase in capital or manpower will not increase production proportionately (five workers may do less than five times the work of one worker; and two workers may do more than twice the work of one worker). When the increase in production is proportionately greater than the addition, there is an increasing return; when production is proportionately less than the addition, the return diminishes.

INCREMENT — An increase or growth, gained or added, such as a population increase.

INCUMBRANCE (ENCUMBRANCE) — A claim, lien, charge, or liability attached to and binding real property. Any right to, or interest in, land which may exist in one other than the owner, but which will not prevent the transfer of fee title.

INCURABLE DEPRECIATION — (See: Economic Obsolescence).

INDEMNITY AGREEMENT — An agreement by which one party agrees to repay another for any loss or damage the latter may suffer.

INDENTURE DEED — A deed executed by both grantor and grantee, containing reciprocal agreements (grants or obligations). (See also: Deed Poll).

INDEPENDENT APPRAISAL — An appraisal by one who has no interest in the property or nothing to gain from a high or low appraisal.

INDEPENDENT CONTRACTOR — The term is most important as used to describe the relationship of broker and salesperson. The salesperson is either an employee or independent contractor. If an employee, the broker must withhold income tax and pay social security, provide workman's compensation when applicable, and may be liable for some negligent acts of the salesperson while on the job, such as automobile accidents. The broker avoids all of these responsibilities if the salesperson is an independent contractor. The greater the control over the salesperson, the more likely the salesperson will be considered an employee. Some examples of this control would be required office hours or attendance at regularly scheduled meetings, as well as payment or reimbursement by the broker for license fees, auto expenses, etc.

INDEXING — To alter mortgage term, payment, or rate according to inflation and/or a suitable mortgage rate index. (See also: Rate Index).

INDEX LEASE — [See: Escalation Clause (2)].

INDIGENT MORTGAGE — (See: County Mortgage).

INDIRECT CONSTRUCTION COSTS — Those costs other than labor and materials, such as administrative costs, financing costs, taxes and insurance, loss of interest on money invested, etc.

INDIRECT LIGHTING — Lighting by means of reflecting the light off the ceiling, wall, or other reflector, in order to soften glare.

INDIVIDUAL RETIREMENT ACCOUNT — (See: IRA).

INDORSEMENT (ENDORSEMENT) — The act of the holder of a note, bill, check, or other negotiable instrument, of assigning said instrument by signing the back of the instrument, with or without qualifications.

INDUSTRIAL DEVELOPMENT BONDS — Bonds issued to finance industrial or commercial real estate developments.

INDUSTRIAL MULTIPLE — A method of promoting property exclusively listed by a member of the American Industrial Real Estate Association (A.I.R.), by making each listing known to all members.

INDUSTRIAL PARK — A subdivision in the pattern of residential subdivisions, except catering to the needs of industry. Off-site improvements may have stronger roads, heavy plumbing and wiring, wider streets for trucks, rail spurs, and other necessities for industry.

INDUSTRIAL PROPERTY — (1) Land which is zoned industrial. (2) Real property improved specifically for industrial use.

INDUSTRIAL SIDING — A railroad siding (spur track) which serves an industrial park or building.

INDUSTRIAL TAX EXEMPTION — An exemption from local property taxes granted to encourage industries to come into an area. Has been used successfully in the South. Usually granted for a definite period.

INFLATION — The expanse or increase in an economy over its natural growth. Usually caused by over printing money and over-extending credit. Marked by a rapid increase in the price of goods.

INGRESS AND EGRESS — A right to enter upon and pass through land.

IN GROSS — Personal rather than attached to land. An easement in gross has no dominant tenement.

INHARMONIOUS — Conflicting surroundings. In appraising, a property not suited to its surroundings is inharmonious, and consequently less valuable than property which is better located.

INHERITANCE — In a legal meaning, real property obtained by law rather than by will; generally misused to mean anything which comes from a deceased person.

INHERITANCE TAX — A tax on the transfer of property from a deceased person; based on the right to acquire the property rather than the property itself.

INITIALS — The first letter of one's first (maybe middle) and last name. May be used as a signature when intended, and usually used to indicate agreement to a change, correction, addition, deletion, or other alteration of a document. Modernly, stricter laws regarding validity of initials and marks to replace a signature have been enacted.

INJUNCTION — An order by a court preventing one from acting or restraining one from continuing some action.

INLAID PARQUET — (See: Parquet Floor).

INLAND WATERS — All bodies of water exclusive of the open sea.

INLET — A narrow waterway extending inland.

INLIQUIDITY — Describing assets not readily convertible to cash.

INNER CITY — A term of no exact meaning but having the connotation of a low economic, high crime area of a large city, rather than merely the geographic central area of a city.

INNOCENT PURCHASER FOR VALUE — Another term for one who purchases in good faith, or a bona fide purchaser. The innocent part refers to no prior knowledge (actual or constructive) of unrecorded interest in the property, such as a prior sale to a third party or a loan secured by the property. The for value part refers to a valuable consideration paid by said purchaser for the property.

IN PERPETUITY — Of endless duration; forever.

IN PERSONAM — Directed at specific persons rather than against property or generally for all people.

IN RE — In the matter of.

IN REM — Pertaining to property or people in general.

INSIDE LOT — Not a corner lot.

INSIDE TRIM — (See: Interior Trim).

INSOLVENCY — Generally applied to a person, corporation, bank, etc., when there is an inability to pay debts as they become due or within a reasonable time thereafter.

INSOLVENT — Incapable of meeting one's current debts.

INSPECTION — An examination of property for various reasons, such as a termite inspection, inspection to see if required repairs were made before funds are released, etc.

INSTALLMENT CONTRACT — A method of purchasing by installment (usually monthly) payments. When referring to real property, it is usually called a land contract.

INSTALLMENT LAND SALES CONTRACT — (See: Land Contract).

INSTALLMENT NOTE — A note calling for payment of both principal and interest in specified amounts, or specified minimum amounts, at specific intervals.

INSTALLMENT SALE — A tax term used to describe a sale which is usually accomplished by use of a land contract. If the seller receives less than 30% of the sale price in the year of the sale (not including interest), the tax on the profit (gain) from the sale may be paid over the installment period, provided the 30% rule is followed each year.

INSTITUTE OF REAL ESTATE MANAGEMENT — The organization conferring the designation of C.P.M. (Certified Property Manager), which is considered the most prestigious designation in the field of property management.

INSTITUTIONAL LENDERS — Banks, savings and loan associations, and other businesses which make loans to the public in the ordinary course of business, rather than individuals, or companies which may make loans to employees.

INSTITUTIONAL PROPERTY — Property, the use of which is created by law, such as schools or hospitals. May also refer to corresponding private properties, such as private schools and hospitals.

INSTRUMENT — Any writing having legal form and significance, such as a deed, mortgage, will, lease, etc.

INSULATION — Materials used for their qualities of hindering the passage or transmission of sound, cold, heat, or electricity.

INSULATION BOARD — Sheets of compressed vegetable pulp, such as sugarcane or cornstalks, which, because of tiny pockets of trapped air throughout its density, provides good insulation.

INSURABLE INTEREST — Concerning real property, an interest which, if terminated, destroyed, or in any other way interfered with, would cause a financial loss to the holder of the interest. May be a mortgagee, owner, lessee, etc.

INSURABLE VALUE — Value of property for insurance purposes. Based on the value of the property, less indestructible parts (land) for fire insurance. For title insurance purposes, the sales price (market value) is used.

INSURANCE — A contract under which, for a consideration, one party (the insurer) agrees to indemnify another (the insured) for a possible loss under specific conditions. May be loss of life, health, property, or property rights.

INSURED MORTGAGE — A mortgage insured against loss to the mortgagee in the event of default and a failure of the mortgaged property to satisfy the balance owing plus costs of foreclosure. May be insured by F.H.A., V.A., or by independent mortgage insurance companies.

INTANGIBLE ASSETS — (See: Intangible Property).

INTANGIBLE PROPERTY — Property which has value but cannot be physically touched, such as a patent, the goodwill of a business, etc.

INTANGIBLE VALUE — The value of intangible property or the intangible portions of tangible property.

INTER ALIA — Among other things.

INTER ALIOS — Between other persons.

INTERCHANGE — A method of connecting highways by ramps and grade level changes, so as to obviate the need for controls (lights, stop signs, etc.).

INTERCHANGE RAMP — A ramp at an interchange. (See also: Interchange).

INTEREST — (1) A share or right in some property. (2) Money charged for the use of money (principal).

INTEREST EXTRA NOTE — A note stating an equal (usually monthly) payment on principal, plus interest. As the interest decreases (based on declining principal balance) the total payment decreases. The amount applied to principal remains the same. (See also: Interest Included Note).

INTEREST INCLUDED NOTE — A note having equal payments (usually monthly). Interest is figured on the declining principal balance. As the principal decreases, interest also decreases, applying more of each payment to principal. (See also: Interest Extra Note).

INTEREST ONLY MORTGAGE — A mortgage under which the principal amount borrowed is repaid in one payment. Periodic interest payments are made.

INTEREST RATE — The percentage of an amount of money which is paid for its use for a specified time. Usually expressed as an annual percentage.

INTEREST RATE CAP — The maximum interest rate increase of an Adjustable Mortgage Loan. For example: a 12% loan with a 5% interest rate cap would have maximum interest for the life of the loan which would not exceed 17%.

INTERIM FINANCING — Temporary financing, usually for construction.

INTERIM LOAN — (See: Interim Financing).

INTERIOR LOT — (See: Inside Lot).

INTERIOR TRIM — All of the moldings on the inside walls of a building.

INTERLOCUTORY DECREE — A provisional or temporary decree, pending some contingency before a final decree. Sometimes the contingency may be only the passage of time.

INTERPLEADER — A court action which may be filed in an existing case to be the initial action. One holding funds which are in dispute, but not having an interest in the funds, would file an interpleader. For example: An escrow agent is holding a deposit of a buyer which funds both buyer and seller claim to be entitled. Escrow is willing to give the funds to either buyer or seller but does not want to be liable for giving the funds to the wrong party. The interpleader filed by the escrow agent asks the court to determine to whom the funds should be awarded.

INTERSECTION — A crossing, usually of roads, but may be lines, such as on a map or survey.

INTERSTATE — Between two or more states.

INTERSTATE HIGHWAY SYSTEM — A federal system of roads which cross the United States, linking its major cities.

INTERSTATE LAND SALES — Sales of land to a buyer in another state. Because the buyer is usually totally dependent on the seller for information regarding the property, federal disclosure laws have been passed to aid the buyer. The buyer also has a period (now 3 days) after signing a purchase agreement, in which to rescind. The laws were passed because of the large promotional land sales of the 50's and early 60's, some of which sold worthless desert and swamp land.

INTER VIVOS — Between living persons. Property transferred between living persons would fall under different laws than property transferred after death or in contemplation of death.

INTER VIVOS TRUST — A trust during the life of the settlor rather than upon death. (See also: Testamentary Trust).

INTESTACY — (See: Intestate).

INTESTATE — Without leaving a will, or leaving an invalid will so that the property of the estate passes by the laws of succession rather than by direction of the deceased.

INTRINSIC VALUE — The value of the thing itself, rather than any special features which make its market value different. For example: The intrinsic value of a painting is the worth of the canvas and paint, rather than the value to an art collector.

INURE — To take effect, to result.

INVENTORY — (1) The goods of a business which are sold in the every day course of business, such as houses by a builder. (2) A detailed list of property, such as of an estate.

INVERSE CONDEMNATION — Condemnation of property near a parcel so as to cause the parcel to lose much of its value. In such a case the parcel is, in effect, condemned and just compensation must be paid to the owner.

INVESTMENT — The putting up of money with the intent to make a profit or receive interest.

INVESTMENT PROPERTY — Generally, any property purchased for the primary purpose of profit. The profit may be from income or from resale.

INVESTMENT TRUST — A company which sells its own stock and invests the money in stocks, real estate, or other investments. (See also: R.E.I.T., Real Estate Investment Trust).

INVESTMENT YIELD — The gain from an investment in real property, including both income and resale. Expressed as a percentage of the amount invested.

INVOLUNTARY CONVERSION — Conversion of real property to personal property (money) without the voluntary act of the owner. This occurs when property is taken by eminent domain (condemnation). The owner is allowed to convert back to real property (buy another property) without paying tax on the gain from the condemnation. This must be done within a set time (3 years) and the prices of the old and new property are considered to form a new tax base.

INVOLUNTARY CONVEYANCE — A transfer of real property without the consent of the owner, such as by a divorce decree, by condemnation, etc.

INVOLUNTARY LIEN — A lien, such as a tax lien, judgment lien, etc., which attaches to property without the consent of the owner, rather than a mortgage lien, to which the owner agrees.

INVOLUNTARY TRUST — (See: Constructive Trust).

IRA (INDIVIDUAL RETIREMENT ACCOUNT) — Savings programs available to individuals. These plans allow for a certain amount to be deposited each year. This money is not subject to income tax for that year or following years as long as it is not withdrawn. The money is taxed as withdrawn upon retirement, usually when the depositor is in a lower tax bracket. During the life of the account, the money may be put into various interest bearing investments. Securities dealers as well as banking institutions now offer IRA's.

IRONCLAD CONTRACT — A term of no legal meaning, being a contract which is considered strong (as iron) and hard to break.

IRON-SAFE CLAUSE — A clause in a policy of fire insurance requiring the insured to keep certain records (usually inventory) in a fire-proof safe.

IRREGULAR CURVE — (See: French Curve).

IRREVOCABLE — That which cannot be revoked or recalled, such as certain trusts, contracts, and other legal relationships.

IRRIGATION — Watering, usually by means of pipes, to increase the fertility of ground in areas where additional moisture is needed for crop growth.

IRRIGATION DISTRICT — A local agency which builds and operates an irrigation system (supplies water to a designated area), and has authority to levy taxes for that purpose.

IRRIGATION DITCH — A ditch, channel, canal, etc., used to carry water to or through a planted area to bring water to the planted crops.

ISLAND — (1) Land surrounded by a body of water. (2) A space between oncoming lanes of a highway, used by pedestrians or as a safety buffer between oncoming traffic.

ISOHYETAL LINE — A line on a map connecting areas which have approximately the same rainfall or thunderstorm activities.

J

JACK RAFTER — A short rafter, used in a hip roof or valley roof, or to simulate a rafter which extends beyond the exterior walls.

JACOB'S LADDER — A hanging ladder, made with wooden steps and sides of rope.

JALOUSIES — Fixed or adjustable horizontal slats, used in doors, windows, shutters, etc., to keep out sun and rain, while letting in light and air.

JAMB — The vertical lining of an opening, such as a doorway, fireplace, window, etc.

JANITOR — One who is hired to take care of a building. Generally associated with cleaning, locking up after closing, and minor repair.

JERRY-BUILT — A structure built of inferior and inexpensive materials. Poorly built.

JETTY — (1) A pier or other structure (usually of stones), built out into a body of water to hinder the currents and so protect a harbor. (2) A part of a building which projects out beyond the exterior walls, such as an overhanging second story, a balcony, etc.

JOINDER — Joining together in some legal proceeding.

JOINT — (1) Meaning two or more, such as joint tenants, joint adventurers, etc. (2) The point of union or connection of two members, whether pipes, boards, or other members.

JOINT ADVENTURE — A combining by two or more persons of their property, skills, efforts, etc., for a specific business purpose. Single purpose partnerships are now most commonly used and are based on the same idea of the single purpose business venture.

JOINT AND SEVERAL — A liability which allows the creditor to sue any one of the debtors (sever one from the others) or sue all together (jointly).

JOINT APPRAISAL — An appraisal by more than one appraiser, but one which states common conclusions of all.

JOINT ESTATE — (See: Joint Tenancy).

JOINT NOTE — A promise to pay, executed by two or more persons, each having equal liability. (See also: Surety).

JOINT PROTECTION POLICY — A policy of title insurance which insures both the owner and the lender under the same policy.

JOINT TENANCY — An undivided interest in property, taken by two or more joint tenants. The interests must be equal, accuring under the same conveyance, and beginning at the same time. Upon the death of a joint tenant, the interest passes to the surviving joint tenants, rather than to the heirs of the deceased.

JOINT TENANTS — Those holding under joint tenancy. (See also: Joint Tenancy).

JOINTURE — A life estate for a wife which takes effect upon the death of her husband. Takes the place of dower, but must be agreed to by the wife and is not an automatic right such as dower.

JOINT VENTURE — (See: Joint Adventure).

JOISTS — Small beams, usually not more than five inches thick, which are in parallel and support floors and ceilings. The joists are supported by larger beams, bearing walls, girders, etc. A joist is rectangular in cross-section, the narrow face being the joist, the wide face the plank.

JUDGMENT (JUDGEMENT) — The decision of a court of law. Money judgments, when recorded, become a lien on real property of the defendant.

JUDGMENT LIEN — A lien against the property of a judgment debtor. An involuntary lien.

JUDGMENT PROOF — One against whom a judgment creditor cannot collect (no assets). If one can show he was defrauded by a "judgment proof" real estate licensee, he may recover from the state fund in states having such a fund.

JUDICIAL FORECLOSURE — Foreclosure through court action rather than by a power of sale. Judicial foreclosure is sometimes necessary to remove certain tax liens.

JUDICIAL SALE — A sale made under court order, by one court appointed, rather than a voluntary sale by the owner, or one appointed by the owner.

JUMBO VA LOAN — A loan for an amount greater than the allowable 100% financed amount. It is determined by subtracting the maximum allowable 100% financed amount from the purchase price and financing 75% of the difference. Example: maximum allowable VA Loan-$110,000. Sale price-$130,000. Difference is $20,000; 75% of the difference is $15,000. Total jumbo loan-$110,000 plus $15,000=$125,000. Required down payment-$5000.

JUNCTION BOX — A metal box used to enclose the meeting (junction) of electrical circuits, wires, and cables.

JUNIOR LIEN — A lien which is subordinate to a prior lien.

JUNIOR MORTGAGE — Any mortgage of lesser priority than a first mortgage.

JUNK VALUE — (See: Salvage Value).

JURAT — (1) The certificate of an officer before whom a writing was sworn to, such as a notary public. (2) That part of an affidavit stating where, when, and before whom, the affidavit was sworn.

JURISDICTION — The extent of the authority of a court, or other governmental branch or agency.

JUST COMPENSATION — In condemnation the amount paid to the property owner. The theory is that in order to be "just", the property owner should be no richer or poorer than before the taking.

K

KAME — A small mound or hill composed of stratified glacial deposits.

KEENE'S CEMENT — An unusually tough and durable gypsum plaster to which alum has been added. Used primarily for walls of commercial buildings.

KEEPER — A term seldom used in the United States. A custodian of a building or grounds.

KELP-SHORE — The shore between the high and low water marks.

KEOGH PLAN — A retirement plan whereby a self-employed person may set aside a certain portion of income (tax deferred) into a retirement account. The money is taxable upon withdrawal at retirement when the person's tax bracket is often lower.

KERF — (1) A notch or slit made by a saw. (2) The width of the cut of a saw blade.

KEYMAN INSURANCE — Insurance through loss (through death or disability) of a "key" (important) person in a company. The liability is the estimated cost of the loss (in business lost, and replacement of the individual). Some lenders require this insurance before lending to small companies which rely on one or a few "key" people.

KICK PLATE — A metal or plastic strip, placed at the lower edge of a door or on a riser of a step to protect it from damage by accidental kicking.

KILN — (1) An oven which reaches high temperatures for baking ceramics, or bricks. (2) A room or shed through which warm, dry air is circulated to dry lumber.

KILO — One thousand; a prefix (kilometer—1000 meters; kilogram—1000 grams).

KILOGRAM — 1000 grams (2.204 pounds).

KILOMETER — 1000 meters. [See also: Meter (1)].

KILOVOLT — 1000 volts.

KILOWATT — 1000 watts.

KILOWATT HOUR — 1000 watt-hours.

KIN — Those related by blood.

KITE WINDER — The steps at the curvature of a circular stairway, which are triangular, or kite-shaped.

KNOCK DOWN — Any parts of a building which can be easily assembled, installed, or removed, such as certain types of window frames, partitions, etc.

KNOLL — A small rounded hill.

KNOT — (1) The hard, irregular shaped defects in boards, caused by cutting at the point where the branch of the tree meets the trunk. (2) A measure of speed, equal to one nautical mile (approximately 6,076 ft.) per hour.

L

LABOR — (1) Work as opposed to materials. (2) A land measure of 177 1/7 acres. Used in Mexico.

LACHES — An unreasonable delay by a party making a claim or bringing an action, so that the rights of said party are waived. Laches are not controlled by a statute of limitations.

LAISSEZ-FAIRE — Leave alone, let proceed. French expression made popular by Adam Smith, and used to describe a theory that free trade promotes a better business climate than government controls.

LALLY COLUMNS — Load-bearing steel columns, which are filled with concrete (lally).

LAMINATE — To cover or construct with thin layers or plies (laminae).

LAMINATED WOOD — Wood such as plywood, which is constructed in sheets, or veneered wood, such as cheaper softwood, covered with a layer of more expensive hardwood, and glued together.

LAND — A general term which includes the ground and those things of a permanent nature such as trees, crops, oil and minerals in the ground, unless specifically excepted.

LAND CERTIFICATE — A certificate given by the federal government enabling one to obtain land by following certain registration processes. Used in the late 1800's.

LAND CONTRACT — An installment contract for the sale of land. The seller (vendor) has legal title until paid in full. The buyer (vendee) has equitable title during the contract term.

LAND GRANT — A gift of public land by the federal government to a state or local government, corporation, or individual.

LANDING — (1) A place for loading and unloading people or cargo from a boat, train, etc. (2) A flat surface adjoining a staircase at the top, bottom, or between flights.

LANDLOCKED PARCEL — A parcel of land surrounded entirely by privately owned land, with no access to a public right of way (road). Condemnation for a limited access highway is a major cause of such parcels.

LANDLORD — An owner of leased real estate.

LANDMARK — Originally, a monument on a boundary line. Modernly, boundary lines are usually established by walls or fences, and these are the landmarks.

LANDOWNER'S ROYALTY — In oil and gas leases, the portion of the value of each barrel of oil which goes to the property owner.

LAND PATENT — (See: Patent).

LAND-POOR — Being short of money because of owning an excess of property which does not produce income.

LAND RECLAMATION — Giving land a higher (more commercial) use by physically changing it (drainage, irrigation, fill, etc.).

LAND RESIDUAL TECHNIQUE — An appraisal technique by which land value is determined by first determining the net return attributable to the building only, and deducting it from the total return to the property (may be estimated); the residual amount is capitalized to find the land value. The building value may be determined by construction costs (new building), depreciated construction costs (if only a few years old), or estimated present construction costs (if an older building).

LANDSCAPE — A picture or single view of inland scenery. In real estate terms, the surroundings of a structure which provide the setting for that structure. To landscape is to modify the natural setting.

LANDSCAPE ARCHITECT — One who, as a profession, plans and designs landscaping. Colleges now offer a degree as a landscape architect.

LANDSCAPE ARCHITECTURE — The designing and planning of landscaping by a landscape architect.

LANDSCAPING — The act of modifying a landscape, or features used in such modification, such as trees, lawns, grade changes, etc.

LAND-SERVICE ROAD — An access road between parcels of land and another public road or highway.

LAND USE MAP — A map of a given area, showing the different land uses in the area.

LAND USE PLANNING — The development of long range plans for the use of land in a given area, such as through zoning plans.

LAND USE REGULATION — A general term encompassing any regulation of land, whether public (zoning) or private (restrictive covenants).

LAND VALUE MAP — An appraisal map showing the value of property in given areas, either in acres, square footage, or front footage.

LAP JOINT — The connection (joint) formed by overlapping two ends or edges and attaching them together.

LAP SIDING — A siding applied in a similar manner to clapboard siding, but utilizing longer boards, usually of better quality.

LARGER PARCEL — A term used in eminent domain proceedings, signifying that the parcel taken is not a complete parcel but part of a "larger parcel"; the owner, therefore, is entitled to damages from the severance as well as the value of the parcel taken. Unity of ownership, use, and contiguity must be present, although federal courts and some states do not require contiguity where there is a strong unity of use.

LATE CHARGE — A penalty for failure to pay an installment payment on time. Usually not allowed as interest for tax deductions. May or may not be included as usury. If not, the amount of late charge is either set by statute or must be "reasonable".

LATENT DEFECT — A hidden or concealed defect. One which could not be discovered by inspection, using reasonable care. In legal descriptions, a latent defect may be corrected, and a totally new description not necessary.

LATERAL — Proceeding from, situated at, directed to, or pertaining to a side. A line branching from a main line (such as a sewer line) is called a lateral line. (See also: Lateral Support).

LATERAL SUPPORT — The right of a landowner to the natural support of his land by adjoining land. The adjoining owner has the duty not to change his land (such as lowering it) so as to cause this support to be weakened or removed. (See also: Subjacent Support).

LATH — The support upon which wet plaster is spread. May be metal (usually a course wire screen) or a solid, cement-like substance (called rock lath).

LATITUDE — North-South distance above a meridian as measured from the equator.

LAUNDROMAT — A business which provides, at its location, laundry equipment (coin operated) for self service use by the public.

LAVATORY — (1) A basin or sink for washing one's hands and face. (2) A room containing a sink and toilet.

LAW DAY — (1) The day (date) in a note, mortgage, etc., when the debt is to be paid. (2) A holiday honoring the law and legal profession.

LAYOUT — (1) The arrangement or plan of any given area, such as the rooms within a structure. (2) The plans (drawings) showing the arrangement of a given area.

LEACHING — Removal of liquid waste material from sewage by filtration through sand, gravel, tiles, stones, etc.

LEACHING TRENCHES — Ducts, either dug in ground having filtration qualities (gravel, sand, etc.), or in which filtration materials are placed to remove the liquid waste from sewage.

LEADER — The metal conduit carrying rainwater from a roof to a sewer or the ground.

LEAN-TO — (1) A shed, abutting the wall of another structure, with three walls and a sloping roof. (2) A free standing structure of three walls and a sloping roof, the open side of which is sheltered from the prevailing winds. Used as a camping shelter.

LEASE — An agreement by which an owner of real property (lessor) gives the right of possession to another (lessee), for a specified period of time (term) and for a specified consideration (rent).

LEASEBACK — (See: Sale-Leaseback).

LEASEHOLD — An estate in realty held under a lease; an estate for a fixed term. Considered in many states to be personal property.

LEASEHOLD IMPROVEMENTS — Improvements made by the lessee. The term is used in condemnation proceedings to determine the portion of the award to which the lessee is entitled. (See also: Tenant Improvements).

LEASEHOLD INTEREST — The interest which the lessee has in the value of the lease itself in condemnation award determination. The difference between the total remaining rent under the lease, and the rent lessee would currently pay for similar space for the same time period.

LEASEHOLD VALUE — The value of a leasehold interest. Usually applies to a long term lease when market rental for similar space is higher than rent paid under the lease. Some states allow the lessee to claim the leasehold value against the landlord in eminent domain proceedings, unless specifically prohibited by the lease itself. Other states, by statute, do not allow for such a claim. (See also: "No Bonus" Clause).

LEASE-PURCHASE AGREEMENT — (See: Lease with Option to Purchase).

LEASE WITH OPTION TO PURCHASE — A lease under which the lessee has the right to purchase the property. The price and terms of the purchase must be set forth for the option to be valid. The option may run for the length of the lease or only for a portion of the lease period.

LEAVES — The panel-like parts of a door, window, table top, etc., which may be removed or moved to a different position by sliding or by hinge attachments.

LEGAL AGE — (See: Majority).

LEGAL DESCRIPTION — A method of geographically identifying a parcel of land, which is acceptable in a court of law.

LEGAL NAME — First and last name. Middle name included, omitted or incorrect will not matter. Today full names (for identification purposes) are required in many instances, but only for identification purposes (to distinguish between two men named John Smith, for example).

LEGAL NOTICE — The notice required by law in a particular case. May be actual notice, constructive notice, etc.

LEGAL OWNER — The term has come to be used as a technical difference from the equitable owner, and not as opposed to an illegal owner. The legal owner has title to the property, although the title may actually carry no rights to the property other than a lien.

LEGAL RATE OF INTEREST — A rate of interest established by law, rather than by agreement (contract).

LEGAL TITLE — Usually title without ownership rights, such as the title placed in a trustee under a deed of trust, or the title in a vendor under a land contract.

LEGATEE — (1) One who receives personal property by will. (2) One receiving any property by will, real or personal.

LENDER — Any person or entity advancing funds which are to be repaid. A general term encompassing all mortgagees, and beneficiaries under deeds of trust.

LENDER'S POLICY — (See: Loan Policy).

LESSEE — The party to whom a lease (the right to possession) is given in return for a consideration (rent).

LESSEE'S INTEREST — In appraising the value of a lessee's interest to determine the value of a potential sublease of assignment (sale) of the lease, the value is the market value of the property, less the interest of the lessor. The lessor's interest would be largely determined by the ratio of the return on the lease to the market value without the lease.

LESSOR — The party (usually the owner) who gives the lease (right to possession) in return for a consideration (rent).

LESSOR'S INTEREST — The present value of the future income under the lease, plus the present value of the property after the lease expires (reversion).

LETTER OF ATTORNMENT — A letter from a grantor to a tenant, stating that the property has been sold, and directing rent to be paid to the grantee (new owner).

LETTER OF INTENT — A formal method of stating that a prospective developer, buyer, or lessee, is interested in property. Not an offer and creates no obligation. However, a builder who wants to build an office building, for example, may influence a lender by showing letters of intent from major prospective tenants.

LETTERS OF ADMINISTRATION — A probate court order appointing an administrator.

LETTERS PATENT — An instrument from the government (federal or state) granting land to an individual.

LETTERS TESTAMENTARY — Order of a probate court granting authority to an executor.

LETTING — A synonym for leasing.

LEVEE — An embankment constructed along a river or stream to prevent flooding. (See also: Causeway).

LEVEL PAYMENT MORTGAGE — (See: Interest Included Note).

LEVERAGE — The use of financing to allow a small amount of cash to purchase a large property investment.

LEVY — A collection, seizure, assessment, etc., such as to levy (assess and collect) taxes.

LIABILITY — A general term encompassing all types of debts and obligations.

LIABLE — Obligated, responsible.

LIBER — The latin word for book. Used instead of the word book in some states when referring to the book and page of a recorded document.

LICENSE — A permission, either express or implied.

LICENSEE — (1) Regarding classifications of people entering upon another's land, a licensee is distinguished from a trespasser, and so has greater legal rights. (2) One who holds a real estate license (a salesperson).

LICENSING ACTS — Laws regulating the granting of real estate licenses. Because these are state laws, the requirements (education, testing, etc.), are not of equal severity. However, generally they are similar, requiring testing and granting exceptions, such as trustees, executors, owners selling property themselves, etc.

LIEN — An encumbrance against property for money, either voluntary or involuntary. All liens are encumbrances but all encumbrances are not liens.

LIEN WAIVER (WAIVER OF LIENS) — For our purposes, a waiver of mechanic's lien rights, signed by subcontractors so that the owner or general contractor can receive a draw on a construction loan.

LIFE — The length of time an improvement will last, either in relation to its physical utility or as an accounting procedure.

LIFE BENEFICIARY — One who receives payments or other rights from a trust for his or her lifetime.

LIFE ESTATE — An estate in real property for the life of a living person. The estate then reverts back to the grantor or on to a third party (remainderman).

LIFE IN BEING — The remaining life of someone already alive. An expression used in rules against perpetuities.

LIFE INTEREST — An interest in real estate for a period of the life of the one having the interest, or the life of another.

LIFE TENANT — One who holds land for the length of his, or another's life.

LIGHT — A single window pane, or opening for a single window pane.

LIGHT AND AIR EASEMENT — An easement restricting the servient tenement from obstructing the light and air (usually the view) of the dominant tenement. For example: A developer builds a resort hotel. He may wish to obtain a light and air easement from adjoining owners so that they may not build tall structures and block the sun from the hotel's swimming pool.

LIGHTER — A flat bottomed boat or barge, used to unload ships not at a quay, and for transporting goods within the harbor.

LIGHT INDUSTRY — Encompassing most light manufacturing, as opposed to factories which tend to produce heavy pollution (air, water, noise, etc.). A zoning designation.

LIGHT WELL — (1) An open space around a basement window, the top of which is at ground level. (2) A shaft designed to provide light and ventilation to inside rooms of a building.

LIKE IN KIND PROPERTY — A tax term used in exchanges. Property may be exchanged for like in kind property and the tax postponed. The term does not refer to the physical similarity of the properties but the purpose and intent (investment) of the taxpayer.

LIME — A white powder, formed by burning limestone, used in making bricks, mortar, plaster and similar materials, and for treatment of sewage, soil, etc.

LIMESTONE — A sedimentary rock, formed mainly from sea shells and coral, and which, when burned, forms lime.

LIMING — To apply lime and water to wood (whitewash), limestone to ground, or in other ways apply lime.

LIMITATION OF ACTION — The time in which a law suit may be begun before it is barred by statute. (See also: Statute of Limitations).

LIMITED ACCESS HIGHWAY — A highway with access only at spaced intervals, usually by the use of ramps. Abutting property occupants have no access other than at the regular stated intervals. Also called a controlled access highway.

LIMITED PARTNER — (See: Limited Partnership).

LIMITED PARTNERSHIP — Used in many real estate syndications; a partnership consisting of one or more general partners who conduct the business and are responsible (liable) for losses, and one or more special (limited) partners, contributing capital and liable only up to the amount contributed.

LINEAL — Concerning a line. A lineal measure is a distance measure rather than an area measure.

LINE FENCE — A fence erected along the property lines of a ranch or farm.

LINE OF CREDIT — An amount of money a borrower may obtain from a bank without a special credit check. The money is generally for business purposes and the amount would not include the borrower's own home loan and other personal secured loans.

LINING — The covering on the interior of a building, as distinguished from the exterior, or casing.

LINK — In surveying, a length of 7.92 inches.

LINOLEUM — A floor covering used in heavy traffic areas (kitchens, bathrooms, entrances, etc.), made of cork, linseed oil, resins and pigments on a canvas or burlap backing, and applied from a roll. A quality material superior to many "tiles".

LINTEL — A horizontal member spanning above an opening, such as a doorway, and usually bearing the load above it.

LIQUID ASSETS — Cash, or assets immediately convertible to cash.

LIQUIDATED DAMAGES — A definite amount of damages, set forth in a contract, to be paid by the party breaching the contract. A predetermined estimate of actual damages from a breach.

LIQUIDATION — The settling of financial affairs of a business or individual, by liquidating (turning to cash) all assets for distribution to creditors, heirs, etc.

LIQUIDATION PRICE — A price paid for property sold to liquidate a debt. Usually less than market value since there is pressure to sell or a forced sale, either of which does not often bring the highest price.

LIQUIDATION VALUE — (See: Liquidation Price).

LIQUIDITY — Having liquid assets (see which).

LIS PENDENS — A legal notice recorded to show pending litigation relating to real property, and giving notice that anyone acquiring an interest in said property subsequent to the date of the notice may be bound by the outcome of the litigation.

LISTING — An agreement between an owner of real property and a real estate agent, whereby the agent agrees to secure a buyer or tenant for specific property at a certain price and terms in return for a fee or commission.

LISTING AGENT — A real estate agent obtaining a listing (see which), as opposed to the selling agent.

LITER (LITRE) — A metric measure of volume, equal to 61.02 cubic inches (slightly more than one quart) liquid measure.

LITERAGE LIMITS — Area in a harbor which is serviced by lighters on a regular basis and standard charge.

LITTORAL — Concerning the shore of lakes and oceans, as opposed to rivers and streams, for which the word riparian is used.

LITTORAL RIGHTS — Rights concerning properties abutting an ocean or lake rather than a river or stream (riparian). Littoral rights are usually concerned with the use or enjoyment of the shore.

LIVABILITY — Minimum standards set by local government for the quality of residential structures (especially rental units).

LIVE — Having force or containing energy, such as a live volcano (one capable of eruption), live wire (one carrying electric current), etc.

LIVE LOAD — (1) Variable weight in a building, such as furniture and people, as opposed to the fixed weight of the building itself (dead load). (2) The weight of cargo in a truck which is taxed by weight. (3) The weight of traffic over a bridge.

LIVING TRUST — A trust which is in effect during the life of the settlor, rather than upon his death (testamentary trust).

LOAD — (1) A weight carried or supported by something, such as supported by "load-bearing" members of a building, or the weight carried in a ship, truck, etc. (2) The power of an electrical charge.

LOAD-BEARING — Supporting weight in addition to its own vertically, or supporting pressure laterally.

LOAD-BEARING WALL — (See: Bearing Wall).

LOAN — A lending of a principal sum of money to one who promises to repay said sum, plus interest.

LOAN BROKER — (See: Mortgage Broker).

LOAN COMMITMENT — (See: Commitment (2)).

LOAN CONSTANT — The yearly percentage of interest which remains the same over the life of an amortized loan, based on the monthly payment in relation to the principal originally loaned. For example: A $1000 loan at 9% interest for 20 years can be amortized at $9.00 per month. The constant interest rate is figured by finding one year's payments ($9.00 × 12 months = $108.00), and expressing this amount as a percentage of the principal originally borrowed (10.8% of $1000).

LOAN ORIGINATION FEE — A one time set up fee charged by the lender.

LOAN PACKAGE — The file of all items necessary for the lender to decide to give or not give a loan. These items would include the information on the prospective borrower (loan application, credit report, financial statement, employment letters, etc.), and information on the property (appraisal, survey, etc.). There may be a charge for "packaging" the loan.

LOAN POLICY — A title insurance policy insuring a mortgagee, or beneficiary under a deed of trust, against loss caused by invalid title in the borrower, or loss of priority of the mortgage or deed of trust.

LOAN RATIO — The ratio, expressed as a percentage, of the amount of a loan to the value or selling price of real property. Usually, the higher the percentage, the greater the interest charged. Maximum percentages for banks, savings and loans, or government insured loans, is set by statute.

LOBBY — An open area immediately inside a building entrance. Most commonly associated with hotels and theaters.

LOCAL GOVERNMENT — City, county, or other governing body at a level smaller than a state. Local government has the greatest control over real property.

LOCATION — The geographical position of real property in relation to its intended use. It is impossible to have a good or bad location without knowing the intended use.

LOCK-IN — The prohibition of prepayment of a loan secured by a mortgage or deed of trust, so that the borrower is "locked in" to the loan for a specified period.

LOCUS SIGILLI — (See: L.S.)

LODGING — A seldom used term meaning a temporary place to stay (lodge).

LOFT BUILDING — A building containing an attic-like upper floor, usually open (without partitions).

LONGITUDE — The East-West circle around the Earth, measured in relation to the meridian or latitude (North-South circle). It is measured from the Greenwich Meridian.

LONGITUDINAL — Pertaining to the length of anything which is measured.

LONG-LIFE PARTS — The most permanent parts of a structure, such as the foundation or bearing walls, as opposed to hot water heaters, roofs, etc.

LONG TERM CAPITAL GAIN — Gain on the sale of a capital asset which has been held for a specified time or longer. Long term capital gain is taxed at a special rate and not as ordinary income.

LONG TERM FINANCING — A mortgage or deed of trust for a term of ten years or more, as distinguished from construction loans or interim loans.

LONG TERM LEASE — A general term which may refer to a lease 10 years or longer in term, or, in some areas, 5 years or longer.

LOSS OF ACCESS — Taking away the right of an owner of property abutting a public road, to come and go to and from said road and his property. Usually happens in condemnation when the abutting road becomes a limited access highway.

LOSS PAYABLE CLAUSE — A clause in a fire insurance policy, listing the priority of claims in the event of destruction of the property insured. Generally, a mortgagee, or beneficiary under a deed of trust, is the party appearing in the clause, being paid to the amount owing under the mortgage or deed of trust before the owner is paid.

LOT — Generally, any portion or parcel of real property. Usually refers to a portion of a subdivision.

LOT AND BLOCK DESCRIPTION — (See: Recorded Map).

LOT BOOK — (See: Plat Book).

LOT LINE — The boundary line of a lot in a subdivision.

LOUVER — Affixed or adjustable formation of slats in a wall, ceiling, door, etc., to let in light and air, allow ventilation of fumes from within, yet keep out rain.

LOVE AND AFFECTION — Loosely called consideration. However, only valid where a valuable consideration is not required, such as a gift. Most contracts to be binding require "valuable consideration".

LOW WATER LINE — Line on the shore marking the lowest ebb of the tide.

L.S. — An abbreviation for "Locus sigilli", the place of the seal. At one time, individuals had seals, and documents were invalid unless the seal was affixed. Modernly, signatures are notarized and only corporations, in certain circumstances, must affix a seal.

LUMBER — A general classification of wood after it passes from the sawmill.

LUMINOUS CEILING — A ceiling emitting light from its entire surface, through the use of fluorescent light above translucent glass or plastic.

M

MADE-LAND — Artificially formed land, either by filling or dredging.

MAGISTRATE — Any civil public officer. Most commonly used to designate an inferior judicial officer, such as a justice of the peace, police justice, etc.

MAGISTRATE'S COURT — Court having jurisdiction over minor matters (small claims), and usually not a court of record.

MAGNESITE FLOORING — A synthetic floor, floated approximately $1\frac{1}{2}$ inches thick, over a concrete floor. Composed of powdered magnesite, magnesium-chloride solution and fillers. Also used for outside steps in areas where cold is not severe.

M.A.I. (MEMBER APPRAISAL INSTITUTE) — The designation given to a member of the American Institute of Real Estate Appraisers. A designation earned through experience, education, and examination.

MAIN — A large conduit or pipe, carrying electricity, sewage, gas, etc., to or from branch lines.

MAIN CIRCUIT — The principal circuit which feeds electric current into smaller circuits (branches) for distribution where needed.

MAINTENANCE — Keeping a property in condition to efficiently serve its intended purpose.

MAINTENANCE FEE — As applied to condominiums and planned developments, the amount charged each unit owner to maintain the common area. Usually a monthly fee paid as part of the budget.

MAINTENANCE RESERVE — Money reserved to cover anticipated maintenance costs.

MAJORITY — The age at which a person is no longer a minor, and is legally entitled to contract and enjoy civic rights, such as voting.

MAKER — One who executes (signs) as the maker (borrower) of a note.

MALL — (1) A shaded walkway or promenade. Modernly, the pedestrian area of a shopping center. May be open or enclosed. (2) A strip between two travelways; may be landscaped or paved. Also called a median strip.

MANAGEMENT — (See: Property Management).

MANAGEMENT AGREEMENT — (See: Property Management Agreement).

MANDAMUS — Latin for "we command". A writ issued by a superior court ordering an inferior court, corporation, or individual, to do or refrain from doing specific acts. The main importance to real estate is that it is a writ commanding a governmental body to do something, such as issue a building permit.

MANSARD ROOF — A four sided roof, each side having two separate slopes of different degree; the lower slope is at a much steeper angle than the upper slope.

MANTEL — (1) The lintel of a fireplace opening, constructed by a post and lintel method. May be of stone, a heavy beam, or other material of strength. (2) A decorative shelf above a fireplace opening, not load-bearing.

MANUFACTURED LOT — A lot upon which construction of a building may begin. Having all off-site improvements and approvals of government agencies.

MAPS AND PLATS — (See: Plat).

MARBLE — A hard, single or multicolored limestone. In construction, used in place of tile in more expensive structures.

MARGINAL — An investment not considered strong. One which barely supports itself.

MARGINAL LAND — (1) Any income producing land which barely covers expenses. (2) Land which is clearly not the best for an intended purpose, but may be adequate.

MARGIN OF SECURITY — [See: Equity (2)].

MARINA — A small harbor or basin, having docks, supplies, and maintenance services for boats.

MARK — An "X" or other symbol used by one who cannot write his or her name. Modernly not used often and laws as to the validity of using a mark should be checked.

MARKETABILITY — Salability. The probability of selling property at a specific time, price, and terms.

MARKETABLE TITLE — Title which can be readily marketed (sold) to a reasonably prudent purchaser aware of the facts and their legal meaning concerning liens and encumbrances.

MARKET DATA APPROACH — (See: Market Value Approach).

MARKET PRICE — The price a property brings in a given market. Commonly used interchangeably with market value, although not truly the same. (See also: Market Value).

MARKET RENT — (See: Economic Rent).

MARKET VALUE — The highest price a willing buyer would pay and a willing seller accept, both being fully informed, and the property exposed for a reasonable period of time. The market value may be different from the price a property can actually be sold for at a given time (market price).

MARKET VALUE APPROACH — Appraising the value of a property by comparing the price of similar properties (comparables) recently sold. The degree of similarity of the properties and circumstances of the sale are the important characteristics to consider.

MARQUEE — A canopy-like projection over the entrance to a building, but not supported by posts or columns. Most commonly found on theaters and hotels.

MARSH — A grassy area of ground which is always soft and wet. Usually distinguished from a swamp by the absence of trees in the marsh.

MASONRY — Anything constructed of the materials used by a mason, such as brick, stone, cement, adobe, etc; anything constructed by a mason of these materials.

MASONRY WALL — A wall, constructed by a mason, of stone, brick, cement, or similar materials.

MASSACHUSETTS TRUST — An unincorporated association, not a partnership, doing business through a trustee. The name comes from authorization of such a trust under the laws of the state of Massachusetts.

MASS APPRAISING — Appraising a whole district or area at the same time, in order to adjust property taxes.

MASTER FORM INSTRUMENT — (See: Fictitious Instrument).

MASTER LEASE — A lease controlling subsequent leases. May cover more property than subsequent leases. For example: "A" leases an office building, containing ten offices, to "B". "B" subsequently leases the ten offices individually. The ten leases from "B" as lessor are controlled by the lease from "A" to "B" (master lease).

MASTER PLAN — A zoning plan for an entire governmental subdivision, such as a city. A comprehensive plan to allow a city to grow in an orderly and sound manner, both economically and ecologically.

MATCHED BOARDS — (See: Tongue and Groove).

MATERIAL FACT — A fact upon which an agreement is based, and without which, said agreement would not be made.

MATERIALMAN — One who supplies construction materials. (See also: Mechanic's Lien).

MATURITY — (1) Termination period of a note. For example: A 30 year mortgage has a maturity of 30 years. (2) In sales law, the date a note becomes due.

MEAN — A middle point between two extremes; or an average, having an intermediate value between two extremes or between several successive values of variable quantity, such as mean low tide and mean high tide.

MEANDER — To follow a winding or flexuous course, usually referring to a river or stream.

MEANDER LINES — Lines run in surveying lands which border navigable rivers to determine the sinuosities of the river.

MEAN HIGH WATER MARK — The point on the shore which the average high tide will reach.

MEAN LOW WATER MARK — The point on the shore which the average low tide will reach.

MECHANIC'S LIEN — A lien created by statute for the purpose of securing priority of payment for the price or value of work performed and materials furnished in construction or repair of improvements to land, and which attaches to the land as well as the improvements.

MECHANIC'S LIEN SURETY BOND — A bond, from a bonding company, indemnifying a title insurer against loss from writing a policy before expiration of the mechanic's lien period.

MECHANIC'S & MATERIALMAN'S LIEN — (See: Mechanic's Lien).

MEDIAN STRIP — A divider, being a strip of land rather than a fence or barrier, between oncoming lanes of a roadway.

MEETING OF THE MINDS — A legal term meaning the mutual agreement necessary to form a contract. It is not based on what may actually be in the minds of the parties, but rather based on whether the acts of the parties and circumstances of the contract indicate that the parties agree.

MEGALOPOLIS — Modern word describing a heavily populated continuous urban area including many cities.

MERGE — To combine two or more entities, so that one survives, the other or others becoming part of the surviving entity, and losing their identity.

MERGE LINE — An appraisal term. The line which arbitrarily splits a lot which fronts on two parallel streets, so that each portion will have the highest value.

MERGER — The combining of two or more entities (businesses) into one surviving entity.

MERGER OF TITLE — A lesser interest in real property being merged (absorbed) into a greater interest. For example: A lessee purchases the property being leased. The interest as a lessee is merged into the interest as an owner, thus ending the leasehold interest.

MERIDIAN — A circle or semicircle around the Earth in a North and South direction, always touching or passing through the poles. Used as a guide in surveying, being placed twenty-four miles apart and running from a base line.

MESNE — Intermediate, intervening.

MESNE ASSIGNMENT — Assignment from A to B to C to D would be described as passing from A by "mesne assignments" to D.

METAL LATH — A heavy coarse screen or slit sheet of metal which is used as a base upon which plaster is spread.

METAL VALLEY — (See: Flashing).

METAMORPHIC ROCK — One of the three major types of rock. A rock formed by metamorphosis (change) caused by heat and/or pressure.

METER — (1) A metric unit of measurement, equal to 39.37 inches. (2) A device for measuring the use of public utilities, such as electricity, gas, etc.

METES AND BOUNDS — Description of land by boundary lines, with their terminal points and angles. Originally metes referred to distance, bounds to direction; modernly, the words have no individual meaning of practical significance.

METROPOLITAN AREA — A major city and surrounding area. The extent of the surrounding area is usually determined by the extent of the influence of the city (commuters for work, shopping, etc.), on the surrounding area.

METROPOLITAN SHOPPING CENTER — (See: Regional Shopping Center).

MEZZANINE — (1) A partial floor between two floors (usually between the first and second). (2) The partial balcony of a theater between the orchestra floor and first balcony.

MICRORELIEF — Minor surface changes, such as channels, dunes, or low hummocks, rather than hills or mountains. The term is used by farm appraisers.

MILE — A linear measurement equal to 5280 feet on land and 6076 feet across water (nautical mile). (See also: Knot (2)).

MILL — Equal to one tenth of a cent. Used in expressing a tax rate. Ten mills would be the same as ten dollars per thousand.

MILL CONSTRUCTION — A type of construction specifically to retard fire. Relies on heavy timbers instead of normal size lumber, extensive use of brick, masonry, and other fire resistant materials.

MILLWORK — Parts of a building produced in a mill, such as doors, window sashes, etc. Differs from cabinet work, which is the work of a finish carpenter, done at the construction site, or precision work done by a cabinet maker, on or away from the construction site.

MINERAL RIGHTS — The ownership of the minerals (coal, gold, iron, etc.) under the ground, with or without ownership of the surface of the land. (See also: Subsurface Rights).

MINERALS — In real estate terms, those minerals of value which may be taken by mining, such as coal, iron, copper, gold, silver, etc. Mineral rights, as well as oil rights, may be sold or leased separately from the land itself.

MINERAL WOOL — A fibrous material produced by the action of steam on molten rock, under pressure, and used as an insulating material. (Also called rock wool).

MINER'S INCH — An indefinite measure of a flow of liquid. Generally agreed to be 1/40th or 1/50th of a cubic foot per second, but which fraction is used depends on area of the country.

MINIMUM LOT — The smallest allowable lot size for development, as stipulated by local zoning laws.

MINIMUM RENTAL — A fixed rental in a lease which contains some formula for a possibly higher rental, such as a percentage lease, overrides, etc.

MINING LEASE — A right to extract (mine) minerals (coal, silver, etc.). (See also: Oil and Gas Lease; Profit a Prendre).

MINOR — Any person under the age of 18. In some states, under age 21 with regard to alcoholic beverages.

MINUTE — [See: Degree (1)].

MISNOMER — A wrong name or mistake in name.

MISPLACED IMPROVEMENTS — An appraisal term indicating an improvement on land which is not the highest and best use.

MISREPRESENTATION — A statement or conduct by a person which represents to another a fact which is not true. A seller, broker, or builder may have a duty to disclose certain defects in property to a buyer or tenant. Failure to disclose is also misrepresentation. The misrepresentation may be deliberate (known to be wrong), negligent (should have known), or innocent (reasonably believed to be true). Depending on the facts and extent of misrepresentation, there may be a suit for damages, recision of a contract, punitive action against the broker (loss of license), etc.

MISSION ARCHITECTURE — A Spanish style of architecture resembling those features of California missions.

MISTAKE — An unintentional, non-negligent error or misunderstanding. A mistake may be of the facts (mistake of fact) or their legal effect (mistake of law).

MITER — To cut two pieces (usually wood) at an angle, to form a joint.

M & M LIEN — (See: Mechanic's Lien).

MOBIL HOME — Originally, a trailer pulled behind a car or truck cab. Now includes large homes which are not truly mobil but are constructed in the same manner as trailers, as opposed to conventional on-site construction.

MOBIL HOME PARK — Originally, a trailer park, having electrical hookups, and water. Modernly, a park-like area having facilities such as complete plumbing and utilities, a recreation center, security guards at the entrance, and mobil homes which are usually attached to foundations and are permanent structures.

MODEL HOME — A home, often decorated, which is shown by a builder to prospective buyers of homes yet to be built. An identical home to the model is then constructed on a lot in the subdivision. The model home is generally sold last.

MODERNIZATION — To make changes to the interior or exterior of a structure for the purpose of reflecting developments of function or design which were not available at the time of the original construction.

MODULAR HOUSE — (See: Prefabricated House).

MOISTURE BARRIER — Insulating materials used to prevent the build up of moisture (condensation) in walls and other parts of a building.

MOLDING — Long, narrow strips of wood or synthetic material, used as a finish piece to cover the crack between the meeting of a wall with a floor or ceiling. Also used for decoration only.

MONEY MARKET — A general term referring to the availability of money for short or long term loans.

MONEY MARKET MUTUAL FUNDS — Funds which invest in the "Money Market", a variety of interest bearing securities such as treasury bills and bank certificates of deposit. None is invested directly into real property or real property securities.

MONTH TO MONTH TENANCY — A tenancy where no written lease is involved, rent being paid monthly. Some obligations as to notice of moving or eviction may exist by statute.

MONUMENT — A visible, permanent object, marked by a surveyor, to indicate the boundaries of land. May be artificial, such as a post, or natural, such as a tree or large stone.

MORATORIUM — A period of suspension of legal rights or remedies. In real estate terms, most commonly used by governmental agenices (usually local) to suspend construction in certain areas until studies are completed to determine the best use for the land involved.

MORTAR — A material used in masonry work as the "glue" holding stones or bricks together. It is composed of lime, cement, sand, and water, and hardens when it dries.

MORTGAGE — (1) To hypothecate as security, real property for the payment of a debt. The borrower (mortgagor) retains possession and use of the property. (2) The instrument by which real estate is hypothecated as security for the repayment of a loan.

MORTGAGE BANKER — A company providing mortgage financing with its own funds rather than simply bringing together lender and borrower, as does a mortgage broker. Although the mortgage banker uses its own funds, these funds are generally borrowed and the financing is either short term or, if long term, the mortgages are sold to investors (many times insurance companies) within a short time.

MORTGAGE BONDS — bonds issued by corporations, which offer first mortgages on real property of the corporation as security for the payment of the bonds.

MORTGAGE BROKER — One who, for a fee, brings together a borrower and lender, and handles the necessary applications for the borrower to obtain a loan against real property by giving a mortgage or deed of trust as security. Also called a loan broker.

MORTGAGE COMPANY — A company authorized to service real estate loans, charging a fee for this service.

MORTGAGEE — The party lending the money and receiving the mortgage. Some states treat the mortgagee as the "legal" owner, entitled to rents from the property. Other states treat the mortgagee as a secured creditor, the mortgagor being the owner. The latter is the more modern and accepted view.

MORTGAGE INSURANCE — Insurance written by an independent mortgage insurance company (referred to as an 'MIC') protecting the mortgage lender against loss incurred by a mortgage default, thus enabling the lender to lend a higher percentage of the sale price. The Federal Government writes this form of insurance through the FHA and the VA.

MORTGAGE LIFE INSURANCE — A term life insurance policy for the amount of the declining balance of a loan secured by a mortgage or deed of trust. The beneficiary under the policy is the mortgagee. In the event of death (some policies also cover disability) of the insured (mortgagor), the mortgage is paid in full.

MORTGAGE POLICY (MORTGAGEE'S POLICY) — (See: Loan Policy).

MORTGAGE POOL — A group or "pool" of mortgages, an interest in which can be purchased through a securities dealer. Because of market changes in interest rates and points (discounts), early payoffs, and foreclosures, pools have different returns and, therefore, different investment values. The rate of payoffs and foreclosures is called the "speed" of the pool.

MORTGAGE SERVICING — Controlling the necessary duties of a mortgagee, such as collecting payments, releasing the lien upon payment in full, foreclosing if in default, and making sure the taxes are paid, insurance is in force, etc. Servicing may be done by the lender or a company acting for the lender, for a servicing fee.

MORTGAGE WAREHOUSING — A system whereby a mortgage company will hold loans which would ordinarily be sold, in order to sell later at a lower discount. These mortgages are used as collateral security with a bank to borrow new money to loan.

MORTGAGOR — The party who borrows the money and gives the mortgage.

MORTISE — A rectangular opening, cut in wood or other material, to receive a bar of wood or other material for the purpose of securing the two parts in a mortise joint.

MOTEL — Originally, a building near a major highway to accommodate travelers, offering a place to sleep and parking. Over the years motels have come to offer most of the features of hotels, such as restaurants, recreation, etc.

M ROOF — A roof constructed of two double pitched roofs, forming a shape similar to the letter M. Utilizes shorter rafters, making construction easier, and allows a lower overall height.

MULLION — A vertical bar separating panes of a window or panels of a door. Also an upright framing member of panels or wainscoting.

MULTIFAMILY DWELLING — (1) A building occupied by more than one family. (2) A building designed as a dwelling for more than four families at the same time.

MULTIPLE DWELLING — (See: Multifamily Dwelling).

MULTIPLE LISTING — An exclusive listing, submitted to all members of an association, so that each may have an opportunity to sell the property.

MUNICIPAL CORPORATION — A town, city, or village, incorporated as a political corporation under state statutes. Would not include a county, or such political divisions as a district.

MUNICIPAL ORDINANCE — (See: Ordinance).

MUNIMENTS OF TITLE — Written evidence (documents) which an owner possesses to prove his title to property.

MUNTIN — A horizontal bar, dividing window panes in a window.

MUTUAL SAVINGS BANK — An institution owned by its depositors, as evidenced by certificates of deposit rather than stock. These institutions are active in long term real estate financing, as opposed to commercial banks, which concentrate more on short term loans.

MUTUAL WATER COMPANY — A company in which the owners are the customers. Stock is issued to the users, who are the organizers of the company.

N

NAME CHANGE — In conveyancing, setting forth both the present name of the grantor and the name under which said grantor acquired title, if different. For example: Joan Doe, a married woman, who acquired title as (or also known as) Joan Smith.

NAR (NATIONAL ASSOCIATION OF REALTORS) — An association of people engaged in the real estate business. Organized in 1908, it currently lists over half a million members. With headquarters in Chicago, it is dedicated to the betterment of the real estate industry through education, legislation, and high ethical standards for its members.

NAREB (NATIONAL ASSOCIATION OF REAL ESTATE BOARDS) — A national trade association whose members include not only real estate brokers, but appraisers, property managers, and other affiliated groups.

NATIONAL ASSOCIATION OF REAL ESTATE BROKERS — An organization dedicated to the betterment of the real estate industry and specifically to the roll of blacks in the real estate industry. It is composed primarily of black real estate brokers who have adopted the term "Realists". Originally founded in Miami in 1947, the association is now based in Washington, D.C.

NATURAL DISASTER — (See: Act of God).

NATURAL FINISH — A finish which retains the color and appearance of the surface covered, such as varnish over wood, rather than paint.

NATURALIZATION — Granting citizenship to an alien. In the United States, a naturalized citizen has the rights of a native citizen, with the exception that the naturalized citizen may not hold the office of president.

NATURAL PERSON — A human being rather than some type of business entity, such as a corporation, partnership, etc.

NATURAL RESOURCES — Resources of an area, such as minerals, oil, timber, water, etc. May also include people.

NAVIGABLE — (1) Capable of carrying commercial shipping, or boats for travel. (2) Any waters put to a public use are "navigable" in some states, giving the word a legal meaning different from its normal meaning.

NAVIGABLE WATERS — A general term which legally differs in different jurisdictions. May mean a body of water capable of carrying a commercial vessel, or a body of water large enough to ebb and flow. In some areas, minor streams have been held to be navigable.

NEAP TIDE — The tide during the first and third quarters of the moon; not as high as in the second and fourth quarters.

NEGATIVE AMORTIZATION — A condition created when a loan payment is less than interest alone. Even though payments are made on time, the amount owing increases.

NEGATIVE CASH FLOW — When the income from an investment property does not equal the usual expenses. The owner must come up with cash each month to meet these expenses. (See also: Cash Flow).

NEGOTIABLE — Capable of being negotiated. Commonly used to mean assignable or transferable in the ordinary course of business, such as negotiable bonds, securities, notes, etc.

NEGOTIABLE INSTRUMENT — According to the Uniform Negotiable Instruments Act, an instrument is negotiable when it is in writing and signed, containing an unconditional promise or order to pay a certain amount of money, on demand, or at a definite future date, to the bearer, to order, or to a named or certain drawee.

NEGOTIABLE ORDER OF WITHDRAWAL CHECKING ACCOUNT (NOW ACCOUNT) — An interest bearing checking account which limits the amount which may be withdrawn over a given period.

NEIGHBORHOOD — A general term describing a contiguous area of similar properties. Since the development of tract housing, the term is not as significant.

NEIGHBORHOOD SHOPPING CENTER — A group of retail stores, usually limited to food and convenience service stores (dry cleaner, barber, etc.) serving a limited area (neighborhood), and having common parking and ownership or management.

NET ACRE — An acre which may be used for building of structures. For example: A builder buys ten acres of raw land on which to build houses. Three acres are used for streets, sidewalks, and other off-site improvements. The remaining seven acres are the net acres of the ten acre site.

NET AFTER TAXES — The net income from property after income tax is paid. (See also: Net Before Taxes; Net Income).

NET BEFORE TAXES — Net income before payment of income tax, but after payment of property taxes. (See also: Net After Taxes; Net Income).

NET EARNINGS — (See: Net Income).

NET GROUND LEASE — A net lease of unimproved land.

NET INCOME — The difference between adjusted gross income and operating expenses. May or may not include depreciation.

NET INCOME MULTIPLIER — The number which, when multiplied by the net income, gives the selling price. Found by dividing the sales price by the net income. Usually, a gross income multiplier is used.

NET LEASE — A lease requiring the tenant to pay, in addition to a fixed rental, the expenses of the property leased, such as taxes, insurance, maintenance, etc. In some states the terms net net, net net net, triple net, and other such repetitions are used. (See also: Gross Lease).

NET LISTING — A listing under which a real estate agent receives any amount over a given net amount to the seller. Illegal in some states.

NET LOSS — The excess of expense over income for a given period. May be more complicated in accounting procedures.

NET NET; NET NET NET — (See: Net Lease).

NET PROFIT — Remainder after deduction of all expenses from income for a given period. Generally classified as either net before taxes, or net after taxes.

NET RENTABLE AREA — (See: Rentable Area).

NET RENTAL — Rental over and above the expenses of the property.

NET SALES AREA — The area (usually expressed in square feet) in a retail store where products are displayed and sold.

NET USABLE ACRE — (See: Net Acre).

NET WORTH — The difference between total assets and liabilities of an individual, corporation, etc.

NEWEL — The post around which winds a circular stairway. In a noncircular stairway, the major post at the bottom of the stairway or at a landing.

"NO BONUS" CLAUSE — A clause under the eminent domain section of a lease, giving the lessee the right to recover only the value of his physical improvements in the event of a taking, and not the value of the leasehold interest (the difference between the fixed rent of the lease and current market rental value). Not applicable in all states.

NOMINAL CONSIDERATION — Consideration in name only, and not related to the market value of the property. Still considered valuable consideration and the purchaser is considered a purchaser for value.

NOMINEE — Most commonly used in a deed, such as to John Doe, or nominee, when the actual grantee is not revealed. Has no legal meaning, other than representative of another.

NONBEARING WALL — A wall used only to separate areas, and which carries only its own weight.

NONCONFORMING USE — A property which does not conform to the zoning of the area. Usually, the property was built in conformity and then the zoning was changed.

NONEXCLUSIVE LISTING — A listing under which the real estate broker has an exclusive listing as opposed to other agents, but the owner may sell the property without using an agent, and not be liable to pay a commission. Also called an agency agreement.

NONJUDICIAL FORECLOSURE SALE — Sale by a trustee under a deed of trust, or mortgagee under a power of sale of a mortgage. There is no court (judicial) proceeding.

NONPROFIT CORPORATION — (See: Eleemosynary Corporation).

NONRECOURSE LOAN — A loan not allowing for a deficiency judgment. The lender's only recourse in the event of default is the security (property) and the borrower is not personally liable.

NONRECURRING EXPENSE — An expense which does not usually repeat itself, such as a fire or other natural disaster.

NORMAL WEAR AND TEAR — (See: Wear and Tear).

NOSING — The edge of a step which projects over the riser below.

NOTARY PUBLIC — One who is authorized by the state or federal government, to administer oaths, and to attest to the authenticity of signatures. A federal authorization may extend the authority to attest to the authenticity of certain documents, and to act as a notary in foreign countries.

NOTE — A unilateral agreement containing an express and absolute promise of the signer to pay to a named person, or order, or bearer, a definite sum of money at a specified date or on demand. Usually provides for interest and, concerning real property, is secured by a mortgage or trust deed.

NOTICE — (See types of notice: Actual; Constructive; Statutory).

NOTICE OF ACTION — A recorded notice that property may be subject to a lien, or even that the title is defective, due to pending litigation. Notice of a pending suit. Also called "Lis Pendens".

NOTICE OF CESSATION — A notice stating that work has stopped on a construction project. Done to accelerate the period for filing a mechanic's lien.

NOTICE OF COMPLETION — A notice, recorded to show that a construction job is finished. The length of time in which mechanic's liens may be filed depends upon when and if a notice of completion is recorded.

NOTICE OF DEFAULT — A notice filed to show that the borrower under a mortgage or deed of trust is in default (behind on the payments).

NOTICE OF NONRESPONSIBILITY — A notice filed by an owner of property to show that work being done has not been contracted for by said owner. If properly done, mechanic's liens will not attach to the property. Often done when a tenant contracts for work on property.

NOTICE OF RECISION — A recorded notice to rescind a notice of default of a mortgage or deed of trust.

NOTICE TO QUIT — A notice by a landlord to a tenant to vacate rented property. There are two types; for nonpayment of rent or a second type for any other reason. Usually the notice for nonpayment allows less time to vacate.

NOTORIOUS POSSESSION — A requirement for adverse possession. Possession so open (notorious) that the owner is presumed to have notice of it and its extent.

NOVATION — Substitution of a new contract, debt, or obligation, for an existing one, between the same or different parties.

NOW — (See: Negotiable Order of Withdrawal).

NUISANCE — A use of property which interferes with the use and enjoyment of other property by excessive noise, odors, fumes, or other harmful or unpleasant emissions.

NULLA BONA — No goods. The name of the return made by the sheriff to a writ of execution, when he has found no goods of the defendant on which to levy within the jurisdiction.

NULL AND VOID — Void. Not legally binding. (See also: Voidable).

NUNC PRO TUNC — Now for then. Applied to acts or entries allowed to be done after they should have been done, with a retroactive effect.

NUNCUPATIVE WILL — An oral will, usually in a deathbed situation, before witnesses who later testify to its authenticity.

NUT — A slang term. (See: Overhead).

O

OAKUM — A fiber used as a caulking, made by pulling apart hemp or rope.

OATH — An attestation by a person which binds him or her legally and morally. Usually attesting to the truth of something, as an affidavit, or the validity of one's signature. A promise to tell the truth. Also, a promise to carry out a duty with high morality (oath of office). An oath has religious connotations and usually involves the word "swear", and may contain the phrase "so help me God", or require the one taking the oath to put his or her hand on a bible. An affirmation (see which) is still legally binding.

OBLIGEE — One to whom an obligation (promise) is owned. (See also: Obligor).

OBLIGOR — One who legally binds (obligates) oneself, such as the maker of a promissory note.

OBSOLESCENCE — An appraisal term meaning that the age of a structure may cause it to become undesirable in use or appearance (old fashioned) and consequently lose income and value.

OCCUPANCY — With reference to land, the word has become synonymous with possession.

OFFER — A presentation or proposal for acceptance, in order to form a contract. To be legally binding, an offer must be definite as to price and terms.

OFFER AND ACCEPTANCE — Necessary elements of a contract to sell real estate. (See also: Offer; Acceptance).

OFFER TO PURCHASE — (See: Purchase Agreement).

OFFICE — A zoning designation allowing businesses to carry on their paperwork rather than manufacturing or sale of inventory to the public on the site. Some businesses may be conducted entirely out of such space, when only paperwork is involved, such as insurance companies, law firms, accounting firms, etc.

OFFSET — (1) A ledge across a wall (usually brick or masonry) formed by reducing the thickness of the wall above the ledge. (2) To balance, as claims in a law suit. Commonly called set-off (when a counter-claim is made to offset damages, the counterclaim being made concerning different subject matter).

OFFSET STATEMENT — (1) A statement given to a buyer of rental property by a tenant, setting forth the amount of rent and terms of the rental agreement. (2) A statement by an owner or lienholder to a buyer, setting forth the balance due on existing liens against the property being purchased.

OFF-SITE — Not on the property to be sold. For example: The developer of a housing tract sells only the house and lot, but must build the streets, sewers, etc., not on the lot.

OFF-SITE IMPROVEMENTS — Development of land to make adjacent property suitable for construction. Includes sidewalks, curbs, streets, sewers, streetlights, etc.

OHM — An electrical measure of resistance of the dissipating of one watt when one ampere passes through it.

OIL AND GAS LEASE — A lease giving the lessee the right to extract oil and gas from land. More like a mining lease than a land lease, in that the lessee has an ownership interest in a portion of the property (the oil and gas) rather than just the use of the property. The lessor is generaly paid based on the oil and gas taken. (See also: Slant Drilling; Profit a Prendre).

OMNIBUS CLAUSE — Clause in a will or decree of distribution passing all property not specifically mentioned.

"ONCE IN A LIFETIME" TAX EXCLUSION — A forgiveness of a portion of the tax due on the sale of a residence by a senior citizen. As the term denotes, the exclusion can be taken only once.

ON CENTER — A construction term referring to a measurement of distance from the center of one structural member to another, such as a stud, joist, etc. Abbreviated on construction drawings as O.C.

ONE HOUR DOOR — A fire resistant door; one which will hold back a fire for a minimum of one hour.

ONE HOUR WALL — A fire resistant wall; one which will hold back a fire for a minimum of one hour.

"ONE, TWO, THREE" FINANCING — A method of "creative" financing by which the buyer (1) assumes an existing loan, (2) secures a second loan from a third party lender, (3) takes a third loan from the seller.

"ON RAIL" — Refers to a property (usually industrial) which is served by a railroad.

ON-SITE IMPROVEMENTS — Structures erected permanently for use on a site, such as buildings, fences, etc.

ON-SITE OFFICE — A real estate branch office specifically for a particular development, and located at said development. May be a sales or leasing office.

OPEN AND NOTORIOUS POSSESSION — (See: Notorious Possession).

OPEN BEAM CONSTRUCTION — A design using heavy roof beams as interior finish, exposed to give a roomy, heavy, rugged appearance to a room.

OPEN-END MORTGAGE — A mortgage permitting the mortgagor to borrow additional money under the same mortgage, with certain conditions, usually as to the assets of the mortgage.

OPEN HOUSE — A house which is open without an appointment to prospective buyers (or tenants) for inspection, during certain hours and days of the week.

OPEN HOUSING — Housing made available to persons without regard to race, religion, sex, color, or national origin.

OPEN LISTING — A written authorization to a real estate agent by a property owner, stating that a commission will be paid to the agent upon presentation of an offer which meets a specified price and terms. However, the agent has no exclusive right to sell and must bring in his offer before any other offer is presented or accepted.

OPEN SPACE LAND — Land used for agriculture, recreation, scenic beauty, natural resources, water shed, or wild life, and so designed on a map.

OPEN SPACE RATIO — Ratio of land area to floor area of an apartment building. Used in zoning requirements.

OPERATING EXPENSES — The cost of operating an income producing property, such as management, utilities, and similar day to day expenses, as well as taxes, insurance, and a reserve for replacement of items which periodically wear out.

OPINION OF TITLE — (See: Abstract of Title).

OPTION — A right, which acts as a continuing offer, given for consideration, to purchase or lease property at an agreed upon price and terms, within a specified time.

OPTIONEE — One who, for consideration, receives an option.

OPTION FOR ADDITIONAL SPACE — An option given to a tenant to rent additional space at a specified rental amount and terms.

OPTIONOR — One who, for consideration, gives an option.

ORAL CONTRACT — A contract, partly written and partly spoken, or not at all reduced to writing.

ORDER CONFIRMING SALE — Court order confirming the terms of a sale of property out of an estate.

ORDINANCE — A law or statute. The term used to designate the enactments of the legislative body of a municipal corporation or a county.

ORDINARY INCOME — A term having meaning only in relation to income tax. The regular graduated scale of tax is paid on income which is called "ordinary", as opposed to capital gains or any other income taxed differently.

ORDINARY REPAIRS — Repairs necessary to keep a property in good condition, against ordinary wear and tear, decay, etc.

ORDINATE — A point along the vertical axis of a curve. When in conjunction with a point on the horizontal axis (abscissas), the point is called the "co-ordinates".

ORIEL WINDOW — A window projecting outward, similar to a bay window. However, an oriel window is supported by brackets or a cantilever, as opposed to a bay window which is supported by the foundation.

ORIENTATION — Planning the most advantageous place on a parcel of land for an improvement to be located.

ORIGINAL COST — The purchase price of property, paid by the present owner. The present owner may or may not be the first owner.

ORIGINAL PAYEE — The person or entity to which a check or promissory note is originally payable.

ORIGINATION FEE — A fee made by a lender for making a real estate loan. Usually a percentage of the amount loaned, such as one percent.

OR MORE CLAUSE — A clause in a note, mortgage, or deed of trust, allowing for additional payments to be made without penalty. The words "or more" come after the specified payment.

OSTENSIBLE AGENCY — An agency created by law when a principal acts (intentionally or negligently) as if one is an agent who in fact is not. (See also: Apparent Authority).

OVERAGE INCOME — Rental from a percentage of the operation of a business in excess of the base rental. (See also: Percentage Lease).

OVERBUILDING — Construction of an excessive number of similar properties (houses, apartments, etc.) so as to cause a surplus of supply over demands.

OVERHANG — An extension of a roof beyond the exterior walls, used as a shading or protection from rain, for a walkway.

OVERHEAD — The expenses of a business or property. Commonly referred to as the "nut".

OVER IMPROVEMENT — An improvement, excessive in cost or size in relation to land value or value of surrounding improvements.

OVERPASS — A bridge or road elevated to avoid intersecting with a roadway, railway, or other traffic carrier.

OVERRIDE — A rental amount paid due to sales of the tenant. For example: A lease for a service station may contain a provision for a certain addition to the rent for every gallon of gasoline over a certain amount sold each month. The amount over is called the override, such as two cents per gallon for every gallon over fifty thousand sold each month.

OVERRIDING ROYALTY — Common in oil and gas leases. A retained royalty by a lessee when the property is subleased.

OVERT — Open, manifest, public; action as distinguished from mere intention.

OWELTY OF EXCHANGE — Money necessary to equalize the value of the properties being exchanged. (See also: Boot).

OWELTY OF PARTITION — Money paid by one co-tenant to another when property is split, but the result is properties of unequal value.

OWNER — One who has the rights of ownership. (See: Ownership).

OWNER OCCUPIED — Property physically occupied by the owner.

OWNER OF RECORD — The owner of property according to the records of the county recorder.

OWNERSHIP — Rights to the use, enjoyment, and alienation of property, to the exclusion of others. Concerning real property, absolute rights are rare, being restricted by zoning laws, restrictions, liens, etc.

OWNER'S POLICY — Title insurance for the owner of property, rather than a lienholder.

OWNER WILL CARRY MORTGAGE — A term used to indicate that the seller is willing to take back a purchase money mortgage. (See: Purchase Money Mortgage (1)).

P

PACKAGE MORTGAGE — Mortgage covering both real and personal property.

PACKAGE TRUST DEED — (See: Package Mortgage).

PANE — The glass portion of a door or window.

PANEL — (1) A section, raised, lowered, or level, of a wall, ceiling, fence, etc., self contained, and usually in a border or frame. (2) Sheets of gypsum, plywood, or other materials in similar form.

PANEL HEATING — Space heating by electric coils, hot air, hot water, or steam pipes, which are built into walls, ceilings, or floor panels. Also called radiant heating.

PANEL WALL — (See: Curtain Wall).

PAPER — A mortgage, deed of trust, or land contract, which is given instead of cash. A seller would take back "paper" if he or she received a mortgage, deed of trust, or land contract as part of the purchase price.

PAR — (1) Average, equal, normal, etc. (2) Face value, as in negotiable instruments.

PARAPET — A short wall along the edge of a platform, such as a roof, terrace, etc., to protect the edge and divert rainwater.

PARCEL — A general term meaning any part or portion of land.

PARGING — Coating cement on a masonry wall, usually for water proofing.

PARISH — A political division in Louisiana, comparable to a county.

PARKWAY — (1) A highway through a park, usually restricting vehicles over a certain weight. (2) A freeway or expressway.

PAROL — Verbal. Usually refers to evidence in a court of law. The "Parol Evidence Rule" governs when such evidence is admissable.

PARQUET FLOOR — Patterned, hardwood flooring, especially parquetry (a geometric design).

PARTIAL RECONVEYANCE — (See: Partial Release).

PARTIAL RELEASE — A release of a portion of property covered by a mortgage. A subdivider will obtain a partial release as each lot is sold, upon payment of an agreed upon amount. In areas where the subdivider is not usually the builder, it may be necessary to sell groups of lots to obtain a partial release. In areas where deeds of trust are used instead of mortgages, a "partial reconveyance" is the document used.

PARTIAL TAKING — The taking of part of an owner's property under the laws of eminent domain. Compensation must be based on damages or benefits to the remaining property, as well as the part taken.

PARTICIPATION — Lender involvement in a development for a percentage of the gross sales or profit, as well as interest on the loan. Usually occurs when money is difficult to obtain.

PARTICIPATION CERTIFICATES — Mortgage securities, rather than mortgages. The advantage of the certificate is that it is readily marketable or pledgeable.

PARTITION — (1) Any division of real or personal property between co-owners, resulting in individual ownership of the interests of each. (2) A wall, sometimes moveable, and not load-bearing, used to divide a room or building.

PARTNERSHIP — As defined by the Uniform Partnership Act, "An association of two or more persons to carry on as co-owners, a business for profit". The business must be lawful and the partners must agree to share in the profit or loss (but not necessarily equally).

PARTY WALL — A wall erected on a property boundary as a common support to structures on both sides, which are under different ownerships.

PAR VALUE — (1) Concerning stock. The face value of a share of stock. (2) With reference to mortgages or trust deeds, the value of the mortgage based on the balance owing, without discount.

PATENT — Instrument of conveyance of title to public (government) land.

PATENT DEFECT — A defect plainly visible or as would be discovered by the exercise of ordinary care. A patent defect in a legal description is one which cannot be corrected on its face, and a new description must be used. (See also: Latent Defect).

PATIO — Originally, a courtyard, enclosed by columns, or an open courtyard. Modernly, a paved area adjoining a house, used for relaxation, outdoor cooking, eating, etc.

PAYMENT CAP — A maximum amount for a payment under an Adjustable Mortgage Loan, regardless of the increase in the interest rate. If the payment is less than the interest alone, negative amortization is created.

PAYOFF — The payment in full of an existing loan or other lien.

PAYOFF ESCROW — An escrow, specifically for the purpose of paying off an existing lien. Usually part of an existing escrow, and called a sub escrow.

PEDESTRIAN OVERPASS — A bridge over a highway, railway, etc., for pedestrian traffic.

PEDESTRIAN TRAFFIC COUNT — (See: Traffic Count).

PEDESTRIAN UNDERPASS — A tunnel, under a highway, used for pedestrian traffic.

PENNY — Most popularly applied to nails. A measure of length, symbolized by the letter "d".

PENSTOCK — (1) A valve to regulate or direct the flow of water. (2) A conduit for a similar purpose.

PENTHOUSE — (1) A condominium or apartment on the roof of a building, used as a residence. (2) A small building on a roof, which houses elevator machinery, ventilating equipment, etc.

PER ANNUM — Yearly, annually.

PER CAPITA — Literally, by heads. Commonly, as individuals. In the right to receive a portion of the estate of a deceased person, one claiming a per capita right would claim an equal share as an individual and not a divided share as part of a family (per stirpes).

PERCENTAGE LEASE — A lease, generally on a retail business property, using a percentage of the gross or net sales to determine the rent. There is usually a minimum or "base" rental, in the event of poor sales.

PERCENTAGE RENT — (See: Percentage Lease).

PERCH — A seldom used unit of measurement equal to $16^1/_2$ feet.

PERCOLATION — The absorption of liquid into soil by seepage.

PERCOLATION (PERK) TEST — The test to determine the capability of the soil to absorb liquid, both for construction and septic systems.

PER DIEM — Daily.

PERFECT ESCROW — A complete escrow. When the escrow agent has all instrument and instructions necessary to carry out the transaction (purpose of the escrow).

PERFORMANCE BOND — A bond posted by a builder to insure completion of a project.

PERIMETER — (1)The boundary lines of a parcel of land. (2)The length of said boundary lines.

PERIMETER HEATING — (See: Baseboard Heating).

PERISTYLE — A colonnade around a building or courtyard.

PERMANENT MORTGAGE — A mortgage on completed construction for a long period of time, usually over ten years. (See also: Take Out Loan).

PERPETUITY — Continuing forever. Legally, pertaining to real property, any condition extending the inalienability of property beyond the time of a life or lives in being plus twenty-one years.

PER SE — By itself; of itself; inherently.

PERSONAL PROPERTY — Any property which is not designated by law as real property.

PERSONAL PROPERTY BROKER — A loan broker operating under a special license to broker personal property loans. The loan broker may be paid in a lump sum or from the monthly interest payment.

PERSONAL PROPERTY LOAN — A loan which is secured by both real and personal property. The minimum ratio of personal to real property is set by law. The credit of the borrower is a major consideration in making the loan. (See also: Equity Loan).

PER STIRPES — As a representative, and not as an individual. In the laws of descent and distribution, one who takes because of a deceased ancestor. For example: A leaves equally to B and C per stirpes. C dies, leaving three children. The estate goes one half to B, one half to be divided among the three children of C. (See also: Per Capita).

PHYSICAL DEPRECIATION — (See: Deterioration).

PHYSICAL LIFE — The normal life of an improvement, if properly maintained.

PI (PRINCIPAL AND INTEREST) — Used to indicate what is included in a monthly payment on real property. If the payment includes only principal and interest, property taxes and hazard insurance would make the total payment higher. (See: PITI).

PICTURE WINDOW — A large window used to let in light and a view, but not air.

PIER — (1) A structure extending from the solid land out into the water of a river, lake, harbor, etc., to afford convenient passage for persons and property to and from vessels along its sides. (2) A heavy, vertical support member, of masonry, wood, or metal.

PIGGYBACK LOAN — A loan made jointly by two or more lenders on the same property under one mortgage or trust deed. A 90% loan, for example, may have one lender loaning 80% and another (subordinate) lender loaning the top 10% (high risk portion).

PILASTER — A pier or column, which partly protrudes from a wall, or is attached to a wall as a decoration. If not strictly decorative, it may be a support member.

PILE — A vertical support member, driven into the ground (or bottom, if in water). May be of concrete, metal, or wood.

PILLAR — A vertical support member, usually the main support. Is not attached at its sides.

PIPELINE — An extended connection of pipes for transporting liquids or gases, such as oil or natural gas.

PITCH — (1) A mixture of resins; a black tar substance. (2) To incline, such as a sloping roof. The rate of incline is the pitch.

PITI (PRINCIPAL, INTEREST, TAXES AND INSURANCE) — Used to indicate what is included in a monthly payment on real property. Principal, interest, taxes and insurance are the four major portions of a usual monthly payment.

PLAINTIFF — The party bringing a civil action against a defendant.

PLANK — Lumber 2″ to 4″ in thickness, 8″ or more in width.

PLANNED (UNIT) DEVELOPMENT — A subdivision of five or more individually owned lots with one or more other parcels owned in common or with reciprocal rights in one or more other parcels. The lots are generally small, being the exact size of the improvements, or slightly larger.

PLANNING COMMISSION — A board of a city, county, or similar local government, which must approve proposed building projects. Often must be confirmed by a higher board, such as a council.

PLANS — All drawings necessary to a construction project, including the subcontractors' drawings. (See also: Specifications).

PLASTER OF PARIS — Gypsum heated to form a fine white powder which, when wet, will dry hard.

PLAT (PLAT MAP) — A map dividing a parcel of land into lots, as in a subdivision.

PLAT BOOK — A book which contains the plat maps for a given area.

PLATE — (See: Wall Plates).

PLEDGE — The depositing (bailment) of goods (personal property) with a creditor as security for a debt.

PLEDGED ACCOUNT LOAN — A loan partially secured by the buyer or third party depositing funds into a savings account as collateral security for the loan. A portion of the monthly payment is drawn from the account over the first years of the loan.

PLEDGEE — The party to whom goods are pledged.

PLEDGOR — The party delivering goods in pledge (pledging).

PLOT — (1) An area of ground for a specific use, such as a cemetery plot. (2) Ground on which an improvement is to be built.

PLOT PLAN — A plan of the location of improvements on a parcel of land. Also called a plot map. Don't confuse with plat.

PLOTTAGE — (See: Assemblage).

PLOTTAGE INCREMENT — The increase in value created by joining smaller adjacent properties into one large parcel, under a single ownership.

PLUMB — (1) To provide plumbing. (2) A weight used on a line (plumb line) to determine the exact right angle to the ground or a floor.

PLUMBING — The pipes, fixtures, etc., necessary for the flow of water to a building, and flow of sanitary waste from a building.

PLY — A layer or fold. Commonly used to describe the thickness of any built-up surface, such as plywood, veneers, tires, etc.

PLYWOOD — A wood sheet made of layers (plies) of thin sheets, glued to a center sheet of thicker wood, the grain running at right angles.

PMI — (See: Private Mortgage Insurance.)

POCKET CARD — A card issued by a state showing that an individual is licensed as a real estate broker or salesperson.

POINT — One percent. When referring to mortgages or deeds of trust, the term is used to describe the percentage of discount rather than interest (for which the word "percent" is used). The points are paid by the seller in F.H.A. and V.A. insured loans, and by either buyer or seller (or both) in conventional loans.

POINT LETTER — A letter from a lender which guarantees the number of points on a loan for a given time.

POINT OF BEGINNING (POB) — A term used in metes and bounds descriptions. The description will start with the words "Beginning at a point" and end with "to the point of beginning".

POLICE POWER — The power of the state which abridges individual rights for the safety, health, and general welfare of society. Condemnation would fall in this category.

POLICY — A general term used to describe all contracts of insurance.

PORCH — An extension from a structure, usually serving as part of the entrance. May be large enough for relaxation, and most often has its own roof, rather than a part of the structure roof.

PORTICO — A colonnade at the front of a building.

POSSESSION — Being in physical control of land or personal property, whether the owner or not. Possession may be lawful or wrongful.

POSSIBILITY OF REVERTER — The term shows no estate (interest) in property, but only the chance that an estate will exist at a future time. If a property were sold on the condition that it be used for a park, and, if not used for a park, would revert back to the seller, the seller would have a possibility of reverter.

POST — (1) To give public notice by attaching to a post or wall or displaying in a public place. (2) After. (3) A vertical support. (4) To enter into ledgers or books, such as posting to an account.

POST AND LINTEL — A system of construction based on vertical supports with horizontal cross beams. No arches are used.

POSTDATED — Dating an instrument after the actual date of execution. Most often thought of in connection with checks, but sometimes used in states where certain days (Sundays and holidays) cannot be used to contract. The contract is still not legal if postdated for this reason.

POSTSTRESSED CONCRETE — Placing cables, in metal casing, in wet concrete. When the concrete dries, the cables are stretched, and the casing filled with grout. When the grout dries, the cables are released, transmitting the stress to the concrete.

POTABLE — Drinkable.

POWER OF ATTORNEY — An authority by which one person (principal) enables another (attorney in fact) to act for him. (1) General power - Authorizes sale, mortgaging, etc. of all property of the principal. Invalid in some jurisdictions. (2) Special power - Specifies property, buyers, price and terms. How specific it must be varies in each state.

POWER OF SALE — Clause in a mortgage or deed of trust giving the mortgagee or trustee the power to sell the property in the event of default. There are laws which govern the sale, which must be at public auction, but there is no court action necessary (judicial foreclosure).

PR — -(1) Slang for the word profit. An expression not nationally used. (2) Public relations.

PRACTICING LAW — The domain of a duly licensed attorney. A real estate or escrow agent may not practice law. What constitutes practicing law varies with state statutes.

PRE-EMPTION RIGHT — The right given to settlers upon the public lands of the United States, to purchase the lands at a limited price in preference to others. Modernly, equivalent to a first refusal right.

PREFABRICATED HOUSE — A house constructed of manufactured components, assembled partly at the site, rather than totally on the site. Also called a modular house.

PREFABRICATION — The manufacturing of parts of a structure, such as walls, roofs, etc., which are assembled at the construction site. More recently called modular housing.

PRELIMINARY TITLE REPORT — A report showing the condition of title before a sale or loan transaction. After completion of the transaction, a title insurance policy is issued.

PREMISES — (1) Buildings and immediately surrounding areas. (2) In conveyancing, the part of a deed giving the names of the grantor and grantee, the consideration, and description of the property conveyed.

PREMIUM — (1) Money paid for an insurance policy. (2) A bonus. The opposite of a discount.

PREPAID INTEREST — Interest paid before becoming due.

PREPAID ITEMS — Those expenses of property which are paid in advance and will usually be prorated upon sale, such as taxes, insurance, rent, etc.

PREPAYMENT — (See: Or More Clause).

PREPAYMENT PENALTY — A penalty under a note, mortgage, or deed of trust, imposed when the loan is paid before it is due.

PREPAYMENT PRIVILEGE — The right to prepay a loan without penalty, either in full or in part. (See also: Lock-in; Or More Clause; Prepayment Penalty).

PRESCRIPTION — Written before.

PRESCRIPTIVE EASEMENT — The granting of an easement by a court, based on the presumption that a written easement was given (although none existed), after a period of open and continuous use of land.

PRESERVATIVE — A chemical covering for wood or metal, preventing insect destruction or rot in the former, and rust in the latter.

PRESTRESSED CONCRETE — Stretching wire or other reinforcement in wet concrete, then releasing it after the concrete has dried, causing the tension (stress) toward compaction of the concrete.

PRESUMPTION — An inference reached by probability and reasoning in the absence of absolute fact. A presumption of law is the required drawing of an inference from existing facts. The presumption may be rebuttable or conclusive. If rebuttable, facts may be presented to refute the presumption. If conclusive, no facts may be presented, as in estoppel.

PRICE — Modernly, the amount of money paid for property which is purchased, although the word is general enough to include anything given (not necessarily money) in exchange for something else.

PRICE TAKE-OFF METHOD — (See: Quantity Survey Method).

PRIMA FACIE — At first sight; on the face of it. Presumed true unless disproved.

PRIME LENDING RATE — The most favorable interest rates charged by a commercial bank on short term loans, (not mortgages).

PRIMER — A coat of sealant or other preparatory substance, applied to a surface before a finish coat.

PRIME TENANT — The major tenant in a building, shopping center, etc. It may be necessary to have a prime tenant in order to obtain construction financing. The tenant may be considered "prime" because of its financial strength, rather than by the amount of space it occupies.

PRINCIPAL — (1) The person who gives authority to an agent or attorney (see attorney-in-fact). (2) Amount of debt, not including interest. The face value of a note, mortgage, etc.

PRINCIPAL MERIDIAN (PRIME MERIDIAN) — The meridian being used as a reference point in a specific property description. (See also: Base Line; Meridian).

PRIORITY — That which comes first in time or importance. Regarding liens, the time of recording establishes priority.

PRIORITY CLAUSE — A clause in a junior lien, acknowledging the priority of a prior lien.

PRIVATE LAND GRANT — A grant of public land to an individual.

PRIVATE MORTGAGE INSURANCE — Insurance against a loss by a lender in the event of default by a borrower (mortgagor). The insurance is similar to insurance by a governmental agency such as FHA, except that it is issued by a private insurance company. The premium is paid by the borrower and is included in the mortgage payment.

PRIVATE PROPERTY — Property owned by a person, group, corporation, or other entity, not a governmental body.

PRIVITY — Mutual or successive relationship to the same rights of property, such as heir and ancestor, assignee and assignor.

PROBATE — Originally, the proving that a will was valid. Modernly, any action over which probate court has jurisdiction.

PROBATE COURT — A court having jurisdiction of estates, whether of a deceased, a minor, or an incompetent person.

PROBATE SALE — Sale of property from an estate. Must be done under supervision and procedures of the probate court.

PROCURING CAUSE — A direct cause of an event, or the direct cause of a series of causes leading to an event. A broker is entitled to a commission under an open listing if proven to be the procuring cause of a sale.

PROFIT — The difference of income less expenses. Further broken down into net profit and gross profit, (see which).

PROFIT AND LOSS STATEMENT — A statement showing the income and expenses of a business over a stated time, the difference being the profit or loss for the period.

PROFIT A PRENDRE — A right to take from the soil, such as by logging, mining, drilling, etc. The taking (profit) is the distinguishing characteristic from an easement, although easement is frequently used as a synonym.

PROMISEE — One to whom a promise has been made, such as the lender under a promissory note.

PROMISOR — One who makes a promise. The borrower under a promissory note.

PROMISSORY NOTE — A promise in writing, and executed by the maker, to pay a specified amount during a limited time, or on demand, or at sight, to a named person, or on order, or to bearer.

PROPERTY — Anything which is owned by someone. (See also: Real Estate).

PROPERTY BRIEF — An expression, not nationally used, meaning a description of a property for sale, which is submitted to a prospective purchaser.

PROPERTY LINE — The boundary line of a parcel of land.

PROPERTY MANAGEMENT — The branch of the real estate business dealing with the management of property. The property may be a rented house or a large office or industrial complex. The duties may range from merely collecting rents to complete management of all maintenance and may also include being leasing agent or sales agent.

PROPERTY MANAGEMENT AGREEMENT — The contract between an owner and property manager (or management company), setting forth the duties of and payment for said manager.

PROPERTY OWNERS' ASSOCIATION — (See: Homeowners' Association).

PROPERTY TAX — Generally, a tax levied on both real and personal property; the amount of the tax is dependent on the value of the property.

PROPRIETARY LEASE — Most commonly used in relation to stock cooperatives, whereby the owners of stock lease units (apartments).

PROPRIETORSHIP — (See: Sole Proprietorship).

PRO RATE — To divide in proportionate shares, such as taxes, insurance, rent, or other items which buyer and seller share as of the time of closing, or other agreed upon time.

PRORATION — To divide (prorate) property taxes, insurance premiums, rental income, etc., between buyer and seller proportionately to time of use, or the date of closing.

PROSCENIUM — Originally the stage of a theater. Modernly, the portion of the stage on the audience side of the curtain.

PROSPECT — A potential buyer, seller, or tenant, rather than one which is actually in the process of buying, selling, or leasing.

PROSPECTUS — A brochure, presenting for a prospective investor the details of an offering.

PROXY — Although the term legally encompasses any agent, it is most frequently used in connection with representation at a meeting, especially when voting is concerned. The written authority to act is called a proxy, as well as the person acting.

PUBLIC DOMAIN LAND — (See: Public Land).

PUBLIC HOUSING — A governmental housing project, usually to accommodate low income families.

PUBLIC LAND — Lands belonging to the federal government, not reserved for government use but subject to sale or other disposal.

PUBLIC LAND SYSTEM — Legal descriptions of land by reference to the public land survey. Often called sectional property descriptions.

PUBLIC OFFERING STATEMENT — (See: Public Report).

PUBLIC RECORDS — Usually at a county level, the records of all documents which are necessary to give notice. The records are available to the public. All transactions for real estate sales should be recorded.

PUBLIC REPORT — A report given to prospective purchasers in a new subdivision, stating the conditions of the area (costs of common facilities, availability of schools, noise factor if near an airport, etc.), issued by the real estate commission.

PUBLIC SALE — Sale at auction, open to the public. May be a foreclosure sale, tax sale, excess state land sale, or other type. A "public" sale generally requires notice (advertising) and must be held in a place accessible to the general public.

PUBLIC UTILITY — A company such as the telephone company, electric company, or gas company, which supplies a necessity in our modern life, and monopolizes the industry. Such companies are under the control of the Public Utilities Commission.

PUFFER — One hired to make false bids at an auction in order to raise the price of the property being sold.

PUFFING — An opinion not made as a representation of fact, but intended to enhance the value of the property.

PUNITIVE DAMAGES — (See: Exemplary Damages).

PUR AUTRE VIE — For (during) the life of another. A life estate measured not by the life of the grantee, but by the life of another person. The life of a famous person is commonly used, such as a young member of a royal family known for its longevity.

PURCHASE AGREEMENT — An agreement between a buyer and seller of real property, setting forth the price and terms of the sale.

PURCHASE AND LEASEBACK — (See: Sale-Leaseback).

PURCHASE MONEY MORTGAGE — (1) A mortgage given from buyer to seller to secure all or a portion of the purchase price. (2)Any mortgage from which the funds are used to purchase the property.

PURCHASE MONEY TRUST DEED — (See: Purchase Money Mortgage).

PURCHASE OFFER — (See: Purchase Agreement).

PURCHASER'S POLICY — (See: Owner's Policy).

PUTTY — A soft clay-like mixture used as a filler for cracks, joints, and to install window panes.

PYLON — (1) A monumental mass which flanks an entrance, such as pillars at a gateway. (2) A tower, such as the steel towers which support high tension wires.

PYRAMID ROOF — A roof resembling a pyramid; having four sloping sides, either forming a point, as a church steeple, or running at a lesser angle to a horizontal ridge, as is common on free standing garages.

Q

QUAD — (See: Quadrant).

QUADRANT — (1) A quarter section of a circle. (2) One of the quarters created by two intersecting roads or streets.

QUANTITY SURVEY METHOD — Also called "price take-off" method. A process of arriving at an estimate of new construction costs by a detailed estimate of quantities of necessary building materials plus labor costs.

QUARTER — (See: Quarter Section).

QUARTER ROUND — A molding which, in cross-section, resembles a quarter circle.

QUARTER SECTION — One quarter of a section. A quarter section (commonly called a quarter) contains 160 acres.

QUASI — Similar to but intrinsically different.

QUAY — A wharf used for loading or unloading ships.

QUESTION OF FACT — Question as to what actually happened. Determined by physical evidence and decided by a jury in a jury trial.

QUESTION OF LAW — Given the facts, what laws, if any, are applicable; decided by a judge, even in a jury trial.

QUICK ASSETS — (See: Liquid Assets).

QUIETUS — Final disposition of a claim or debt.

QUIET ENJOYMENT — (See: Covenant of Quiet Enjoyment).

QUIET TITLE — (See: Action To Quiet Title).

QUITCLAIM DEED — A deed operating as a release; intended to pass any title, interest, or claim which the grantor may have in the property, but not containing any warranty of a valid interest or title in the grantor.

R

RABBET — A method of joining or fitting together wood by cutting a deep groove in one piece to allow the other to be fitted against it.

RACEWAY — A pipe carrying electrical wiring, having outlets at close intervals.

RADIANT HEATING — A heating system using electrical coils, or pipes in the ceilings, walls, or floors, which heat with steam, hot water, or hot air.

RADIATOR — An old fashioned, cast iron, ribbed heating fixture using hot water. Most modern systems use air for heating, because water or steam systems are more expensive.

RAFTERS — Load-bearing timbers of a roof. Flat roof rafters are usually called joists.

RAIL — (1) A horizontal bar, such as the cross member of a fence. (2) Tracks on which a train runs.

RAKE — Sloping members, such as a cornice, which run parallel to the inclination of a roof.

RAMP — (1) An inclined, concrete or wooden path, used instead of steps. (2) A roadway used as an entrance or exit to a limited access highway.

RANCH — Traditionally, a place for raising horses or cattle, which feed on a grazing range. More modernly, the term has been applied to the raising of other animals under controlled conditions, such as mink, chickens, etc.

RANCH STYLE HOUSE — Modernly, any one story house is called a ranch style. A true ranch style house is rambling, with low pitched gable roofs, and an interior of open design.

RANCH UNIT — The ranch itself plus public lands used as part of the ranch operation, under permits.

RANDOM SHINGLES — Roof or siding shingles of different sizes.

RANGE — (1) A division of land in the government survey, being a six mile wide row of townships, running North and South, and used in legal descriptions. (2) Land used for grazing livestock.

RATABLE ESTATE — Property capable of being rated (assessed), taxed).

RATE INDEX — An index used to adjust the interest rate of an adjustable mortgage loan. For example: the change in U.S. Treasury securities (T-Bills) with a 1 year maturity. The weekly average yield on said securities, adjusted to a constant maturity of one year, which is the result of weekly sales, may be obtained weekly from the Federal Reserve Statistical Release H.15 (519). This change in interest rates is the "index" for the change in the specific Adjustable Mortgage Loan.

RATE OF RETURN — The annual percentage of return on investment on income property.

RATIFICATION — Affirming a prior act which was not legally binding; the affirmation gives the act legal effect. Occurs when an unauthorized agent acts, and the principal later affirms the action, giving authority retroactively.

RAT WALL — A wall only a few inches above ground, but to a specified depth (according to local code) below ground, around a house to prevent rats from going under the house. Not used in all parts of the country, and only necessary where there is not a full basement or slab construction.

RAW LAND — Land in its natural state. Land which has not been subdivided into lots, does not have water, sewers, streets, utilities, or other improvements necessary before a structure can be constructed.

RAZE — To tear down or demolish.

READY, WILLING, AND ABLE — Capable of present performance. A broker supplying an offer from a ready, willing and able buyer, which meets the price and terms of the listing, is entitled to a commission, even though the seller is not bound to accept the offer. A standard listing agreement would state this.

REAL ESTATE — (1) Land and anything permanently affixed to the land, such as buildings, fences, and those things attached to the buildings, such as light fixtures, plumbing and heating fixtures, or other such items which would be personal property if not attached. The term is generally synonymous with real property, although in some states a fine distinction may be made. (2) May refer to rights in real property as well as the property itself.

REAL ESTATE BOARD — A board composed of regular members (real estate brokers and salespersons), and affiliate members (lenders, title companies, etc.). for the purpose of furthering the real estate business in a given area.

REAL ESTATE BROKER — (See: Broker).

REAL ESTATE COMMISSION — (See: Department of Real Estate).

REAL ESTATE LICENSE — A state license granted to one as a broker or salesperson, after passing an examination. Some states have educational requirements before the brokers' examination may be taken.

REALIST — A member of the National Association of Real Estate Brokers.

REAL PROPERTY — (See: Real Estate).

REALTOR — A designation given to a real estate broker who is a member of a board associated with the National Association of Real Estate Boards.

REALTY — Real estate.

REASSESSMENT — Re-estimating the value of all property in a given area for tax assessment purposes.

REBATE — A discount or reduction in price of a product or interest, not given in advance, but handed back because of prompt payment or other reason. Many states regulate gifts and educational aids given to real estate brokers by supporting companies such as title companies, calling these in effect, a price discount (rebate).

RECAPTURE — The return of monies invested in property, through reduction of the loan amount and appreciation; it is realized when the property is sold.

RECAPTURE OF DEPRECIATION — Taxing as ordinary income, upon the sale of property, the amount of depreciation taken above straight line depreciation.

RECEIPT — A written acknowledgment or admission that something has been received. Has no other legal effect, and does not in itself affirm any contractual obligation.

RECEIVER — A court appointed person who holds property which is either in dispute or cannot competently be handled by its owner.

RECIPROCITY — A mutual exchange of privileges by states, allowing attorneys, real estate brokers, and others to practice in one state while being licensed in another.

RECITAL — Setting forth in a deed or other writing some explanation for the transaction. For example: A deed may state that the property is being transferred in lieu of foreclosure.

RECLAMATION — The process of bringing economically unusable land to a higher dollar value by physically changing it. For example: draining a swamp, irrigating a desert, replanting a forest.

RECONDITIONING — Restoring a property to good condition without changing its plan or character, as distinguished from remodeling. Also called renovation, rehabilitation.

RECONVEYANCE — An instrument used to transfer title from a trustee to the equitable owner of real estate, when title is held as collateral security for a debt. Most commonly used upon payment in full of a trust deed. Also called a deed of reconveyance or release.

RECORDATION — Filing instruments for public record (and notice) with a recorder (usually a county official).

RECORDED MAP — A map recorded in a county recorder's office. May be a subdivision map or describe a non-subdivided parcel. Reference to a recorded map is commonly used in legal descriptions.

RECORDED PLAT — A subdivision map filed as a matter of public record.

RECORDER'S OFFICE — The county office where instruments are recorded, giving public notice.

RECORDING — Filing documents affecting real property as a matter of public record, giving notice to future purchasers, creditors, or other interested parties. Recording is controlled by statute and usually requires the witnessing and notarizing of an instrument to be recorded.

RECORDING ACTS — State statutes enacted to cover the public recording of deeds, mortgages, etc., and the effect of these recordings as notice to creditors, purchasers, and other interested parties.

RECORDING FEE — The amount paid to the recorder's office in order to make a document a matter of public record.

RECORD OWNER — (See: Owner of Record).

RECOURSE — The right of the holder of a note secured by a mortgage or deed of trust to look personally to the borrower or endorser for payment, not just to the property.

REDDENDUM — Technical name for a clause in a conveyancing instrument or lease, creating a reservation to the grantor or lessor.

REDEMPTION — The process of canceling a defeasible title to land, such as is created by a mortgage foreclosure or tax sale.

REDEMPTION PERIOD — A time period during which a mortgage, land contract, deed of trust, etc., can be redeemed. Usually set by statute, and after judicial foreclosure.

REDEVELOPMENT — Generally, the improvement of land in accordance with an urban renewal project.

"RED LINING" — The outlining on a map of certain "high risk" areas for real estate loan purposes. This means lenders will not extend credit in these areas for real property loans, regardless of the qualifications of the applicant. Some states have passed laws against this practice. The use of a red pen or pencil for the outlining gave rise to the term.

RE-ENTRY — The right to resume possession reserved when the possession was given to another. Not automatic and court action may be necessary.

REFEREE — One appointed by a court to take testimony and report back to the court. May be in bankruptcy or other proceedings.

REFERRAL — In the real estate business, generally the act of a past client recommending a real estate broker or agent to one currently a buyer or seller. Also, any recommendation by one real estate agent of another for a referral fee.

REFINANCE — (1) The renewing of an existing loan with the same borrower and lender. (2) A loan on the same property by either the same lender or borrower. (3) The selling of loans by the original lender.

REFORMATION — An action to correct a deed or other document which, through mistake or fraud, does not express the real agreement or intent of the parties.

REGIONAL SHOPPING CENTER — The largest type of shopping center, having one or more major department stores, a variety of retail stores, usually a bank or savings and loan, and common parking and management.

REGISTER — A grid-like opening in a wall, ceiling, or floor, thorugh which hot or cold air flows for heating or air.conditioning.

REGISTRAR OF DEEDS — A term used in some states to describe the person in charge of recorded instruments. More commonly called a recorder.

REGULATION Z — Federal Reserve regulation issued under the Truth-in-Lending Law, which requires that a credit purchaser be advised in writing of all costs connected with the credit portion of the purchase.

REHABILITATION — Synonymous with reconditioning, except when used in connection with urban renewal, at which time it encompasses all types of changes, including structural and even street changes.

REINFORCED CONCRETE — Concrete strengthened by reinforcing (addition of steel bars, mesh, etc.).

REINFORCED CONCRETE CONSTRUCTION — The use of reinforced concrete in the load-bearing members, such as the frame, foundation, walls, floors, etc.

REINFORCING — (1) The strengthening of concrete by positioning metal rods, mesh, etc. in said concrete when wet. (2) The strengthening of any members by propping or adding additional material.

REINSTATEMENT — (1)Payment of a note, mortgage, deed of trust, etc., to bring it from default to good standing. (2)Restoring the previously used entitlement of a veteran to enable the veteran to purchase property under a VA program. (Also called Restoration of Eligibility).

REINSURANCE — The transferring of a portion of the liability to other insurers. Example: Insurer A insures for $200,000. A insures for $100,000 and reinsures the "second" $100,000 through B insurer. The "first" $100,000 is called "primary liability".

REISSUE RATE — A charge for a title insurance policy if a previous policy on the same property was issued within a specified period. The reissue rate is less than the original charge.

R.E.I.T. (REAL ESTATE INVESTMENT TRUSTS) — A method of investing in real estate in a group, with certain tax advantages. Federal and state statutes dictate procedure.

RELEASE — An instrument releasing property from the lien of the mortgage, judgment, etc. When a trust deed is used, the instrument is called a reconveyance. In some areas, a "discharge" is used instead of a release.

RELEASE CLAUSE — A clause in a blanket encumbrance allowing for the "release" of certain parcels upon payment of a specified amount. Example: A builder mortgages an entire subdivision under one loan. As the builder sells each house, the lender releases the lien upon that house upon a specified payment by the builder.

RELICTION — An increase of land by the permanent withdrawal of the sea, a river, lake, or other body of water.

RELIEF — (See: Topography).

RELIEF MAP — A map showing the topography of an area.

REMAINDER — (1) An estate which vests in one other than a grantor, after the termination of an intermediate estate. Example: A grants land to B for life, then to C, his heirs or assigns. If A grants to B for life, then back to A, it is not a remainder, but reversion. (2) The portion of a property remaining after a taking under eminent domain.

REMAINDERMAN — The one entitled to the remainder.

REMAINING ECONOMIC LIFE — Number of years between the time of an appraisal and the point in time when an improvement becomes economically valueless.

REMISE — To give up or remit. Used in a deed, especially a quitclaim deed.

REMNANT — An appraisal term. A parcel of land, after a partial taking by eminent domain, so small or poorly shaped as to have practically no value.

REMODELING — Improving a structure by changing its plan, characteristics, or function, as opposed to reconditioning.

RENDERING — (See: Artist's Conception).

RENEGOTIABLE RATE MORTGAGE — A real property loan calling for an adjustment in the interest rate at a given time. Example: A loan with a 15 year amortization is adjusted to current interest rates after 2 years. The lender agrees to make the adjusted loan at the new rate as long as the old loan is not in default. The Federal Reserve Board allows the original loan to be treated either as a balloon payment loan or a variable rate loan. However, points must be figured into the A.P.R. based on the time or renegotiation (2 years rather than 15).

RENEGOTIATION — An attempt to agree on new terms to an existing contract (in real estate, usually a lease). A lease, for example, may call for renegotiation of rent after 5 years. Since renegotiation needs agreement of the parties, a set formula to determine the rent, such as an escalation clause, would not be renegotiation. Arbitration may be provided for in the event renegotiation fails.

RENEWAL — (1) To cause a lease to begin again for another term. (2) To rebuild, as in urban development (urban renewal).

RENEWAL OPTION — The right of a tenant to renew (extend the term of) a lease for a state period of time and rent which can be determined.

RENOVATION — (See: Reconditioning).

RENT — Consideration paid for the occupancy and use of real property. A general term covering any consideration (not only money).

RENTABLE AREA — The area (square footage) for which rent can be charged. For example: An office building would not rent the space used for stairways, elevators, public washrooms, hallways, etc.

RENTAL AGENT — One who (for a fee) aids a landlord to find a tenant or a tenant to find property. Generally concerned with residential property and may not require a real estate license (or may require a special license) in some states.

RENTAL AGREEMENT — A lease. The term is mainly used when concerning residential property.

RENTAL VALUE — The fair rental value of a property; the market rental value.

RENT CONTROLS — A legal maximum on rental price. Used extensively during World War II. Modernly, a control on subsidized housing, where the rent is paid partly by a governmental agency, and a maximum rent is established, not by the landlord, but by the agency.

RENT SUBSIDY — (See: Subsidy).

REPAIRS — The general upkeep of property without major replacement or change of the plan or characteristics of the building.

REPLACEMENT — The substitution of a portion of a structure with one of substantially the same nature, such as a new furnace, new roof, etc.

REPLACEMENT COST — In appraising, the cost of a substitute property, either identical to or of equivalent utility.

REPLEVIN — A legal action to recover goods wrongfully taken, where damages are not satisfactory.

REPRODUCTION COST — The cost of reproducing a property (usually one which has been destroyed) at current prices using similar materials.

REQUEST FOR RECONVEYANCE — A request by a beneficiary under a deed of trust to the trustee, requesting the trustee to reconvey the property (release the lien) to the trustor, usually upon payment in full.

RERECORDING — The recording of a deed for a second time to correct an error contained in the deed when originally recorded. Also called a correction deed, confirmation deed, or reformation deed.

RESCIND — To void or cancel in such a way as to treat the contract or other object of the recision as if it never existed.

RECISION OF A CONTRACT — Annulling or abrogating a contract and placing the parties to it in a position as if there had not been a contract.

RESERVATION — (1) A right created and retained by a grantor. The reservation may be temporary (such as a life estate) or permanent (such as an easement running with the land). (2) Public land reserved for a special purpose, such as an Indian reservation.

125

RESERVE — A setting aside of funds, usually for indefinite contingencies, such as future maintenance of a structure, or to pay future claims, such as insurance claims.

RESERVOIR — A body of water used as household water (drinking, washing, etc.), irrigation, or other domestic or commercial uses. The water is usually treated and its purity is monitored.

RESIDENCE — A place where someone lives. [See also: Domicile (1)].

RESIDENTIAL BUILDING RATE — The rate of residential construction in a given area. Determined by housing starts per 1,000 population.

RESIDENTIAL PROPERTY — Land designated by zoning ordinances as "residential". May be vacant or improved.

RESIDENT MANAGER — A manager of an apartment project who lives on the property. Some states require a resident manager in apartment projects above a certain number of units. The manager is not required to have a real estate license.

RESIDUARY ESTATE — That property of a deceased after expenses of administration, and after all bequests and devises.

RESORT PROPERTY — Generally, any property where people would go for purposes of fun and vacations. In some states the term may have legal significance, and regulations may exist regarding advertising and selling property as resort property.

RESPA (REAL ESTATE SETTLEMENT PROCEDURES ACT) — A federal statute effective June 20, 1975, requiring disclosure of certain costs in the sale of residential (one to four family) improved property which is to be financed by a federally insured lender.

RESPONDEAT SUPERIOR — Doctrine of responsibility of a principal for the wrongful acts of an agent arising from the authorized acts of said agent. In real estate, one of the reasons for the status of independent contractor.

RESTRAINT OF ALIENATION — Restrictons placed against the transfer (vesting) or sale of property. Certain restrictions are allowed but must conform to the rule against perpetuities and free right of an owner to sell. For example: Selling on the condition that the grantee could resell only to members of a certain family would be too restrictive and not valid.

RESTRICTION — Most commonly used to describe a use or uses prohibited to the owner of land. Restrictions are set forth by former owners in deeds or in the case of a subdivision, a declaration of restrictions is recorded by the developer. A limitation on use of the property by law (zoning ordinances) may also be termed a restriction.

RESTRICTIVE COVENANT — (See: Restriction).

RESUBDIVISION — Subdividing an existing subdivision. (1) Frequently done when the original subdivision was not built upon, and the present builder wishes to change the size or shape of the lots. (2) Recently, some states have held that one who buys several properties in the same subdivision (even if already with buildings) must resubdivide before selling. This has been carried to the point of including one who buys two condominiums in the same subdivision. However, a simpler and less costly procedure has been provided in such cases.

RESULTING TRUST — (See: Constructive Trust).

RETAINING WALL — A wall used to contain or hold back dirt, water, or other materials of a similar nature.

REVALUATION — (See: Reassessment).

REVALUATION CLAUSE — A clause in a lease calling for a periodic revaluation (appraisal) of the leased property, and subsequent adjustment of rent.

REVENUE STAMPS — Formerly federal tax on sale of real property. Cancelled and replaced by state tax stamps. The stamps (similar to postage stamps) are affixed to the conveyancing instrument (deed), or a rubber stamp is used to show the amount of the tax.

REVERSION — The right to possession of the residue of an estate in a grantor or successors of a grantor or testator, commencing upon the termination of a particular estate, granted or devised.

REVERSIONARY INTEREST — An interest held in a reversion (future right to property in possession of another).

REVOCABLE — Capable of being revoked.

REVOKE — To cancel, annul, reverse, take back, etc.

RIBBON — (1) A narrow strip; a strip of wood to add support to studs and joists. (2) A driveway consisting of two cement strips, the same distance apart as tires on a car.

RIDER — (See: Addendum).

RIDGE — The meeting of the roof rafters of a gable or other roof with two sloping sides.

RIDGEBOARD — The highest horizontal member of a roof, running along the ridge, and receiving the rafters at right angles.

RIGHT OF FIRST REFUSAL — (See: First Refusal Right).

RIGHT OF SURVIVORSHIP — The right of a survivor of a deceased person to the property of said deceased. A distinguishing characteristic of a joint tenancy relationship.

RIGHT OF WAY — A strip of land which is used as a roadbed, either for a street or railway. The land is set aside as an easement or in fee, either by agreement or condemnation. May also be used to describe the right itself to pass over the land of another.

RIGHTS — A General term which encompasses those things a person may do unopposed, even though a burden on another occurs, as in the right of a tenant, holder of an easement, etc.

RILL EROSION — Erosion caused by heavy rainfall on freshly cultivated ground, which produces channels in the loose soil.

RIPARIAN — Belonging or relating to the bank of a river or stream. Land within the natural watershed of a river or stream.

RIPARIAN OWNER — One who owns land along the bank of a river or stream.

RIPARIAN RIGHTS — Rights of an owner to riparian lands and water.

RIPARIAN WATER — Water within the normal flow of the stream or river. An abnormal flow (flood) is not riparian water.

RIPRAP — A loosely composed wall of rocks and stones used to hinder the flow of water, thereby preventing erosion.

RISE — The vertical measurement of a slope in relation to its horizontal measurement, such as a rise of three feet vertically over a horizontal distance of fifty feet.

RISER — (1) The vertical board rising from the back of each step in a stairway. (2) A warm air duct rising from a furnace.

RIVER — A large, natural stream of water, which flows in a permanent channel or bed, and may empty into a lake or the sea.

RIVER BED — The land between the banks of a river during its normal course.

ROAD — (1) A rural travelway for the use of pedestrians and/or vehicles. (2) Any travelway for the use of pedestrians and/or vehicles.

ROCK WOOL — A fibrous insulation material made from molten rock.

ROD — A unit of linear measure equal to $16\frac{1}{2}$ feet.

ROLL-OVER PAPER — Short term notes which may be extended (rolled over) or converted to installment payments, after the initial due date.

ROLL ROOFING — An asphalt paper or fiber material, which is used in rolls, being unrolled and fastened to the roof surface, under the shingles.

ROMAN BATH — A bathroom constructed to resemble the public baths of ancient Rome. Usually there is a large sunken tub and a use of marble or marble-like tiles as the principal covering of the floors, vanities, etc.

ROMAN BRICK — Brick which shows a narrower face than standard building brick.

ROOF — A general term meaning the top of a building. (See specific types for more detail).

ROOF SHEATHING — (See: Sheathing).

ROOM — A fully enclosed section of the interior of a building, having access through a door or doorway. In residential property, rooms are described specifically, such as living room, dining roon, etc.

ROOM COUNT — The number of rooms in a residential property. There is no national method of counting but, generally, bathrooms are specified and counted separately.

ROTUNDA — A room or building, shaped in a circle, and usually with a domed roof.

ROW HOUSES — A method of construction of individual houses with common side walls and a common roof. Modernly called townhouses.

ROYALTY — A fraction or percentage of the value of a natural resource (oil, sand, etc.) paid to the owner of the resource by those extracting and selling it.

RRM — (See: Renegotiable Rate Mortgage).

RULE AGAINST PERPETUITIES — Principle that a property interest is void unless it must vest not later than the remaining time of a life or lives in being, plus gestation time, plus twenty-one years. (The time has been modified by statute and should be checked in each state).

RUNNING WITH THE LAND — Usually concerned with easements and covenants. Passing with the transfer of the land.

RURAL — Concerning the country, as opposed to urban (concerning the city).

S

SAFETY CLAUSE — A clause in a listing protecting the broker from having buyer and seller wait until the listing expires to make a deal, thereby avoiding the payment of commission. The clause states that if the property is sold during a specified period after the expiration of the listing (or any extension theraof) to a buyer provided during the listing period by the broker, the commission shall be paid.

SALARY — A compensation for services, usually paid at specified intervals, and of a set amount.

SALE-LEASEBACK — A sale and subsequent lease from the buyer back to the seller. Although the lease actually follows the sale, both are agreed to as part of the same transaction.

SALES-ASSESSMENT RATIO — The ratio of the assessed value of a property to its selling price, which is presumed to be market value. This shows the percentage of assessed value to market value.

SALES CONTRACT — Another name for a sales agreement, purchase agreement, etc. Not to be confused with a land contract, which is a conditional sales contract.

SALES KIT — Materials carried by a salesperson to aid in listings and sales. This is the "tool kit" of real estate, containing forms, maps, tape measure, amortization schedules, pens, paper, etc.

SALESPERSON — One who is licensed to work in real estate under a licensed broker.

SALVAGE VALUE — The value of a building or portion of a building to be moved from one location for use at another site. Most often occurs in condemnation, especially for highway purposes, where large areas must be cleared. (See also: Scrap Value).

SAM — (See: Shared Appreciation Mortgage).

SANDWICH BEAM — (See: Flitch Beam).

SANDWICH LEASE — A lease between the primary lease and the lease to the user or party in possession.

SANITARY SEWER — A sewer carrying waste products, as opposed to rainwater. (See also: Storm Sewer).

SASH — Wood or metal framing around a door or window opening.

SATELLITE CITIES — A concept designed to stop urban sprawl to the suburbs. The satellite city leaves an undeveloped area between itself and a major city, rather than the gradual expansion of the major city. Satellite cities must be self-contained in order to be effective.

SATISFACTION — Discharge of an obligation by payment of the amount due, as on a mortgage, trust deed, or contract; or payment of a debt awarded, such as satisfaction of a judgment. Also the recorded instrument stating said payment has been made.

SATURATION ZONE — The layer of ground which serves as a reservoir, feeding springs, wells and streams, rather than feeding vegetation or evaporating. Below the aeration zone.

SAVINGS AND LOAN ASSOCIATION — Originally an association chartered to hold savings and make real estate loans. Federally insured and regulated. Active in long term financing rather than construction loans. Recent changes in federal controls have enabled these associations to offer checking accounts, consumer loans, and other services traditionally offered by banks.

SAW-TOOTH ROOF — A series of single pitched roofs, resembling the sharp edge of a saw. Usually used in factories and contains windows in each facing to allow maximum lighting. Not used in modern construction.

SBA (SMALL BUSINESS ADMINISTRATION) — A federal agency authorized to make loans to small businesses, including loans for land purchase and construction. To be eligible, the borrower must have been refused the loan by a private lender.

SCALE — Used in maps, blueprints, and other diagrams where the drawing represents a large area. Example: One inch on a road map may equal ten miles actual distance. This ratio is the scale.

SCANTLING LUMBER — Boards used in construction which are from 2" to 6" and 8" or less wide.

SCOPE OF AUTHORITY — The authority of an agent to bind a principal. An agent may bind a principal not only when the agent has actual authority, but also implied or apparent authority.

SCRAP VALUE — The value of a building or part of a building based on the value of the material alone, and not its function. Example: Plumbing for the melted down value of the metal, walls for the value of the bricks, wood, etc. (See also: Salvage Value).

SCRATCH COAT — A term used in wet plastering, meaning the first coat applied to the lath.

SCRIBING — Cutting wood precisely to fit an area. The term is used because the carpenter marks (scribes) before he makes his cut.

SEAL(S) — A physical impression made on a document to attest to a signature. Most common are corporate seal and notary seal.

SEA LEVEL — The level of the sea, at mean tide.

SEARCH — (See: Title Search).

SEASONED — A term referring to a land contract or mortgage, indicating that payments have been made regularly over a period of time, and that the contract or mortgage is not a new one.

SEC (SECURITIES AND EXCHANGE COMMISSION) — The federal agency which regulates the stock market. It gets involved in real estate when the real estate development is one which sells shares.

SECOND — [See: Degree (1)].

SECONDARY FINANCING — A loan secured by a mortgage or trust deed, which lien is junior (secondary) to another mortgage or trust deed.

SECONDARY LOCATION — A location not considered the best (prime) for the the purpose intended.

SECONDARY MORTGAGE MARKET — The buying and selling of first mortgages or trust deeds by banks, insurance companies, government agencies, and other mortgagees. This enables lenders to keep an adequate supply of money for new loans. The mortgages may be sold at full value (par) or above, but are usually sold at a discount. The secondary mortgage market should not be confused with second mortgage.

SECOND FOOT — A measure of water; a flow of one cubic foot per second (almost seven and one half gallons).

SECOND GROWTH — In lumbering, the trees of a forest which grow after the original stand has been cut or otherwise destroyed.

SECOND MORTGAGE — A mortgage which ranks after a first mortgage in priority. Properties may have two, three, or more mortgages, deeds of trust, or land contracts, as liens at the same time. Legal priority would determine whether they were called a first, second, third, etc. lien.

SECTION — A division or parcel of land on a government survey, comprising one square mile (640 acres). Thirty-six sections comprise a township.

SECURED PARTY — Mortgagee, beneficiary (under a deed of trust), pledgee, or any other party having a security interest.

SECURITY — Real or personal property pledged or hypothecated by a borrower, as additional protection for the lender's interest.

SECURITY AGREEMENT — A "catch all" term used to describe many different types of debtor-creditor relationships, such as a chattel mortgage, trust receipt, inventory liens, etc.

SECURITY DEPOSIT — Commonly a deposit of money by a tenant to a landlord to secure performance of a written or oral rental agreement.

SECURITY INTEREST — The interest of the creditor (secured party) created by a security agreement.

SECURITY (INSTALLMENT) LAND CONTRACT — A form used in California which combines a land contract with a deed of trust, creating a land contract in order to defeat a first lender's "due-on sale" (alienation) clause but having the foreclosure provisions of a deed of trust.

SEDIMENT — Any matter which settles to the bottom in a liquid. (See also: Sedimentary Rock).

SEDIMENTARY ROCK — One of the three major classifications of rocks. Rocks formed from sediment, such as suspension in water. Sandstones, limestones, and shales, are some examples.

SEISEN (SEIZEN) — Originally the completion of feudal investiture, it has come to mean possession under a legal right (usually a fee interest).

SELF-SUPPORTING WALLS — Walls which support only their own weight. Not load-bearing.

SELLER TAKE BACK MORTGAGE — (See: Purchase Money Mortgage (1)).

SELLING AGENT — The real estate agent obtaining the buyer rather than listing the property. The listing and selling agent may be the same person or company.

SEMI — A prefix meaning partly; one half, or twice in a time period. For example: A semicircle is one half of a circle; semiannual is twice in one year. (See also: Bi).

SEMICIRCULAR ROOF — A roof resembling an extended arch. Usually found on barns or barracks type buildings.

SEPARATE PROPERTY — Property owned by a husband or wife in which the other has no legal ownership interest.

SEPIA — A master of a construction plan, from which prints are made. Called a sepia because of its brown color.

SEPTIC SYSTEM — A sewage system, whereby waste is drained through pipes and a tile field into a septic tank. Found in areas where city or county sewers have not yet been installed.

SEPTIC TANK — An underground tank into which a sanitary sewer drains from a building. The sewage is held until bacterial action changes the solids into liquids or gases, which are then released into the ground.

SEQUESTRATION, WRIT OF — The taking custody of one's property (real or personal) to force compliance with a court order.

SERVICE — Notice given to one by delivery of a writ, subpoena, injunction, etc., by one duly authorized, giving notice to the person served of some court action or other proceeding with which he or she is involved (as defendant, witness, etc.).

SERVICE INDUSTRY — An industry which sells the knowledge or work of its people, rather than a tangible product. Example: A real estate broker is paid for his service. The product (property) does not belong to the broker.

SERVICE LINE — The gas or water line which runs from the main line (usually at the street) to each property to be served.

SERVICE ROAD — A road running alongside a limted access highway, for use by abutting owners, and as a transition road from the highway to local streets. Also called a frontage road.

SERVICE STATION — A place where gasoline and other automobile products and services are sold. A gas station.

SERVICING — (See: Mortgage Servicing).

SERVIENT TENEMENT — An estate burdened with a servitude. Most commonly a parcel of land burdened by an easement. (See also: Easement Appurtenant; Easement In Gross).

SERVITUDE — In relation to easements, "easements" refer to the advantage of the dominant tenement, while "servitude" describes the burden of the servient tenement.

SET BACK ORDINANCE — Part of a zoning ordinance. Regulates the distance from the lot line to the point where improvements may be constructed.

SET-OFF — (1) A construction term relating to the reduction of the thickness of a wall, or any recess or sunken panel of the wall. (2) A legal term meaning a counter demand to a claim. In condemnation, the benefits to the remaining property in a partial taking may in some jurisdictions be "set-off" against the value of the land taken. Example: part of land taken for a freeway; residue now more valuable because of freeway. Increased value is "set-off" against value of land taken.

SETTLEMENT STATEMENT — A statement prepared by broker, escrow, or lender, giving a complete breakdown of costs involved in a real estate sale. A separate statement is prepared for the seller and buyer.

SETTLING — The compaction of the soil by the weight of a newly built structure. If severe, cracks in the structure may result.

SETTLOR — One who creates a trust.

SEVERALTY — An estate in severalty is property held by one person alone.

SEVERANCE — Partition or separation.

SEVERANCE DAMAGE — Damage to the remaining property in condemnation, caused by the partial taking and subsequent construction of the road, building, or other use for which the taking took place.

SEWAGE — Liquid or solid waste material of humans, animals, or industry.

SEWER — A pipe or other conduit, generally underground, which carries either waste materials or water from rainfall, or melting snow to a point of disposal.

SHAKE — To split or crack wood.

SHAKE SHINGLE — Shingle composed of split wood. Used as a roofing or siding material.

SHARE CROP — Crop raised by a tenant farmer who gives a portion of the crop to the landlord as rent.

SHARE CROPPER — One who farms as a tenant, sharing his crop with the owner as payment of rent.

SHARED APPRECIATION — The gaining or retaining of equity in a property by someone other than the buyer. For example: the seller retains a 25% interest in the property. This makes the buyer responsible for only 75% of the purchase price and, therefore, lowers the necessary financing by 25%. This obviously makes the property more affordable. By agreement, expenses are shared as well as any increase in value when the property is sold.

SHARED APPRECIATION MORTGAGE(SAM) — A financing arrangement under which the lender offers a lower interest rate in return for a percentage of the appreciation (profit) when the property is sold.

SHAREHOLDER — Commonly, one who owns stock (shares) in a corporation.

SHEATHING — The covering over the outside studs (or rafters) of a roof. May be wallboard, plywood, etc.

SHEET EROSION — The loss of soil in even amounts over a given area, through the action of water.

SHELTER BELT — A row of trees planted so as to shelter a building from severe weather conditions. Usually found in open areas which receive heavy snowfall.

SHERIFF'S DEED — Deed given at sheriff's sale in foreclosure of mortgage. The giving of said deed begins a statutory redemption period. Also given at court ordered sale, pursuant to the execution of a judgment.

SHINGLES — Roof or wall surfacing of overlapping small sheets of wood, slate, tile, asphalt, or other waterproof material.

SHOE — A trim molding, covering the juncture of baseboard and floor.

SHOPPING CENTER — A general term, covering a number of types of clustered retail stores with common parking and ownership or management. (See specific shopping centers: Strip; Neighborhood; Community; Regional).

SHORE LINE — The lands alongside navigable waterways, between the high and low water marks.

SHORT FORM DOCUMENT — A document which refers either to another document not of record containing the total agreement, or incorporates by reference a document of record.

SHORT TERM CAPITAL GAIN — Profit from the sale of a capital asset not held long enough to qualify as a long term capital gain. Taxed as ordinary income.

SHORT TERM LEASE — A general term, indicating a lease under five years in some states, under ten years in others.

SHOULDER — The land adjacent to the travel lanes of a road, used for vehicles having difficulty. May be paved or unpaved.

SIDE DITCH — A ditch running alongside a highway to carry off excess rainfall. May be paved, contain portions of large metal or clay pipe, or simply be of dirt or grass.

SIDING — (1) A surfacing for exterior walls, such as wood siding, aluminum, asphalt, etc. (2) A railroad track connected to a main track, and used for storage of cars, passing of trains, or other reasons to clear the main track.

SIGN — An advertisement placed on a property showing that the property is availble for "sale", "lease", "exchange", etc. Signs have been shown by studies to be the second best advertising in terms of attracting buyers, only slightly behind classified newspaper advertising. Many local governments restrict signs as to size and location on the property.

SIGNATURE — The act of putting one's name on an instrument. Although legally, a signature must not necessarily be hand written (may be typed, stamped, etc.), recording statutes may be very specific regarding allowable signatures, even as to the color ink used (must be capable of being photocopied).

SIGNED, SEALED, AND DELIVERED — A phrase indicating that everything necessary to convey has been done by the grantor. Modernly, signed and delivered are still necessary, but the only seals commonly used are by governments, corporations, and notaries.

SILL — The lowest member of a frame (usually wood or metal), which supports the uprights of a frame. Most commonly used to describe the lowest horizontal member of an opening, such as a door sill or window sill.

SILO — Generally, a tall, cylindrical structure, used for storage of corn, etc.

SIMPLE INTEREST — Interest computed on principal alone, as opposed to compound interest.

SIMULTANEOUS ISSUE — A simultaneous issuance by a title insurance company of policies insuring both an owner and a lender. The lender's policy is issued at a reduced rate.

SINGLE — (1) One who has never been married. (2) Commonly, one who is not married, but may have been married.

SINGLE FAMILY HOUSE — A general term originally used to distinguish a house designed for use by one family from an apartment house. More recently, used to distinguish a house with no common area from a planned development or condominium.

SINGLE PITCH ROOF — A roof pitched entirely at the same angle, usually over 20 degrees.

SINGLE PURPOSE PROPERTY — (See: Special Purpose Property).

SINKING FUND — A fund (often invested) which will be used to replace improvements as needed. Most commonly set aside from the income of income producing property.

SINKING FUND METHOD OF DEPRECIATION — A process of recovering the value of an asset by setting up a sinking fund.

SITE — A general term signifying a plot of land suitable or set aside for any specific use.

SITE ANALYSIS — The study of a specific parcel of land (and the surrounding area) to determine its suitability for a specific use.

SITE DEVELOPMENT — All improvements made to a site before a building may be constructed, such as grading, utility installation, etc.

SITUS — Location, place.

SKELETON — The frame, especially the supporting parts.

SKIN — A construction term, meaning the outer covering of a building.

SKY LEASE — A lease of air space above a parcel of land. A structure which is cantilevered or a bridge can be used in such a lease.

SKYLIGHT — A window in a roof or ceiling.

SLAB — (1) A concrete floor used as a foundation in homes without a basement. (2) Any concrete floor, even if an upper story.

SLANDER OF TITLE — The making of malicious, untrue statements, regarding one's title or interest in property. The statements must be made to a third party and must cause injury to the party against whom the statements are made.

SLANT DRILLING — A method of drilling for oil or gas from adjoining property when surface rights have not been granted. (See also: Subsurface Rights; Surface Rights).

SLIDING WINDOW — (See: Traverse Window).

SLIP — A place between two piers or docks, where a boat is kept.

SLOPE — The angle of a grade as measured from a level surface.

SMALL CLAIMS COURT — A court having limited jurisdiction to hear cases up to a statutory limit (generally between $300 - $750, depending on the state). Cases are heard quickly, attorneys are usually not allowed unless a party to the action, and most cases are decided on fairness rather than fine legal points.

SNOW FENCE — A portable barrier placed along the side of a road to prevent snow from drifting onto the road.

SOFFIT — The undersurface of an arch, overhang, stairway, or other such part of a building.

SOFTWOOD — Wood such as pine or fir, as distinguished from hardwood such as maple or oak. In construction, especially in flooring, softwoods and plywoods have become more popular because they cost less than the traditional hardwood flooring.

SOIL — The top layer of earth in which plants grow and through which water drains.

SOIL BANK — A federal program of conservation, under which farmers are paid for not growing crops, or growing non-commercial vegetation, in order to preserve the quality of the soil, as well as to avoid surpluses.

SOIL EROSION — (See: Erosion).

SOIL MAP — A map showing the different types of soil in a given area.

SOIL PIPE — A sanitary sewer pipe, from a building to the sewer main.

SOIL PROFILE — A vertical cross-section showing the different horizons (layers) of the Earth's surface.

SOLAR HEATING — Heating by use and control of the energy of the sun.

SOLE PLATE — The plate on which the studs rest. Usually a two by four, laid horizontally at floor level.

SOLE PROPRIETORSHIP — Individual ownership of a business as opposed to a partnership or corporation.

SOLVENT — (1) Financially able to meet one's current debts. (2) A liquid used to dissolve a substance, usually to remove it.

SOUND VALUE — A synonym for depreciated costs. Used in fire insurance evaluation. Depreciation due to use up to the time of a fire.

SPACE DESIGN — The planning of interior space of a building to meet the needs of the user. Involves a layout and construction drawings. There are companies which specialize in space design, from construction to color coordination. Need not be architects.

SPACE HEATER — (See: Heater).

SPAN — The spread (distance) between load-bearing members, such as walls or girders.

SPANDREL — (1) The triangular space between the exterior curve of an arch and the enclosing right angle above it. (2) The triangular space beneath the string of a stair. (3) The space between the top framing of a window to the bottom framing of a window above it.

SPANDREL STEP — A step, such as in a circular staircase, which is triangular in shape.

SPANDREL WALL — A wall which fills the spandrel space of an arch.

SPANISH ARCHITECTURE — Copying the houses of Spain and Mexico, a home with a courtyard, tiled roof, and usually constructed of adobe or stucco.

SPECIAL ASSESSMENT — Lien assessed against real property by a public authority to pay costs of public improvements (sidewalks, sewers, street lights, etc.), which directly benefits the assessed property.

SPECIAL BENEFITS — Benefits to the remaining property after a partial taking by eminent domain.

SPECIAL PARTNER — A limited partner. (See also: Limited Partnership).

SPECIAL POWER — [See: Power of Attorney (2)].

SPECIAL PURPOSE PROPERTY — A building which, by its design, cannot be used for other than the original purpose intended, without extensive remodeling, such as a hospital or church. Also called a single purpose property.

SPECIFICATIONS — Written, detailed, drawings which show a contractor how to proceed with construction, whether in new construction or remodeling.

SPECIFIC PERFORMANCE — An action to compel the performance of a contract, when money damages for breach would not be satisfactory.

SPECULATOR — One who buys property, not for his use, but with only the intent to sell at a profit.

SPENDABLE INCOME — Net income after taxes.

SPENDTHRIFT TRUST — A trust created to give an income to the beneficiary while protecting the principal from the beneficiary and creditors of the beneficiary. The beneficiary may, therefore, not be able to sell or encumber the trust property.

SPITE FENCE — A fence built for the purpose of causing a problem for one's neighbor. May ruin the view, make access of a vehicle difficult, etc., or simply be ugly.

SPLIT-LEVEL HOUSE — A house with different levels, none of which is a complete story higher than another.

SPLIT-RATE — Capitalization rate applied separately to land and improvements, to determine the value of each.

SPOT ZONING — Zoning on a parcel by parcel basis, rather than a comprehensive general or master plan. Considered poor planning.

SPOUSE — One's husband or wife.

SPREADER DAM — A dam built in such a way as to divert water to either side, thus causing the water to spread over a given area.

SPRINKLER SYSTEM — (1) When used in reference to residential property, a system of pipes under a lawn, used for watering the grass. (2) In commercial or industrial property, a system of pipes and valves in the ceiling, sensitive to ambient temperatures, which automatically sprinkles water or a chemical in case of fire.

SPUR TRACK — A segment of railroad track, connected at only one end to a main track, which services an industrial building or buildings.

SQUARE — A unit of measurement in roofing or siding, 10' × 10' (100 sq. ft.).

SQUARE FOOT COST — The cost of one square foot of floor space in a building or of land. Usually used to determine rental price of a building. When used for land, usually to determine a sale price.

SQUATTER — One who lives on another's land without authority or claim of a right to possession. The land may either be private or public.

SQUATTER'S RIGHTS — Commonly confused with adverse possession. A squatter has no ownership rights and cannot, under the definition of a squatter, acquire any since he claims no interest adverse to the owner.

SRA (SOCIETY OF REAL ESTATE APPRAISERS) — One gaining membership, through education, experience, and examination, receives the designation SRA.

STAIN — An oil paint used to coat wood, which has little thickness or gloss.

STANDARD COVERAGE POLICY — A title insurance policy used in several states, not having as broad a coverage as the nationally recognized American Land Title Association (A.L.T.A.) policies.

STANDARD DEPTH — Depth of a lot considered to be the normal depth for appraisal purposes. Traditionally, one hundred feet for a residential lot.

STANDARD PARALLELS — East-West survey lines, establishing township boundaries at twenty-four mile intervals, and correcting inaccuracies in the government survey, due to the curvature of the Earth.

STANDBY COMMITMENT — A commitment to issue a loan, usually for a term of one to five years, after completion of construction, in the event a permanent loan cannot be obtained. The standby loan is usually at a higher interest rate than a permanent loan, and a standby fee is charged.

STAND CRUISE — (See: Cruise).

STANDING LOAN — A loan requiring interest payments only, the principal being paid in full at maturity.

STANDING TIMBER — Timber still uncut. Trees.

START CARD — A file card used as a record of the opening of an escrow. It lists the date the escrow opened, escrow number, name of escrow officer, names of parties to the escrow, lender, title company, legal description of property, consideration, and type of transaction (sale, loan, etc.).

STARTER — A copy of the last policy issued by a title insurer, which describes the condition of title to land upon which a new policy is to be written. In some states this is furnished to an attorney for his opinion as to the condition of title, and is called a back title letter or back title certificate.

STARTS — Units on which construction has begun.

STATEMENT OF IDENTITY — (See: Statement of Information).

STATEMENT OF INFORMATION — A confidential form filled out by buyer and seller to help a title company determine if any liens are recorded against either. Very helpful when people with common names are involved. Also called a statement of identity.

STATE ROAD — A highway under the control of the state, which may eliminate it if desired, as opposed to a federal (interstate) highway.

STATUTE — A law which comes from a legislative body. A written law, rather than law established by court cases.

STATUTE OF FRAUDS — State laws, requiring certain contracts to be in writing. All contracts for the sale of real property must be in writing. Leases (personal property) for more than one year must be in writing.

STATUTE OF LIMITATIONS — A law which limits the bringing of a court action (civil or criminal) to within a specified period of time.

STATUTORY DEDICATION — The giving of private land for public use under a procedure dictated by statute.

STATUTORY LIEN — An involuntary lien (created by law rather than by contract). Includes tax liens, judgment liens, mechanic's liens, etc.

STATUTORY NOTICE — Notice given by legislative enactment (laws or statutes).

STATUTORY REDEMPTION PERIOD — (See: Redemption Period).

STATUTORY RESERVE — Reserves of funds which must be kept by banks, savings and loans, insurance companies, and like businesses, to insure their ability to meet demands for funds in their course of business.

STEP-UP LEASE (GRADED LEASE) — A lease calling for set increases in rent at set intervals.

STIRPES — (See: Per Stirpes).

STOCK COOPERATIVE — A corporation formed for the purpose of holding title to real estate, physically similar to an apartment house. Each shareholder receives the right to exclusive occupancy of a dwelling unit. A forerunner of the condominium.

STORM SASH (STORM WINDOW) — An extra window on the outside of an existing window, as additional protection against cold weather.

STORM SEWER — A sewer carrying off rainwater. May also carry off industrial waste, such as chemicals, although many areas now forbid this.

STRAIGHT LEASE (FLAT LEASE) — A lease calling for the same amount of rent to be paid periodically (usually monthly) for the entire term of the lease.

STRAIGHT LINE DEPRECIATION — A method of replacing the capital investment of income property, by reducing the value of the property by a set amount annually from the income, over the economic life of the property.

STRAIGHT NOTE — A promise to repay a loan, signed by the debtor and containing the date executed, amount owing and to whom, date due (or on demand), rate of interest and how it is payable. A straight note is not amortized.

STRAIGHT-TERM MORTGAGE — A mortgage calling for principal to be paid in a lump sum at maturity.

STRAW MAN — One who acts for another, not openly, but as a principal to hide the identity of the party for whom acting.

STREAM — Any water course, including a river, brook, channel, etc.

STREET — A general term which includes any urban roads, usually paved.

STREET IMPROVEMENT BONDS — Interest bearing bonds, issued by a local government, to secure assessments for street improvements. The owners of the property assessed may pay in a lump sum or pay installments on the bonds, including interest.

STREET IMPROVEMENTS — Improvements connected with a street, such as paving, sidewalks, curbs, etc.

STRESS — The pressure of weight against a structural member. Materials are tested to determine the amount of stress they may hold before bending or breaking.

STRINGPIECE — A heavy timber used as a horizontal support for cross members.

STRINGS — The sides which support stair treads.

STRIP CENTER — Any shopping area, generally with common parking, comprised of a row of stores. Usually does not contain major department stores or grocery chain stores.

STRUCTURAL LUMBER — Lumber used for its strength, 2″ X 4″ or greater.

STRUCTURE — Any man-made building or edifice.

STRUT — A construction member, usually wood, placed between other members to support a load vertically, or pressure horizontally.

STUCCO — A wet plaster finish, specificaly designed for exterior use, very popular as an outside wall surface in warm, dry areas.

STUDS (STUDDING) — Vertical supports (wood or metal) in walls and partitions.

SUBBASE — The base under a slab or roadway, usually of crushed rock, sand, and gravel.

SUBCHAPTER "S" CORPORATION — An entity receiving the protection of the corporate form, but being taxed as a partnership.

SUBCONTRACTOR — One who works under a general contractor (builder), such as an electrical contractor, cement contractor, etc.

SUBDIVIDER — (See: Developer).

SUBDIVISION — Commonly, a division of a single parcel of land into smaller parcels (lots) by filing a map describing the division, and obtaining approval by a governmental commission (city or county). The exception is a condominium, which is sometimes called a "one lot subdivision".

SUBDIVISION MAP — A map submitted by a subdivider to the proper governmental body for approval in order to establish a subdivision. When the map is approved and recorded, it becomes the basis for the legal description of the subdivision.

SUBFLOOR — Underflooring laid on joists, over which finish flooring is laid.

SUBJACENT SUPPORT — The right of an owner to have the surface of his land supported by the land under it, so that it does not collapse. Work on adjoining land (mining, excavating, etc.) could cause this problem. (See also: Lateral Support).

"SUBJECT TO" CLAUSE — A clause in a deed, stating that the grantee takes title "subject to" an existing mortgage. The original mortgagor is alone responsible for any deficiency, should there be foreclosure of the mortgage. Differs from an "assumption" clause, whereby the grantee "assumes" and agrees to pay the existing mortgage.

SUBLEASE — A lease, under which the lessor is the lessee of a prior lease of the same property.

SUBORDINATE — To make subject or junior to.

SUBORDINATION AGREEMENT — An agreement by which an encumbrance is made subject (junior) to a junior encumbrance. For example: A loan on vacant land is made subject to a subsequent construction loan.

SUBPOENA — A legal process (writ) used to require the appearance of a person or documents into court.

SUBROGATION — The substitution of one person for another, so that the former may exercise certain rights or claims of the latter. used primarily when a surety relationship exists, as in insurance.

SUBSCRIBE — To write under or below. To sign at the end of a document.

SUBSIDENCE — Settling of the ground surface from loss of support in the ground beneath. May be caused by mining, lowering of the water table, etc.

SUBSIDY — A grant to aid in any work or enterprise, or to reduce the cost of a product. The federal government, for example, aids certain low income families by subsidizing rental payments.

SUBSTITUTION OF TRUSTEE — A document which is recorded to change the trustee under a deed of trust. A simple procedure in some states; more regulated in others.

SUBSURFACE EASEMENT — (See: Subsurface Rights).

SUBSURFACE RIGHTS — The rights, whether by fee or easement, to oil, gas, or minerals, below a certain depth beneath the surface of land. The right of surface entry may or may not be excluded, and is important to the value of the surface land for improvement purposes. (See also: Slant Drilling).

SUBURBAN — The area around a city. Usually residential with small businesses, although modernly an attraction for large industrial and commercial complexes.

SUCCESSION — The passing of real property by will or inheritance, rather than by grant of a deed or any other form of purchase.

SUITE — A group of rooms in a hotel, rented as one unit. Usually contains a minimum of one bedroom, a sitting room, and bathroom.

SUMP — A pit or similar storage area in a basement for collecting drained liquid waste.

SUMP PUMP — A pump used to force the collected liquids from a sump.

SUPERSTRUCTURE — That part of a building or other structure above the ground or foundation.

SUPPLEMENTAL ABSTRACT — An abstract covering a search of the public records between given dates.

SUPPORT — (See: Lateral Support; Subjacent Support).

SURETY — One who voluntarily binds himself to be obligated for the debt or obligation of another. For example: A co-maker of a note; an insurance carrier. Surety differs from guarantor, although commonly (and mistakenly) used interchangeably.

SURFACE RIGHTS — The rights (easements) to use the surface of land, including the right to drill or mine through the surface when subsurface rights are involved.

SWEAT EQUITY — A program which allows a purchaser to do work on the property in place of all or part of the down payment and other costs of purchase.

SURFACE WATER — Water caused by precipitation, which spreads over land and stays on the surface (a swamp) or percolates through the ground.

SURRENDER — The giving up of an estate, such as a lease. A contractual agreement, having the consent of both parties, such as lessor and lessee, as opposed to abandonment.

SURVEY — The measurement of the boundaries of a parcel of land, its area, and sometimes its topography.

SURVIVORSHIP — Gaining an interest in property by outliving (surviving) another who had the interest.

SWAMP — Soft, wet land, usually containing heavy vegetation and under water much of the time.

SYNAGOGUE — Meaning "to bring together", it is a building where Jews assemble to worship.

SYNDICATE — An association of individuals, formed for the purpose of carrying on some particular business venture in which the members are mutually interested.

T

TACKING — (1) Annexing a lien to one superior to it in order to gain the priority of the superior lien and defeat an intermediate lien. Generally not allowed. (2) Annexing periods of possession to add up to enough time for successful adverse possession. For example: A begins adverse possession. A dies and A's son takes up possession, adding A's time to his own. Not always allowed.

TAKE OUT COMMITMENT — Agreement by a lender to place a long term (take out) loan on real property after completion of construction.

TAKE OUT LOAN — The "permanent" (long term) financing of real estate after completion of construction.

TALUS — Rocks at the foot of a hill or other slope, which accumulate by sliding or rolling down the slope from the action of wind, rain, and gravity.

TANDEM PLAN — A method of keeping home financing active by the purchase of mortgages by GNMA (Government National Mortgage Association) at face value (par), for resale to FNMA (Federal National Mortgage Association), a private corporation, at a discount.

TANGIBLE PROPERTY — (See: Corporeal Property).

TANGIBLE VALUE — Value in appraisal of the physical value (land, buildings, etc.), as opposed to the value of an intangible, such as a favorable lease.

TAX BASE — The assessed valuation of real property, which is multiplied by the tax rate to determine the amount of tax due.

TAX BOOK — (See: Tax Roll).

TAX BRACKET — The percentage of income tax which one pays, based on graduated tax tables.

TAX DEED — (1) Deed from tax collector to governmental body after a period of non-payment of taxes according to statute. (2) Deed to a purchaser at a public sale of land taken for delinquent taxes. The purchaser receives only such title as the former owners had, and strict procedures must be followed to prevent attachment of prior liens.

TAX DISTRICT — An area over which a governmental body has authority to levy property taxes; may contain one or more assessment districts.

TAXES — A mandatory contribution of money to meet the expenses of a government, whether federal, state, or local.

TAX EXEMPTION — Freedom from payment of property or other taxes, granted to religious, educational, and similar organizations. Partial property tax exemptions are granted in some states to individuals, such as veterans and senior citizens.

TAX LIEN — (1) A lien for nonpayment of property taxes. Attaches only to the property upon which the taxes are unpaid. (2) A federal income tax lien. May attach to all property of the one owing the taxes.

TAX RATE — Traditionally the ratio of dollars of tax per hundred or per thousand dollars of valuation. Modernly, has become to be expressed as a percentage of valuation.

TAX ROLL — A list, usually published by a county, containing the descriptions of all parcels in said county, the names of the owners (or those receiving the tax bill), the assessed value, and tax amount.

TAX SALE — Public sale of property at auction by governmental authority, after a period of nonpayment of property tax.

TAX SEARCH — A part of a title search which determines if there are any unpaid taxes or assessments which may be a lien against the property being searched.

TAX SHELTER — A general term used to include any property which gives the owner certain income tax advantages, such as deductions for property taxes, maintenance, mortgage interest, insurance, and especially depreciation.

TAX STAMPS — (See: Documentary Tax Stamps).

T-BILLS — (See: Treasury Bills).

TAX TITLE — [See: Tax Deed (2)].

TEMPERA — A process of painting, using a base of albuminous or colloidal materials, instead of oil.

TEMPLE — A place of worship, usually thought of as being large and ornate.

TENANCY BY THE ENTIRETY — A form of ownership by husband and wife whereby each owns the entire property. In the event of the death of one, the survivor owns the property without probate.

TENANCY FOR YEARS — (See: Estate For Years).

TENANCY IN COMMON — An undivided ownership in real estate by two or more persons. The interests need not be equal, and, in the event of the death of one of the owners, no right of survivorship in the other owners exists.

TENANT — (1) A holder of property under a lease or other rental agreement. (2) Originally, one who had the right to possession, irrespective of the title interest.

TENANT AT SUFFERANCE — One who comes into possession lawfully, but holds over after the termination of his interest.

TENANT AT WILL — One who holds possession of premises by permission of the owner or landlord, but without agreement for a fixed term of possession.

TENANT CHANGES — (See: Tenant Improvements).

TENANT FARMER — One who operates a farm but is a tenant rather than the owner. Rent may be in cash, a share of the crops, or both.

TENANT FOR LIFE — (See: Life Estate; Life Tenant).

TENANT IMPROVEMENTS — Improvements to land or buildings to meet the needs of tenants. May be new improvements or remodeling, and be paid for by the landlord, tenant, or part by each.

TENANT IN SEVERALTY — One who owns property alone, without any other person being joined in said ownership.

TENANT IN TAIL — (See: Fee Tail).

TEN DAY ESCROW LAW — (See: Bulk Sales Act).

TENDER — The offer of money or performance in connection with a contract. If unjustifiably refused, places the party who refuses in default and gives rise to an action for breach of contract.

TENDON — The materials used to reinforce concrete, such as cable and wire, which resemble human tendons.

TENEMENT HOUSE — A term now seldom used. A run-down apartment house, such as those which were common after World War II; overcrowded, cold water, etc.

TENEMENTS — Commonly used to refer to certain types of property of multiple dwellings. Legally, any property, or property rights, which are of a permanent nature.

TENTATIVE MAP — A map submitted by a subdivider to a planning commission for approval; approval is usually conditioned upon changes. The final map, embodying the changes, is recorded.

TENURE — Manner of holding title subordinate to a superior interest. Derived from feudalism; the superior title was seisin.

TERM — A period of time, such as the term of a lease.

TERMINABLE INTERESTS — Property interests which are not perpetual but liable to terminate, such as a leasehold. Also called "terminable property".

TERMINATE — To end. To cause to stop or end.

TERMITE INSPECTION — An inspection required in certain types of sales of property, to determine if termites are present within a building.

TERMITES — Insects, similar to ants, which feed on wood, causing destruction to wooden structures.

TERMITE SHIELD — Metal shields at the foundation of a structure or around pipes to prevent the entrance of termites.

TERM MORTGAGE — (See: Straight-Term Mortgage).

TERMS — The considerations, other than price, in a sale, lease, mortgage, etc. For example: the way the money will be paid, time to take possession, conditions, etc.

TERRACE — (1) A common synonym for a balcony in a residence. (2) A series of flat cuts bulldozed into a slope, on which houses are constructed. (3) The natural levels of sloping ground, usually alongside water and indicating the levels of the water over different eras.

TERRA COTTA — Literally "baked earth". A hard baked, glazed or unglazed, ceramic material used architecturally as a decorative surface for facings and tiles.

TERRA COTTA LUMBER — Very porous earthenware which can hold a nail and be cut without breaking or shattering.

TERRAZZO — A flooring made by embedding small pieces of marble or granite into cement and polishing to a high gloss.

TESTAMENT — Commonly synonymous with "will", but technically only the disposition of personal property. (See also: Will).

TESTAMENTARY TRUST — A trust created by a will.

TESTATE — Having written a last will and testament.

TESTATOR (F. TESTATRIX) — One who dies leaving a testament or will.

TESTIMONIUM CLAUSE — Clause in a deed or other instrument of conveyance which states that the proper parties are signing the document: "In witness whereof, the parties to these presents have hereunto set their hands and seals".

THERM — A measure of heat equal to one hundred thousand British thermal units (B.T.U.'s).

THERMAL — Heat. Having to do with heat or temperature.

THERMAL WINDOW — An insulating window of two panes of glass with air between.

THERMOSTAT — The part of a heating or air conditioning system which controls the heating or cooling unit by adjusting to bring ambient air to a pre-set temperature.

THIRD PARTY — A general term which includes anyone not a party to a contract, agreement, instrument, etc. However, statutes or court decisions may limit the definition in certain cases to, for instance, exclude representatives of the parties to a contract, etc.

THREE PHASE WIRING — A method of wiring, used in industrial buildings, allowing a series of heavy machines to be used at the same time, without overload.

THRESHOLD — A wooden strip under an outside door; the entrance to a building being over the threshold.

TIDAL BASIN — A bay or inlet without water gates. The water level varies directly with the ebb and flow of the tide.

TIDE — The ebb and flow of the sea. The tide reaches its ebb (low tide) and its flow (high tide) twice in each day (actually 24 hours 51 minutes).

TIDE LANDS — Lands which are covered at the highest point of the tide. These lands are state property and cannot be used for private purposes. Even though the tide may lower over a period of years, the land still remains state property.

TIE BEAM — A beam which acts to hold other structural members together, as a beam of a roof. Also called a collar tie.

TIER — A group of townships which form a row across a map, running East and West.

TIL — (See: Truth In Lending).

TILE — A general term used to describe ceramic materials used for floors, facing of walls, and trim; also square, flat materials of many varieties of both composition and usage, such as acoustical ceiling tile, carpet tile, field tile, sewer tile, etc.

TILE FIELD — (See: Disposal Field).

TILL — Unstratified glacial deposits, composed of clay, sand, gravel, rocks, in any proportion.

TILLABLE LAND — Land which may be plowed and planted without special preparation, such as cutting trees, removing boulders, etc.

TILL PLAIN — Level or rolling land covered by till.

TILTH — (1) Land which has been cultivated (tilled). (2) The crop produced from tilled land.

TIMBER — A general term applied to trees, standing or cut. Wood of a large size. Usually a piece of wood larger than 4″ X 4″ in cross-section.

TIME CERTIFICATE OF DEPOSIT (T.C.D.) — (See: Certificate of Deposit).

TIME INTERVAL MAPS — Maps showing a given area, indicating certain changes over a given period.

"TIME IS OF THE ESSENCE" — Clause used in contracts to bind one party to performance at or by a specified time in order to bind the other party to performance.

TIME-SHARING — A concept of ownership increasing in popularity as real estate prices rise. The purchase of an undivided interest (usually in a resort area condominium) for a fixed or variable time period. For example: Fifty-two different purchasers buy one condominium; each agrees to possession for one week per year. Costs (taxes, insurance, maintenance, etc.) are shared equally. Possession may be fixed, or by reservation, by lease, license, etc. Some developers provide several projects in different parts of the world, so that a person owning one week in a project in Hawaii could elect to spend that week in a connected project in France or other area.

TITLE — The evidence one has of right to possession of land.

TITLE DEFECT — (See: Defective Title).

TITLE INSURANCE — Insurance against loss resulting from defects of title to a specifically described parcel of real property. Defects may run to the fee (chain of title) or to encumbrances.

TITLE INSURANCE COMPANY — A company which issues insurance regarding title to real property.

TITLE ORDER — An order for a search of the title to some parcel of property, eventually leading to the issuance of a policy of title insurance.

TITLE PAGE — The page in a subdivision map which is signed by all parties having an interest in the land, agreeing to the subdivision.

TITLE PLANT — A filing of all recorded information to real property, paralleling the records of the county recorder's office, although the filing system may be different.

TITLE REPORT — (See: Preliminary Title Report).

TITLE SEARCH — A review of all recorded documents affecting a specific piece of property to determine the present condition of title.

TOENAILING — Nailing at a slant for greater gripping into a second member.

TOLL — (1) Money paid for the use of a road, bridge, etc. (2) To take away, stop, or defeat. Commonly used to indicate the defeating of the statute of limitations.

TOLL BRIDGE — A bridge, the crossing of which requires a fee to be paid.

TOLL ROAD — A highway over which a motorist may travel, for a specified fee.

TOMBSTONE TITLE — Information to validate title taken from tombstones, such as the death of an owner, date of death, names of survivors, etc.

TON — (1) A measure of weight; two thousand pounds. (2) A measure of capacity of an air conditioner. One ton equals twelve thousand British thermal units (B.T.U.'s).

TONGUE AND GROOVE — A method of joining (usually lumber) by cutting a tongue (protrusion) in one board and a corresponding groove in the other.

TOPOGRAPHICAL SURVEY — Survey showing the differences in grade of a parcel of land. Grades are measured in relation to sea level.

TOPOGRAPHY — The contour of land surface, such as flat, rolling, mountainous, etc.

TOPSOIL — The surface or upper layer of soil, which determines its suitability for farming.

TORRENS TITLE — A system by which title to land is registered with a registrar of land titles, instead of being recorded. Originally established by Sir Robert Torrens in Australia in 1858.

TORT — A civil wrong committed against person or property, independent of any contractual agreement.

TOWN — A term varying in meaning, depending on the area of the country. May be a county, city, or unincorporated village.

TOWNHOUSE — Originally a house in a city as opposed to a country estate. More recently the term is applied to certain types of row houses, whether planned unit developments or condominiums.

TOWNSHIP — A territorial division of land established by federal survey, being six miles square and containing thirty-six sections, each one mile square.

TOWNSHIP LINES — Survey lines which divide townships at their Northern and Southern boundaries. The East and West boundaries are called Range lines.

TOWNSHIP ROAD — A road under the jurisdiction of, and maintained by a town or township.

TRACK RECORD — A general term referring to the past record of performance of one applying for a loan, developing a project, asking for a listing, etc.

TRACT — A parcel of land. In some states, synonymous with a subdivision.

TRACT HOUSE — A house built using the plan of the builder, as one of many similar homes in a subdivision, as opposed to a custom house, which is built to the specifications of the owner.

TRADE AREA — The area from which a commercial development can expect to draw customers.

TRADE FIXTURES — Personal property used in a business, which is attached to the property, but removable upon sale as part of the business and not the real estate.

TRADE-IN — Sale of a house by an owner to a real estate broker in order for the owner to purchase another house. The house is put on the market at market value. If not sold in a specified time, the broker guarantees to buy the house at a lower price.

TRAFFIC — (1) The transporting of goods in trade or business. (2) The movement of air, sea, or land vehicles, people, or animals, along a route.

TRAFFIC COUNT — The number of pedestrians or vehicles moving past a given point in a given period of time. The counts are used to determine business potential, patterns for redesigning streets, etc.

TRAFFIC DENSITY — The number of vehicles moving across a portion of a road at a given time. Usually expressed as vehicles per mile of road.

TRAILER — Anything from a carrier used to haul small loads, boats, etc., to a complete mobile home, may be called a trailer.

TRAILER PARK — A site containing two or more parking spaces for trailers (mobile homes) with minimum facilities of water, sewer, electricity, laundry and bathing facilities. The more modern are called mobile home parks and have all the conveniences of an apartment complex.

TRANSFER — The act by which the title to property is conveyed from one person to another.

TRANSFER TAX — State tax on the transfer of real property. Based on purchase price or money changing hands. Check statutes for each state. Also called documentary transfer tax.

TRAP — (1) The lowest curved portion of pipe under a sink (or other fixture using water) to catch and hold objects dropped into the drain. (2) A term used among sales agents of tract houses to describe the barriers which guide potential buyers through the sales offices on their way to and from the model homes.

TRAVERSE WINDOW — A window popular in modern construction, having sashes which open horizontally, sliding on separate grooves past each other.

TREAD — The middle or center line of a road or stream.

TREADS — The width of a step in a staircase, being the horizontal distance between consecutive risers.

TREASURY BILLS — Interest bearing U.S. Government obligations sold at a weekly sale. The change in interest rates paid on these obligations is frequently used as the Rate Index of Adjustable Mortgage Loans.

TREBLE DAMAGES — Three times the amount of actual damages. Given when damages were caused by a deliberate or grossly negligent act of the defendant. (See also: Compensatory Damages; Exemplary Damages).

TRESPASS — Legally covers a variety of wrongs against person or property. Most commonly used to describe the wrongful entry of a person onto another's land, although encroachment of an inanimate object, such as a building or fence, is a form of trespass.

TRIM — Decorative or finish materials in a building as interior moldings, and exterior moldings around doors and windows.

TRIMMER — The vertical side members of a doorway, opening for a stairway, opening for a chimney, etc., to which a header is attached.

TRIPLE NET — (See: Net Lease).

TRUCK HIGH — A platform at the height of a truck bed, usually about four feet high.

TRUCK INDENTURE — A recessed platform allowing a truck to back into a building to unload.

TRUCK WELL — A slope which brings the level of a truck bed to the level of a loading platform.

147

TRUNK TITLE — (See: Dresser Drawer Title).

TRUSS — A frame to support a roof, bridge, or other span.

TRUSS HEIGHT — The height of the trusses (roof beams), as measured from the floor.

TRUST — A fiduciary relationship under which one holds property (real or personal) for the benefit of another. The party creating the trust is called the settlor, the party holding the property is the trustee, and the party for whose benefit the property is held is called the beneficiary.

TRUST ACCOUNT — An account used by brokers, escrow agents, or anyone holding money in trust for another. (See also: Commingling).

TRUST AGREEMENT — The writing which sets forth the terms of a trust.

TRUST DEED — (See: Deed of Trust).

TRUSTEE — (1) One who is appointed, or required by law, to execute a trust. (2) One who holds title to real property under the terms of a deed of trust.

TRUSTEE IN BANKRUPTCY — One appointed by a bankruptcy court, and in whom the property of the bankrupt vests. The trustee holds the property in trust, not for the bankrupt, but for the creditors.

TRUSTEE'S DEED — A deed by a trustee under a deed of trust, issued to a purchaser at auction, pursuant to foreclosure.

TRUSTEE'S SALE — A sale at auction by a trustee under a deed of trust, pursuant to foreclosure proceedings.

TRUST INSTRUMENT — Any writing which creates a trust. May be a will, court order, trust agreement, or similar writing.

TRUSTOR — The borrower under a deed of trust. One who deeds his property to a trustee as security for the repayment of a loan.

TUCK POINTING — The finishing of joints of brick, block, or similar material, with putty or mortar. Most commonly used in chimney repair.

TURN KEY — Referring to an owner making a property ready for a tenant to begin business by having the tenant furnish only furniture, phone, and inventory, if any. Ready to "turn the key" in the front door and begin business.

TURN-OVER — In business opportunities, refers to the sale of one average inventory of a business within a specified time. For example: A business having an average inventory worth $10,000, and having gross sales of $5,000 per month, would "turn-over" the inventory once every two months.

TURNPIKE — A toll road. Modernly, a road across a large portion of a state, having limited access, maximum speeds, and for the use of which a toll is charged.

TURPENTINE — An oil distilled from pine and other trees, used to thin paint and as a solvent for varnish.

TWO HOUR DOOR — A door with a resistance to fire, so that it would take a fire two hours to burn through it.

TWO HOUR WALL — A wall with a resistance to fire, so that it would take a fire two hours to burn through it.

ULTRA VIRES — Originally acts of a corporation beyond or against its charter. Now includes illegal acts. An officer of a corporation may be personally liable for an ultra vires act of the corporation.

UNAVOIDABLE CAUSE — A cause which reasonable prudence and care could not have prevented, such as death, illness, papers lost in the mail, etc.

UNBALANCED IMPROVEMENT — An appraisal term describing an improvement not in conformity with the surrounding area, and so, not suited to its location. May be an underimprovement or overimprovement.

UNCONSCIONABLE CONTRACT — So unfair that a court will not allow it. So one sided that no one in his right mind would agree on one side, and no fair and honest person would agree on the other side.

UNDERCOATING — A "prime" or first coat before the finish or "top coat" of paint or other finish.

UNDERFLOOR WIRING SYSTEM — A system of electrical wiring built into the floor of a building through conduits, ducts, and raceways.

UNDERIMPROVEMENT — An improvement which is deficient in size or quality in relation to the site on which it is built.

UNDER-LEASE — A sub-lease for either less than the remaining term on the master lease or less than the total property covered by the master lease.

UNDERLYING FINANCING — A mortgage, deed of trust, etc., prior to (underlying) a land contract, mortgage, etc., on the same property.

UNDERPASS — A passageway under a road, railway, or other right of way. May be for pedestrian traffic, automobiles, or any other method of transportation.

UNDERPINNING — (1) Temporary load-bearing beams used during construction. (2) Permanent load-bearing supports, added to an existing structure.

UNDERWRITER — One who insures another. A small title company may buy insurance from a larger one (the underwriter) for all or part of the liability of its policies. A larger title company may buy part of the insurance from another company on high liability policies.

UNDISCLOSED PRINCIPAL — A principal whose identity is not revealed by an agent.

UNDIVIDED INTEREST — A partial interest by two or more people in the same property, whether the interest of each is equal or unequal.

UNDUE INFLUENCE — Influence used to destroy the will of another so that his decision is not his free act.

UNDULATING LAND — Rolling land composed of compound slopes (two or more slopes of different grades).

UNEARNED INCREMENT — An increase in value to real property due to some change in the area rather than an improvement in the property itself.

UNEARNED PREMIUM — That unused portion of an insurance premium which is returned to the policy holder upon cancellation.

UNENCUMBERED — Free of liens and other encumbrances. Free and clear.

UNFINISHED BUILDING SPACE — Not completed. A general term not specifying how much has not been completed. May need paint, floor covering, or other minor completions. May need plumbing, electricity, floors, or other major completions.

UNIFORM COMMERCIAL CODE — A code (laws) which regulates the transfer of personal property; it took the place of the various state statutes covering chattel mortgages, conditional sales, trust receipts, etc.

UNIFORMITY — In taxation, equality in the burden of taxation, implying equality in the method of assessment as well as the rate of taxation.

UNIFORM LAWS — Laws approved by the National Conference of Commissioners on Uniform State Laws. Many have been adopted in one or more states. Among these are the Uniform Commercial Code, Uniform Negotiable Instruments Act, Uniform Partnership Act, Uniform Residential Landlord and Tenant Act, etc.

UNILATERAL CONTRACT — A contract under which one party expressly makes a promise; the other party, although making no reciprocal promise, may be obligated by law or may have already given consideration.

UNIMPROVED LAND — Most commonly land without buildings; it can also mean land in its natural state.

UNINCORPORATED AREA — An area of a county which has not formed a municipal corporation (become a city).

UNIT — (1) One of any group. (2) An apartment, condominium, house in a subdivision, etc.

UNIT COST — In relation to real estate, a cost per square foot. Also called unit price.

UNIT COST IN PLACE METHOD — An appraisal method. The cost of construction by estimating the cost of each component part in place, including labor cost and overhead.

UNITIES — The peculiarities necessary to form a valid joint tenancy. Unity of time, title, interest, and possession.

UNIT PRICE — (See: Unit Cost).

UNITY OF INTEREST — In joint tenancy, the joint tenants must acquire their interest by the same conveyance and said interest must be equal.

UNITY OF POSSESSION — In joint tenancy, the joint tenants must have equal rights to possession.

UNITY OF TIME — To have a valid joint tenancy, the joint tenants must acquire title at the same time.

UNITY OF TITLE — In joint tenancy, the holding by the joint tenants under the same title.

UNLAWFUL DETAINER — The unjustifiable possession of property by one whose original entry was lawful but whose right to possession has terminated; usually a tenant.

UNMARKETABLE TITLE — Not saleable. A title which has serious defects.

UNRECORDED INSTRUMENT — A deed, mortgage, etc., which is not recorded in the county recorder's office and, therefore, not protected under recording statutes. Valid between the parties involved, but not against innocent third parties.

UPLANDS — Land bordering bodies of water but above the high water mark.

UPSET PRICE — A legal term signifying the minimum price at which a property can be sold at auction, usually foreclosure.

URBAN — Pertaining to a city or town.

URBAN RENEWAL — Razing and rebuilding of obsolete sections of cities through financing by federal, state, and local governments.

USE DENSITY — The relationship of the number of buildings of a particular use to a given land area.

USEFUL LIFE — (1) In appraisal for sale purposes, the true economic value of a building in terms of years of use to the owner. (2) For tax purposes, the life set for depreciation. At any time during that period, a new life could begin for a new owner.

USE VALUE — The value of a single purpose property or building. Also called value-in-use.

UNSUFRUCT — The right to use and profit from property vested in another, so long as the user (usufructuary) does not change the substance of the property. Would include an easement but not a profit a prendre.

USUFRUCTUARY — One who has a usufruct.

USURY — Charging an illegal rate or amount of interest on a loan.

UTILITIES — Public utility companies, under the control of the Public Utilities Commission, such as the telephone, gas, and electric companies.

UTILITY ROOM — A room used for laundry, heating equipment, telephone wiring, or janitorial purposes.

V

VACANCY — A place which is empty (vacant). The term is generally used to describe a property available for rent.

VACANCY FACTOR — The estimated percentage of vacancies in a rental project. May be based on past records of the property, or a professional guess if a new project. Surrounding area buildings, if similar, may be used for comparison.

VACANT LAND — Land without buildings. May or may not have improvements, such as grading, sewers, etc.

VACATE — (1) To move out. (2) A legal term meaning to set aside or annul, as to vacate a judgment.

VA ESCAPE CLAUSE — A clause stating that the buyer (borrower) shall not be obligated to buy nor shall any deposit be lost if the appraisal is less than the agreed upon amount.

VALID — Legally binding. Properly carried out in accordance with legal procedures.

VALLEY — (1) The concave angle formed by the two sloping sides of a roof. (2) Low land between hills or mountains.

VALLEY FLASHING — Waterproofing (flashing) applied to the concave joint (valley) of a roof.

VALLEY RAFTER — A rafter (beam) which forms the apex of the interior angle of a valley roof.

VALLEY ROOF — A roof, the exterior surface of which forms a concave angle, having the edges higher than the center.

VALUABLE CONSIDERATION — A legal term meaning any consideration sufficient to support a contract. The word "valuable" does not mean of great value but merely having value.

VALUATION — The estimating of value. Appraisal.

VALUATOR — (See: Appraiser).

VALUE — (1) The usefulness of an object. (2) The monetary worth of an object. (3) A shortening of the term valuable consideration, as in a purchaser "for value".

VALUE AFTER THE TAKING — In the case of a partial taking under eminent domain, the value of the part not taken.

VALUE BEFORE THE TAKING — The market value of a property before condemnation.

VALUE-IN-USE — (See: Use Value).

VALVE — A device, operated automatically or manually, to regulate the flow of a gas or liquid, or to prevent the return of the gas or liquid to its source.

VAPOR BARRIER — The placing of moisture retarding material, such as paints, foil, treated paper, etc., on or in walls to prevent condensation.

VARA — A Spanish or Portuguese unit of measure of approximately 33 inches.

VARIABLE INTEREST RATE — An interest rate which fluctuates as the prevailing rate moves up or down. In mortgages there are usually maximums as to the frequency and amount of fluctuation. Also called "flexible interest rate".

VARIABLE RATE MORTGAGE — (See: Adjustable Mortgage Loan).

VARIANCE — Change of a portion of zoning requirements without changing the zoning.

VARNISH — A finish for wood which gives a transparent protective covering. Composed of resins dissolved in oil.

VAULT — (1) An arched ceiling or roof. (2) A room or enclosure used for the storage of valuables.

VENDEE — Purchaser or buyer, especially on a land contract.

VENDOR — The person who transfers property by sale. Another word for "seller". Commonly used in land contract sales.

VENEER — Thin sheets of wood or other material, such as brick, usually covering less costly material.

VENEERED CONSTRUCTION — The placing of a facing material over the external surface of a structure.

VENT — An opening, usually a pipe or duct, which allows the passage of air or gas to release undesirable fumes from a building.

VENTILATION — A system, natural or artificial, of providing fresh air circulation through a structure.

VENT PIPE — A pipe used for the elimination of sewer gases by allowing these gases to move from plumbing fixtures to a vent stack.

VENT STACK — A small chimney-like stack allowing ventilation through a roof.

VENUE — (1) The county (or other geographical division) in which an action or prosecution is brought for trial and which is to furnish the panel of jurors. (2) The county in which an acknowledgement (notarization) is made.

VERANDA — An open porch alongside a building. Usually covered by a roof for protection from the sun or rain.

VERGEBOARD — (See: Barge-board).

VERIFICATION — Confirmation of truth, correctness, or authenticity. Done by affidavit, oath, or deposition, all of which require sworn statements.

VERIFY — To confirm, substantiate, or prove to be true.

VERTICAL — Up and down. Perpendicular to the surface of the Earth.

VEST — To give an immediate interest, as opposed to a contingent or future interest.

VESTED — Present ownership rights, absolute and fixed. Modernly, ownership rights, even though on a land contract or subject to a mortgage or deed of trust.

VETERAN'S ADMINISTRATION (V.A.) LOANS — Housing loans to veterans by banks, savings and loans, or other lenders which are insured by the Veteran's Administration, enabling veterans to buy a residence with little or no down payment.

VETERAN'S TAX EXEMPTION — A state exemption for property taxes granted qualified veterans or their widows. Not in every state.

VICINAGE — (1) A neighborhood, vicinity. (2) A legal term signifying the county where a trial is held.

VILLAGE — A small community.

VILLA LOT — A term of no legal significance, used to describe a large lot upon which would be built an expensive house.

VIOLATION — Breach of any law or agreement.

VISUAL RIGHTS — The right to be able to see clearly as a general welfare right taking priority over a property right. Example: Restriction of structures or trees, shrubs, etc., at intersections if visibility is restricted as to cause a danger.

VITAL STATISTICS — Data regarding births, deaths, marriages, health records, etc., and usually kept by a governmental bureau. Federally, the Bureau of Vital Statistics.

VITREOUS — Relating to or resembling glass. Glassy.

VITRIFIED TILE — Clay pipes used in a disposal field.

VOID — Having no legal force or binding effect.

VOIDABLE — May be voided, but not void in itself.

VOLT — A term in electronics, being the force necessary to cause one ampere to flow through a conductor with a resistance of one ohm. Common household current is 110 volts, with a 220 volt circuit used for some heavy appliances. Industrial uses may require higher voltage.

VOLUNTARY LIEN — A lien placed against real property by the voluntary act of the owner. Most commonly, a mortgage or deed of trust.

W

WAGES — A general term encompassing all pay given a hired person for his or her services, whether paid as a salary, commission, fee, etc.

WAINSCOT — (See: Wainscoting).

WAINSCOTING — The covering of an interior wall with wood (usually panels), tiles, etc., from the floor to a point about half way to the ceiling; the remaining portion is painted, wallpapered, or covered with another material different from the lower portion.

WAIVE — To knowingly abandon, relinquish, or surrender a right, benefit, or claim.

WAIVER — The relinquishment of a right. In construction, most commonly the waiver by subcontractors of their mechanic's lien rights in order for the owner to obtain draws under a construction loan.

WALL — A vertical structure erected to divide, enclose, support, or secure an enclosure, such as a room or building. (See also: Party Wall).

WALL-BEARING — (See: Bearing Wall).

WALL-BEARING CONSTRUCTION — Weight of roofs and floors supported entirely by the exterior walls, with no load-bearing partitions. Posts and pillars are used at points where the span is too wide for exterior wall support.

WALLBOARD — A sheet, usually 4' by 8', of gypsum or similar material, which is attached to the studs (frame) of a wall and forms a surface which can be finished (painted, wallpapered, etc.).

WALL FURNACE — A small furnace, usually electric, fitting between the studs of a wall, and heating without ducts by using a small fan for circulation. More commonly called a "heater" than a "furnace".

WALL PANEL — An exterior wall which bears no load; the load is carried by girders or beams of the framing skeleton. Used primarily in high-rise office buildings.

WALL PLATES — (1) The horizontal members at the top and bottom of a wall, to which the studs are attached. (2) In a mine, a heavy, framed timber used for support.

WALL TILE — Tile placed on a wall as a finish material, usually in bathrooms and kitchens of homes, but sometimes throughout, as in mobile homes and trailer homes.

WAREHOUSE — A structure used for the storage of goods, either for short or long periods of time.

WAREHOUSEMAN — One who, for compensation, stores the goods of others.

WAREHOUSING — The depositing of loans by a lender such as a mortgage company, in a bank, for sale at a later date. The mortgage company then borrows against these loans. This is done when the mortgage company wishes to assemble a block of loans for sale, or when the company believes that the discount rate is dropping and the loans may be sold for a higher price in the future.

WARM AIR HEATING SYSTEM — Also called hot air heating system. A heating system whereby air is heated in a furnace and moves through ducts to the areas to be heated. (See also: Forced Air Furnace; Gravity Furnace).

WARRANT — To legally assure that title conveyed is good and possession will be undisturbed.

WARRANTY — A legal, binding, promise, given at the time of a sale, whereby the seller gives the buyer certain assurances as to the condition of the property being sold. Warranties as to real property have taken on a lesser role with the increase of the use of title insurance.

WARRANTY DEED — A deed used in many states to convey fee title to real property. Until the widespread use of title insurance, the warranties by the grantor were very important to the grantee. When title insurance is purchased, the warranties become less important as a practical means of recovery by the grantee for defective title.

WASTE — (1) A destruction of property by one who holds possession rightfully, but either is not the owner or does not own the property free and clear. (2) A change made in property, even if the value is increased by the change. This is called ameliorating waste.

WASTING ASSETS — Assets which, by use or lapse of time, are consumed or reduced in book value, irrespective of market fluctuation. Includes oil, minerals, patent rights, franchises for a fixed term, etc. Also called "diminishing assets"; "wasting property".

WASTING PROPERTY — (See: Wasting Assets).

WATERFRONT — Property (improved or unimproved) fronting on a body of water. More loosely, a neighborhood near a large body of water which has a commercial port.

WATER-GAGE — A sea wall to restrain water from overflowing.

WATER-HOLDING CAPACITY — The amount of water a given type and amount of soil will absorb and hold under normal conditions. The capacity is expressed as a percentage of the soil's own weight when dry.

WATER LEVEL — The surface height of a body of water as measured by a point on the shore. (See also: Water Mark).

WATER MARK — A mark on the shore indicating the highest point to which a body of water will normally rise (high-water mark) and also the lowest point (low-water mark) to which it will recede.

WATER POWER — The power created by the fall of a stream across one's land, the riparian owner being entitled to its utilization.

WATERPROOF — Capable of withstanding absorption of water; treating a material to give it this capability.

WATER REPELLANT — A chemical compound, in liquid form, which penetrates wood or other materials and prevents absorption of moisture or water into said materials.

WATER RIGHTS — (See: Riparian Rights).

WATERSCAPE — An aqueduct.

WATERSHED — An area formed by natural barriers, such as a mountain range, which separate two river systems. The term may be used to describe the drainage area or the barrier.

WATER TABLE — (1) The depth, measured from the surface, at which natural underground waters are found. (2) A ledge to aid the run-off of rainwater, built at or above the top of the foundation wall.

WATT — A unit of electrical power equal to the flow of one ampere caused by the pressure of one volt.

WATT-HOUR — The basis used to determine electric bills. Example: A 100 watt light bulb means if the bulb burns for one hour, it will use 100 watts of electricity.

"WEAR AND TEAR" — The deterioration or loss in value caused by the normal and reasonable use of the property. In leases, the tenant is not usually responsible for "normal wear and tear".

WEATHERING — (1) Commonly, the deterioration of the exterior of a structure caused by exposure to weather. (2) A step in the refining of gasoline.

WEATHERSTRIPS — Strips of felt, metal, etc., installed between a door or window and its casing, to keep out wind, moisture, dust, or other elements of the weather.

WEEP HOLES — Small holes in a retaining wall or other wall where it may be necessary to drain off excess water to avoid pressure build-up.

WEIR — (1) A dam used to divert water to a pond, mill, or similar use. (2) A device for measuring the flow of water past a given point.

WEIR BOX — A box set in an irrigation ditch to measure the flow of water. The box (usually of wood or concrete) is open at both ends and contains a measuring device (weir).

WELL — A hole or shaft which is sunk (usually by drilling) into the ground to obtain water, oil, natural gas, etc.

WESTERN FRAMING — A type of framing in which the studding for each floor rests on a separate sill rather than ground to roof as in balloon framing.

WET PLASTER — Plaster mixed with water and spread wet over a lath. The plaster dries hard to form the surface of a wall, ceiling, etc.

WHARF — A structure used for loading and unloading ships. May be constructed, as a dock or pier, or simply a piece of ground prepared for the same use.

WIDOW'S QUARANTINE — Old English law. Forty days during which a widow could stay in her husband's house, rent free, after his death.

WIFE — A woman who is legally married to a living man.

WILD INTEREST — An interest of record which cannot be traced in the chain of title. Frequently occurs when an incorrect legal description appears on a document. An apparent wild interest may occur if a woman who changes her name through marriage after acquiring property, sells the property using her married name only.

WILD LAND — Land not being used for cultivation or construction. Land completely in its natural state.

WILL — A written expression of the desire of a person as to the disposition of that person's property after death. Must follow certain procedures to be valid.

WINDBREAK — Any natural or artificial structure which shelters by breaking the force of the wind.

WINDOW — An opening in a wall or roof of a building to provide light, air, view, etc., but containing glass to keep out the weather.

WINDOW SILL — The bottom framing member of a window casing.

WING — A portion of a building which projects from the main area of the structure as a bird's wing projects from its body.

WIRE GLASS — A pane of glass embedded with wire to strengthen it and prevent flying glass.

WIRE LATH — A coarse mesh upon which plaster is spread.

WITHOUT RECOURSE — A finance term. A mortgage or deed of trust securing a note without recourse allows the lender to look only to the security (property) for repayment in the event of default, and not personally to the borrower.

WITNESS — (1) To sign a deed, note, or other document, to attest to its authenticity, or to prove its execution. (2) The person attesting.

WOOD FRAME CONSTRUCTION — Buildings in which the walls, roof, and floors are framed with wood, although metal, stucco, or other material may cover the framing.

WORKING CAPITAL — Cash, or assets which are readily convertible to cash, used to carry on a business.

WORKING DRAWING — Drawing used by workman in construction. Shows all structural detail such as electric, plumbing, partitions, etc.

WORKINGHOUSE — A structure on top of a grain elevator which houses the mechanical operating equipment for the elevator.

WORTHIER TITLE — A doctrine of common law which held that if one devised (left by will) the same interest as the devisee would inherit (no will), the title by inheritance would prevail, and the person would take as heir rather than devisee.

WRAP-AROUND MORTGAGE — A second or junior mortgage with a face value of both the amount it secures and the balance due under the first mortgage. The mortgagee under the wrap-around collects a payment based on its face value and then pays the first mortgagee. It is most effective when the first has a lower interest rate than the second, since the mortgagee under the wrap-around gains the difference between the interest rates, or the mortgagor under the wrap-around may obtain a lower rate than if refinancing.

WRIT OF EJECTMENT — Writ in an action for the recovery of real property, generally from a tenant.

WRIT OF EXECUTION — A writ to carry out the judgment or decree of a court.

WROUGHT IRON — An easily molded form of iron used for decorative railings, gates, furniture, etc. The term is loosely used to describe steel or aluminum used in the same manner.

WYE — The joining of railway tracks, the branches coming to the main track from different angles so as to form the shape of the letter Y.

WYTHE — A partition in a chimney which contains more than one flue, separating the flues.

X

X — (See: Mark)

Y

YACHT BASIN — A system of docks and channels used for the keeping of yachts and similar boats.

YARD — (1) A measure of 36″. (2) The area between the building and property line of a residential property (back yard, side yard, front yard). (3) An enclosure, in or out of a building, used for a business purpose (lumber yard, etc.).

YARD LUMBER — Lumber generally found in a lumber yard, that is, lumber graded for general building purposes.

YIELD — Ratio of income from an investment to the total cost of the investment over a given period of time.

Z

ZANJA (SPANISH) — An irrigation ditch.

ZERO LOT LINE — The construction of a building on any of the boundary lines of a lot. Usually built on the front line, such as a store built to the sidewalk. (See also: Zero Side Yard).

ZERO SIDE YARD — The building of a subdivision with each house built on a side boundary line. This gives more usable yard space on narrow lots. An easement for maintenance is given over a portion of the lot adjoining each house.

ZONE — (1) An area of a county or city in which the use of the land is restricted by law (zoning ordinance). (2) An area designated by a number for the delivery of mail. Zip codes incorporate the zones.

ZONING — The division of a city or county by legislative regulations into areas (zones), specifying the uses allowable for the real property in these areas.

ZONING MAP — A map of a community showing the zones of permitted use under zoning ordinances.

ZONING ORDINANCE — A law (generally at the city or county level) controlling the use of land and construction of improvements in a given area (zone).

ZONING VARIANCE — (See: Variance).

ZYGOCEPHALUM — In civil law an inaccurate measure of land. The area of land a yoke of oxen could plow in one day.